Digital Infrastructure for Science Advancement

Digital Infrastructure for Science Advancement

RAFEAL MECHLORE

Readers Publications

CONTENTS

INDEX 1

INTRODUCTION 3

1 | Chapter 1 19

2 | Chapter 2 46

3 | Chapter 3 71

4 | Chapter 4 95

5 | Chapter 5 123

6 | Chapter 6 146

7 | Chapter 7 171

8 | Chapter 8 193

9 | Chapter 9 216

10 | Chapter 10 240

INDEX

Introduction

1. The role of digital infrastructure in scientific progress
2. The need for an updated and robust digital infrastructure
3. The scope and goals of the book

Chapter 1: The Evolving Landscape of Science

1.1 Historical perspective on scientific research
1.2 The digital revolution's impact on science
1.3 The current state of scientific infrastructure
1.4 The challenges and opportunities presented by digitalization

Chapter 2: Foundations of Digital Infrastructure

2.1 Defining digital infrastructure in the context of science
2.2 Hardware and software components
2.3 Data storage and management
2.4 Network connectivity and communication

Chapter 3: Data Management and Sharing

3.1 Importance of data in scientific research
3.2 Data collection, curation, and preservation
3.3 Open science and data sharing
3.4 Data ethics and privacy concerns

Chapter 4: High-Performance Computing

4.1 The role of supercomputing in scientific breakthroughs
4.2 Parallel processing and distributed computing
4.3 Cloud computing in scientific research

Chapter 5: The Internet of Things (IoT) in Science
5.1 IoT applications in scientific research
5.2 Sensor networks and data collection
5.3 Real-time monitoring and control
5.4 Challenges and security considerations

Chapter 6: Artificial Intelligence and Machine Learning
6.1 Leveraging AI/ML for scientific discovery
6.2 Data analysis and pattern recognition
6.3 Predictive modeling and simulations
6.4 Ethical considerations and transparency in AI

Chapter 7: Virtual Labs and Collaborative Platforms
7.1 The concept of virtual laboratories
7.2 Online collaboration tools for researchers
7.3 Remote experimentation and simulations

Chapter 8: Cybersecurity and Research Integrity
8.1 The importance of cybersecurity in science
8.2 Protecting research data and intellectual property
8.3 Ensuring research integrity in a digital age
8.4 Ethical dilemmas and the responsible use of technology

Chapter 9: Funding and Policy Considerations
9.1 Government and private sector investments in digital infrastructure
9.2 Policy frameworks and regulations
9.3 International collaboration in science infrastructure
9.4 The role of academia in shaping policy

Chapter 10: Future Prospects and Challenges
10.1 Emerging technologies and trends in science infrastructure
10.2 Sustainability and environmental impacts
10.3 Addressing the digital divide in science
10.4 Preparing for unforeseen challenges

INTRODUCTION

In a time when the limits of human knowledge are still being pushed further and further at a rate that seems to be accelerating at an exponential rate, the role that science plays in sculpting our reality has never been more obvious. The vast number of discoveries and technologies that have been made by science have impacted every part of our lives and have transformed them. The importance of scientific progress is difficult to overstate, as it has been responsible for everything from medical advances that have increased human life expectancy to technology advances that have brought the globe closer together. However, these ground-breaking accomplishments would not have been possible without a crucial enabler of scientific progress known as digital infrastructure, which is sometimes concealed from the view of the general public but is more important than ever.

Even if it may not be as eye-catching as a spectacular laboratory discovery or a ground-breaking medical therapy, the digital infrastructure for science is the essential component that underpins the development of modern scientific knowledge. It is the technological framework that modern research and innovation rely on to function. To achieve greater heights of knowledge, scientists of today rely on digital infrastructure, just as ancient architects used sturdy foundations to build towering marvels.

The phrase "digital infrastructure" refers to a sophisticated network of technologies and systems that are designed to assist scientific study in a variety of fields, ranging from physics and chemistry to biology and environmental science. This network was created to facilitate the advancement of scientific knowledge. It encompasses a variety of instruments, resources, and platforms that promote and expedite scientific investigation, such as high-performance computers, data storage, machine learning techniques, and collaborative research spaces.

The purpose of this book, titled "Digital Infrastructure for Science Advancement," is to shed light on the significant part that digital infrastructure plays in determining the trajectory of contemporary scientific inquiry and its associated landscape. Within these pages, we shall set out on a trip through the complex maze of technology, policy, and practice in order to untangle the intricate tapestry of the digital infrastructure's contributions to the advancement of scientific knowledge. We are going to investigate the fundamental elements that are driving this digital revolution, as well as the obstacles that it must surmount and the boundless opportunities that it paves the way for in the future of science.

The beginning of the digital age marked the beginning of a new era for scientific inquiry, ushering in a new era for scientific inquiry that redefined the methods in which research is carried out, data is obtained, and knowledge is disseminated.

In the pages that are to come, we will get started on an in-depth investigation of the shifting environment of science and the digital infrastructure that drives its advancement.

The Ever-Changing Terrain of Scientific Research

Before we can fully comprehend the enormous effect that digital infrastructure has had on the scientific community, we need to first recognize the shifts that have taken place in the scientific landscape. In this chapter, we will take a trip back in time to trace the historical history of scientific research and the role that digitization has played in changing the frontiers of scientific inquiry.

Since the beginning of our journey, the pursuit of knowledge through scientific inquiry has been an indispensable component. The scientific endeavor can be summed up in one word: understanding. From the earliest observations of celestial bodies to the most recent achievements in gene editing and artificial intelligence, the scientific endeavor is defined by its unrelenting pursuit of comprehending the world around us. Over the course of several generations, scientists have pushed the boundaries of human knowledge and uncovered significant discoveries that have brought about fundamental changes in our world.

In the early days of science, the researchers had access to a substantially less number of methodologies and tools than they do today. The conduct of scientific research was traditionally characterized by arduous, hands-on experiments, thorough data recording, and tardy sharing of conclusions. The number of people involved in scientific research was very low, and the only way information could be shared was through handwritten manuscripts or restricted editions of printed literature. Even though numerous scientific ideas and discoveries were made during this time period, it was simply the tip of the iceberg in terms of scientific advancement.

The beginning of the Digital Revolution, which started in earnest in the middle of the 20th century, is considered to be a watershed moment in the development of science. It was the impetus for a paradigm shift in the manner in which research was carried out and knowledge was disseminated. The scope of possible scientific investigations has significantly broadened thanks to the development of computers, capacity for more sophisticated data storage and processing, as well as global communication networks. These technological advancements created the framework for a new era of science, which would be characterized by the vast volume of data collected, the speed at which analysis could be performed, and the global collaboration that was made possible.

The capacity of the Digital Revolution to bring about transformation is becoming more and more obvious as we progress farther into the 21st century.

One of the most obvious results of this revolution is the fact that modern scientific investigation is increasingly focused on collecting and analyzing data. Researchers working in fields as diverse as genomics and environmental science are now producing enormous datasets that are orders of magnitude larger and more complicated than those produced by researchers working in previous generations. These databases have important information that can be used to solve some of the most critical problems we face at this juncture, find a cure for diseases, and uncover the mysteries of the universe.

On the other hand, the sheer volume and complexity of this data present both previously unimaginable opportunities and tremendous obstacles. This is the point at which the role of digital infrastructure turns into an absolute need. Scientists are able to process, analyze, and derive useful insights from these huge datasets thanks to the computational power and storage capacity provided by high-performance computing systems and data centers. These capabilities, when combined with improved data management approaches, enable the scientists to do so.

In addition to the administration of data, the Digital Revolution has also resulted in the development of new methods for doing scientific research. Researchers now have access to invaluable aids in the form of machine learning algorithms and artificial intelligence technologies. These aids automate hard operations, recognize trends, and even propose new hypotheses. These technologies, which are integrated into the digital infrastructure of the scientific community, are hastening the rate of discovery in a variety of different fields.

Beyond the confines of the laboratory lies the transformation. Additionally, collaboration and exchange of information have advanced over time. The proliferation of the internet and virtual platforms for collaborative work has led to a democratization of scientific research. This has made it possible for specialists from all over the world to collaborate, share data, and jointly find solutions to difficult problems on a global scale. The development of digital infrastructure has made it possible for unprecedented levels of scientific cooperation to take place on a worldwide scale, and this trend is expected to continue.

However, despite the fact that we are on the cusp of a new age in science, the breadth and depth of the role that digital infrastructure plays in the advancement of scientific knowledge are not yet well recognized by the majority of people. The hidden complexities of the digital infrastructure that underpin the achievements of modern science are the subject of this book, which aims to shed light on those complexities. The objective of this project is to shed light on the underlying technologies, data management methodologies, and collaboration platforms that form the backbone of the scientific endeavor.

In the chapters that are to come, we are going to delve into the complexities of digital infrastructure and investigate the essential contributions that it has made to the development of science. In this section, we will discuss the fundamental components of this infrastructure, the obstacles it must overcome, and the ethical and policy issues that drive responsible utilization of this infrastructure. In the end, one of our goals is to provide a complete grasp of the ways in which digital infrastructure is transforming the landscape of scientific investigation and opening doors to new frontiers of knowledge.

In the following chapter, we will look deeper into the fundamental aspects of digital infrastructure, such as the hardware, software, and networking components that make contemporary scientific investigation possible. By gaining a grasp of the components that make up this infrastructure, we can have a deeper appreciation for its revolutionary power as well as its ability to rethink the manner in which scientific research is carried out.

1. **The role of digital infrastructure in scientific progress**

Science, which may be defined as the methodical pursuit of information about the natural world, has always been an essential part of human advancement and the growth of our contemporary society. It has not only increased our comprehension of the cosmos, but it has also resulted in a vast number of advancements that have resulted in an improvement in the standard of living of people all over the world. In spite of this, the advent of digital infrastructure over the course of the last several decades has caused a dramatic shift in the general course of scientific advancement. The application of cutting-edge technology and information networks in scientific investigation has fundamentally altered the way in which scientific inquiry is carried out. This has resulted in a significant acceleration in the rate at which new discoveries are made, the facilitation of collaborations on a scale never before seen, and an improvement in our capacity to deal with difficult problems on a worldwide scale.

In the course of this investigation into the part that digital infrastructure plays in the progression of science, we will investigate the ways in which technology has emerged as the primary motivating factor behind a variety of scientific advances. The incorporation of digital infrastructure has fundamentally altered the nature of the scientific landscape in a variety of ways, including the management and analysis of data, high-performance computing, artificial intelligence, and the development of virtual collaborative platforms.

1. **Methods of Data Management and Evaluation**

Data, both huge and intricate, can be found at the core of a variety of scientific disciplines. The sheer volume of data generated has expanded tremendously in recent years, presenting researchers in fields such as genetics, climate science, and astronomy with both an opportunity and a challenge. The management and analysis of this data is made significantly easier by the presence of digital infrastructure.

Scientists now have the ability to collect and store enormous datasets in a secure manner thanks to modern data storage options such as data centers and cloud computing. This is of the utmost importance in the field of genomics, since the human genome consists of billions of base pairs, as well as in the field of climate science, as the outputs of climate models require terabytes for research purposes.

In addition, sophisticated data analysis techniques, which frequently make use of machine learning and artificial intelligence, make it possible for researchers to draw useful conclusions from the vast amounts of data at their disposal. For example, in the field of healthcare, AI-powered algorithms can sift through patients' medical histories to recognize trends and make predictions about patient outcomes, which can lead to more individualized treatment options.

2. **Computing with a High Performance Level**

    In many cases, intricate simulations, mathematical models, and computational modeling are required for scientific inquiry. In order to successfully complete these activities, you will require high-performance computing (HPC) equipment. These systems come outfitted with potent processors and large memory. Researchers are able to model the behavior of complicated systems, simulate the behavior of materials, and examine sophisticated physical processes because to the availability of these tools.

    High-performance computing is an essential component in many scientific disciplines, including astrophysics, where it is used to model the behavior of galaxies, black holes, and the early cosmos. In the same vein, these supercomputers are utilized in the field of drug development as well as materials research in order to model the behavior of materials on an atomic level and screen millions of possible compounds for usage in novel therapies.

    In this way, high-performance computing (HPC) not only quickens the pace of research but also enables scientists to tackle issues that were previously insurmountable. It paves the way for brand new discoveries, breakthroughs, and answers to some of the world's most intractable problems.

3. **A.I. and ML (Automated Learning and Machine Intelligence)**

    In recent years, the fields of machine learning (ML) and artificial intelligence (AI) have developed into extremely useful research tools. They are exceptional at recognizing patterns, optimizing processes, and making decisions, which makes them invaluable in a variety of fields.

    In the field of medicine, artificial intelligence may examine medical pictures like

X-rays and MRIs to look for abnormalities or to provide radiologists with assistance when making diagnosis.

In the field of climate science, artificial intelligence has the potential to improve weather forecasting and climate models by more effectively managing enormous datasets. Particle physicists are also benefiting from AI thanks to its ability to recognize patterns in massive volumes of data collected by particle colliders.

In addition, machine learning algorithms are utilized in domains such as genomics in order to read the genetic code and comprehend the role that particular genes play in both health and sickness. In the field of astronomy, artificial intelligence is contributing to the identification of new heavenly bodies and the classification of galaxies.

Not only can these tools make research more efficient, but they also have the ability to unearth insights that may, under different circumstances, continue to be masked by the onslaught of data. The future of scientific investigation is being shaped by a cooperation between artificial intelligence and human knowledge working together.

4. **Virtual Laboratories and Platforms for Collaborative Work**

The digital era has seen the rise of virtual laboratories and collaborative platforms, both of which make it possible to conduct scientific research in fresh and original ways. These virtual environments provide the option to carry out experiments and research remotely, removing geographical restrictions and making it possible for a scientific community from across the world to collaborate.

Researchers can now carry out experiments remotely in a variety of subjects, including biology, chemistry, and physics, by making use of specialized equipment that is capable of connecting to the internet. Experiments may be run, data can be shared, and real-time collaboration can take place thanks to these virtual labs, which are accessible from a variety of locations. For instance, chemists are able to conduct experiments at many locations throughout the world while concurrently monitoring the progress of each experiment. Not only does this help save time, but it also makes it possible to share both equipment and experience.

On the other hand, collaborative platforms bring together scientists and researchers from a wide variety of fields and locations. They provide venues for the exchange of data, the discussion of discoveries, and the coordination of research projects. Interdisciplinary research has flourished as a result of the proliferation of these platforms, which bring together researchers from a variety of fields in an effort to solve difficult challenges.

5. **Openness in Science and the Exchange of Data**

A significant cultural change toward open science has been made possible as a result of the advent of digital infrastructure. Open science is a scientific methodology that promotes the dissemination of research findings, data, and methodologies to the larger scientific community. This not only encourages transparency but also has the effect of speeding up the rate at which scientific progress is made.

In the past, data was frequently kept in isolation within individual research organizations or laboratories, which prevented it from being shared with other parties. The proliferation of digital technology has made it significantly simpler to exchange data. Researchers are able to make their data and discoveries available to the general public through the use of platforms and repositories that support open access. This provides a wide variety of advantages:

Replicability means that the outcomes of study may be verified by other scientists, which increases the dependability of scientific discoveries.

Interdisciplinary research is made possible by increased opportunities for collaboration among researchers coming from a variety of institutions and fields of study.

Reusing Data: It is possible to save time and resources by reusing previously collected data in new research projects.

Open science projects are particularly noticeable in the field of genomics, which makes enormous information freely accessible to academics all around the world. Researchers in genomics have been able to speed up the process of discovering new genetic markers that are connected with diseases by exchanging data, which has enabled customized medicine to advance more quickly.

6. **Protecting the Integrity of Research and Cyberspace**

   The growing reliance on digital infrastructure in scientific research has elevated the importance of cybersecurity to a position of preeminence among concerns. It is absolutely necessary, in order to keep the credibility of scientific endeavors intact, to take precautions against cyber attacks on research data and intellectual property.

   The security and integrity of research can be put at risk by data breaches and cyberattacks, which can also result in the loss of essential data. Theft of drug research data, for instance, can result in lost earnings and put public health in jeopardy, both of which are problems for the pharmaceutical business.

   For the purpose of protecting the results of research, it is essential to implement cyber security measures such as encryption, secure data storage, and access controls.

   In addition, the integrity of research in the digital era extends well beyond the realm of cybersecurity. Growing significance is being given to ethical problems about the application of technology in research, including the ethical use of data, the responsible application of artificial intelligence, and the transparency of algorithms. These issues need to be addressed by researchers, institutions, and politicians in order to guarantee that the benefits of digital infrastructure are maximized while at the same time avoiding the potential for unethical errors.

7. **Factors to Consider Regarding Funding and Policy**
Significant financial investments are required for both the installation and on-going upkeep of digital infrastructure. Funding initiatives for digital infrastructure that are essential to scientific research is provided by a variety of sources, including government agencies, groups from the corporate sector, and charitable organizations.

Research endeavors receive major financial backing from government agencies like the National Institutes of Health (NIH) in the United States and the European Space Agency (ESA) in Europe. Both of these organizations are located in the United States. It is common practice to direct these monies toward the creation of high-performance computer clusters, the launch of data centers, and the promotion of open science initiatives.

Companies in the private sector, particularly those in the information technology and cloud computing industries, are essential contributors to the development of digital infrastructure. Because of their resources, researchers can gain access to cutting-edge tools and platforms, which in turn helps advance scientific knowledge.

In addition, charitable organizations contribute to the development of the digital infrastructure necessary for scientific research. Many organizations, such as the Bill & Melinda Gates Foundation, have made investments in global health efforts that are largely reliant on digital infrastructure in order to solve concerns such as disease control and the creation of vaccines.

In the process of reshaping the landscape of digital infrastructure in the scientific community, policymakers and regulators play an important role as well. They set criteria for the ethical use of technology in research, as well as for the sharing of data, cybersecurity, and other concerns. Their choices have the potential to advance scientific research in either a positive or negative direction.

8. **Prospects for the Future and Current Obstacles**

In the coming years, the significance that digital infrastructure plays in the advancement of scientific knowledge is expected to grow even more. Both fresh opportunities and new obstacles will present themselves as technological advancements continue.

New technologies, such as quantum computing, hold the potential to bring about a sea change in high-performance computing as well as the analysis of complicated datasets. It is particularly interesting for traditional computing-based subjects like chemistry, materials science, and encryption that quantum computing may one day be able to tackle issues that are currently unsolvable using traditional computing methods.

In addition to this, the incorporation of digital infrastructure into the routine research methods of scientists will continue to expand. When it comes to storing data, doing analyses, and working together, researchers will increasingly rely on tools and platforms that are hosted on the cloud. Both the presentation of data and the modeling of experiments could potentially benefit from the use of virtual reality and augmented reality.

The swift development of digital infrastructure, on the other hand, is not without its share of difficulties. As the demand for energy from high-performance computer centers and data centers continues to rise, sustainability is becoming an increasingly pressing topic. One of the most important things to think about for the future is how to mitigate the negative effects that digital infrastructure has on the surrounding environment.

In addition, it is vital to bridge the digital gap in order to ensure that all scientists, regardless of

the resources they have access to or the area they work in, may benefit from digital infrastructure. In parts of the world where there is less access to technology and less connectivity, this presents a huge difficulty.

The importance of digital infrastructure to the advancement of science is a driving force behind the changing nature of the scientific landscape. The development of digital infrastructure has been a primary factor in the majority of recent advances in several scientific fields, including data management and analysis, high-performance computing, artificial intelligence, and virtual collaborative platforms. It quickens the pace of research, makes it possible for scientists from around the world to collaborate, and throws open the door to new discoveries and breakthroughs.

When we consider the future, we see that the ongoing incorporation of digital infrastructure into scientific study holds the prospect of even more significant improvements.

The possibilities are practically endless, but so are the obstacles. The trajectory of the role that digital infrastructure plays in the progression of scientific knowledge will be shaped by issues of sustainability, accessibility, and ethics.

The digital infrastructure is not merely a supporting actor in the scientific drama; rather, it is an essential component of the storyline in a world that is becoming increasingly data-driven and networked. Not only does it play a transformative role, but it also serves as a foundational one, serving as the driving force behind the modern scientific endeavor and propelling it to new horizons of knowledge and comprehension.

B. The need for an updated and robust digital infrastructure

The digital infrastructure that supports modern society has evolved into the central pillar of our fast-paced, technology-driven society. Not only does it establish the framework that supports the functioning of enterprises and governments, but it also forms the structure that supports the crucial sectors of healthcare, education, and research. On the other hand, the ever-increasing demands placed on our digital infrastructure have brought to light the system's weaknesses and constraints. There is an immediate and pressing need for a modernized and resilient digital infrastructure in order to keep up with the ever-changing requirements of our globally networked world. This article delves into the factors that make it necessary for us to make such an upgrade both now and in the future.

1. **Rapid Increases in the Development of New Technologies**
   The rapidity with which new technological capabilities are being developed is nothing short of amazing. Artificial intelligence, quantum computing, and the Internet of Things are examples of ideas that were previously considered to be the purview of science fiction but have now emerged into the real world and become a vital part of our everyday life. These developments call for the establishment of a digital infrastructure that is equipped to meet the enormous data processing and networking requirements they impose.
   For example, quantum computing has the potential to transform the way difficult problems are solved, which might have implications for everything from the search for new drugs to cryptography. We need a digital infrastructure that is capable of supporting quantum communication and quantum computing networks in order to fully harness its power. In a similar manner, the Internet of Things (IoT) is linking billions of devices and sensors, ranging from smart home appliances to industrial machinery. In order to function properly, these connected gadgets require a solid and dependable underlying infrastructure.
2. **The challenge posed by the explosion of data and big data**
   One of the qualities that best characterizes the modern age is the exponential growth of available data. Massive amounts of data are produced from a wide variety of sources on a daily basis, including social networking platforms, online shopping, scientific research, and the Internet of Things. This data offers insightful knowledge that has the potential to revolutionize entire sectors, enhance process efficiency, and make better decisions.
   Nevertheless, the process of managing, storing, and analyzing these huge databases is a challenging endeavor. The digital infrastructure needs to be outfitted with data centers that have a high capacity, storage solutions that are efficient, and data analysis tools that are powerful in order to fully tap into the potential of big data. In addition, the protection of personal information and data privacy are of the utmost importance, necessitating the implementation of stringent cybersecurity protocols.
3. **Connectivity and communication on a global scale**
   The fluid transmission of information, the promotion of international partner-

ships, and the maintenance of economic growth throughout the world are all dependent on the robustness of the world's communication networks. The COVID-19 pandemic brought to light the significance of digital infrastructure in maintaining social relationships and safeguarding the continuity of businesses in times when there were less opportunities for face-to-face contact.

The requirement for connectivity that is both high-speed and reliable is ever increasing. With the proliferation of 5G networks and the investigation of 6G technology, the digital infrastructure needs to keep pace with the need for faster and more resilient networks. This is essential not just for enhancing the experiences of consumers, but also for making possible remote work, telemedicine, and the mass use of smart technologies.

4. **Electronic Administration and Public Services**

   Digital solutions are becoming an increasingly popular option for governments all over the world as they seek to modernize public services, simplify administrative procedures, and increase transparency. E-government initiatives have the potential to make public services more user-friendly and convenient for citizens. However, in order for them to function properly, they require a solid digital infrastructure that is able to enable the secure movement of data, online authentication, and the storing of huge amounts of data held by the government.

   The COVID-19 epidemic has hastened the transition to the use of digital public services like as online schooling, consultations with healthcare professionals, and transactions with the government.

   The government must make investments in dependable and up-to-date digital infrastructure in order to guarantee the continued provision of these services and guarantee that they are available to all of its residents.

5. **Healthcare and Electronic Medical Record Systems**

   Another industry where digital infrastructure is becoming increasingly important is the healthcare industry. The proliferation of telemedicine and other forms of remote patient monitoring has made it easier for people to obtain medical care, particularly in more remote or underdeveloped locations. Patients are now able to consult with healthcare providers without having to leave the convenience of their own homes, which relieves some of the pressure on traditional healthcare institutions.

   However, telemedicine is extremely dependent on a high-speed internet connection and the transfer of data in a secure manner. By maintaining an up-to-date digital infrastructure, medical professionals are guaranteed to be able to provide high-quality care, safely exchange patient records, and get access to cutting-edge diagnostic tools and research. Because of the expected increase in demand for telemedicine and other digital health services, it is essential to continually modernize the infrastructure.

6. **Educational Opportunities and Online Learning**
   E-learning has emerged as the industry standard as a direct result of the pandemic, which has fundamentally altered the educational landscape. All levels of education, from elementary schools to colleges and universities, have transferred their operations to online platforms to ensure that students are able to keep up with their coursework during times of emergency.
   However, in order for e-learning to be effective, students need access to a stable internet connection, tools for high-quality video conferencing, and online platforms that are safe for material distribution. Students are able to learn without disruption thanks to an up-to-date and powerful digital infrastructure, which also enables teachers to deliver education in an efficient manner.

7. **Engaging in Creative and Scholarly Activity**
   It is impossible to exaggerate how important digital infrastructure is to the processes of research and innovation. The availability of high-performance computers, data storage, and collaboration tools is becoming increasingly important to the advancement of science in areas ranging from the discovery of new drugs to the modeling of climate change. The processing of enormous datasets, the running of simulations, and the analysis of complicated systems are all made possible thanks to these resources.
   In addition to the management and processing of data, digital infrastructure also supports virtual laboratories and collaborative research platforms. These platforms give researchers from different areas of the world the ability to work together on the solution of difficult problems. This both quickens the rate at which new discoveries are made and increases our capacity to find solutions to problems on a global scale.

8. **Continuity of Business Operations and Resilience**
   The COVID-19 pandemic brought to light the significance of maintaining corporate operations and remaining resilient in the face of unforeseen disturbances. Because businesses were forced to quickly adjust to online operations and remote labor, the digital infrastructure was put under a significant amount of strain.
   It is absolutely necessary to have an up-to-date infrastructure that has redundancy, failover systems, and scalability in order to guarantee business continuity. Even in the face of unanticipated disruptions or cyberattacks, organizations need to have the ability to maintain their operations and react to changing conditions.

9. **Sustainability and the Future of Smart Cities**
   The idea of "smart cities," in which technology is utilized to improve the quality of life in urban areas, is gaining popularity. In order to monitor and control the many facets of urban life, including transportation, energy consumption, and waste management, smart cities rely on the infrastructure provided by digital

technologies.

This infrastructure makes it possible to collect and analyze data in real time, which in turn helps cities become more efficient, sustainable, and responsive to the demands of its citizens. Nevertheless, in order to construct smart cities, it is necessary to have a digital infrastructure that is both current and strong.

10. **The Difficulty of Maintaining Cybersecurity**

    The difficulty of ensuring digital infrastructure's safety increases in tandem with the growing dependence we have on it. The more connected we are to one another, the more susceptible we are to cyberattacks, data leaks, and other forms of digital danger. Enhanced security mechanisms, encryption methods, and continuous monitoring are some of the components of an up-to-date infrastructure that are included to protect against growing cyber threats.

11. **Bridging the Gap in Digital Technology**

In spite of the fact that the proliferation of digital infrastructure has made many elements of contemporary life more accessible and efficient, it has also brought to light inequities in access.

Not everyone has the same level of access to digital devices, high-speed internet, or the digital literacy skills necessary to successfully traverse the digital world.

It is imperative that efforts be made to bridge the digital divide in order to provide equal access to and participation in digital activities in this age. A modernized infrastructure should include programs that offer underserved communities with access to the internet that is both inexpensive and dependable as well as programs to improve digital literacy, which equip persons with the skills necessary to flourish in the digital era.

The requirement for a modernized and reliable digital infrastructure is of the utmost importance in a world that is becoming more data-driven and networked. It is the foundation upon which our technological advancements are built, enables global connectivity and communication, supports e-government and public services, improves healthcare and telemedicine, facilitates e-learning, accelerates research and innovation, ensures business continuity and resilience, and contributes to the development of smart cities and sustainability.

In order to meet the problems of handling enormous datasets, maintaining cybersecurity, and closing the digital divide, major investments need to be made, and novel solutions need to be developed. To construct a digital infrastructure that is capable of meeting the ever-evolving requirements of our linked world, governments, entities from the private sector, and international organizations will need to work together. Our ability to adapt and improve the digital foundations of our communities, economies, and scientific advancements will determine their respective destinies in the future.

C. The scope and goals of the book

It is vital, as we get started on this investigation of "Digital Infrastructure for Science Advancement," to establish the scope and goals of this work. By outlining the parameters of our trip and articulating our goals, we can provide the audience with a clear picture of what to anticipate and what it is that we hope to accomplish. This book dives into the complex relationship that exists between digital infrastructure and the growth of science, illuminating the many of facets, obstacles, and opportunities that constitute the dynamic junction of these two fields.

The Topics Covered in the Book

Foundations of Digital Infrastructure In this section, we will investigate the primary aspects of digital infrastructure, such as its hardware, software, data storage, and network connectivity. These components serve as the foundation upon which scientific advancement can be built in the modern era.

Management of Data and Information Exchange The administration of data is an essential part of scientific study. This book will go into the fundamentals of data gathering, curation, and preservation, as well as the ever-increasing significance of open science and the exchange of data.

High-Performance Computing High-performance computing is an essential tool for conducting research in a variety of scientific disciplines. We are going to have a conversation on the significance of supercomputing, parallel processing, and cloud computing, as well as the impact that these technologies have had on a variety of scientific fields.

Exploring the Applications of the Internet of Things (IoT) in Science We will investigate the IoT's applications in scientific research, sensor networks, real-time monitoring, and difficulties connected to security and privacy.

AI and ML: This book will study how AI and ML are altering scientific discovery by making data analysis, pattern recognition, and predictive modeling easier to perform.

Virtual Laboratories and Online Collaboration technologies The way in which scientific research is carried out is being revolutionized by the use of virtual laboratories and online collaboration technologies. We are going to investigate their influence, as well as various use cases and successful implementations.

Integrity of Research and Cybersecurity Given the ever-increasing reliance of the scientific community on digital infrastructure, cybersecurity has emerged as a significant concern. In this lesson, we will discuss the significance of protecting research data, intellectual property, and the integrity of research in the age of digital technology.

Considerations Regarding Funding and Policy The funding and policy environment of digital infrastructure in science is an essential component to the success of the endeavor. During this session, we will talk about investments made by the government and the private sector, policy frameworks, international collaboration, and the role that academics plays in the process of making policy.

In the section titled "Future Prospects and Challenges," topics such as emerging technologies and trends in science infrastructure, sustainability, bridging the digital divide, and becoming ready for unanticipated problems will be discussed and analyzed.

Case Studies: Throughout this book, we will highlight the practical applications of digital infrastructure in real-world contexts by incorporating case studies from a variety of scientific disciplines. These case studies will be taken from a variety of sources.

The Objectives of the Book

Education and Awareness: Our primary objective is to raise awareness among readers about the vital part that digital infrastructure plays in the progression of scientific knowledge. We hope to promote a greater appreciation of the ways in which digital infrastructure enables scientific advancement by raising knowledge of the technological underpinnings of scientific inquiry. This will allow us to achieve our goal of increasing awareness.

Components and Functions of Digital Infrastructure in the Context of Scientific Research This book's overarching goal is to provide a complete understanding of the many components and functions of digital infrastructure as they relate to scientific research. Our mission is to shed light on the complex network of technology and organizational structures that facilitates the quest of knowledge by scientific researchers.

We give practical counsel and insights to anybody interested in technology, including scientists, researchers, policymakers, and enthusiasts. Whether you are interested in securing your research data, establishing a virtual lab, or utilizing AI in your research, our goal is to give you with helpful assistance and recommendations for best practices.

Ethical Considerations The consideration of ethical issues is at the forefront of our conversations at the moment. Our mission is to find solutions to the moral conundrums raised by evolving technologies and to promote the proper utilization of digital infrastructure. We hope to promote more responsible behavior in the scientific community by investigating these concerns.

Inspiring Innovation: Our intention is to encourage innovation by demonstrating the potential for digital infrastructure to undergo significant transformation. The book will focus on success stories, research that is on the cutting edge, and the frontiers of digital technology in a variety of scientific fields.

Policy Insights: When it comes to the expansion and long-term viability of digital infrastructure for science, policy and financial concerns are of the utmost importance. Our mission is to shed light on the current policy landscape and discuss the various ways in which stakeholders and policymakers can influence the future of scientific infrastructure.

A Conscious Understanding of the Obstacles Facing You In order to successfully navigate the intricate landscape that is digital infrastructure, one must have a conscious understanding of the obstacles and dangers that it presents. Our mission is to arm readers with the information they need to combat cybersecurity risks, close the digital divide, and ensure the ethical application of technology in research.

Getting Ready for the Future Getting ready for the future is of the utmost importance in a field that is constantly undergoing change. This book will talk about new technologies, trends, and the necessity of having a digital infrastructure that is both sustainable and egalitarian so that it can meet the challenges of the future.

Fostering an Interdisciplinary Perspective On the Role of Digital Infrastructure Our goal is to create an interdisciplinary perspective on the role of digital infrastructure by investigating a wide variety of scientific fields and the specific requirements of each. With this approach, collaboration and the sharing of knowledge are encouraged across a variety of fields.

The scientific method does not recognize national boundaries, and the global perspective is something that will be reflected in our book. We will investigate the worldwide cooperation and collaborations that are necessary for the continued development of scientific research through the utilization of digital infrastructure.

Chapter 1

The Evolving Landscape of Science

From the earliest contemplations of celestial bodies by ancient astronomers to the complicated gene-editing tools of the present age, the voyage of science is an odyssey that spans centuries. This journey begins with ancient astronomers and ends with modern gene-editing technology. This interesting journey has resulted in a number of technologies that affect our everyday lives and has changed the way we see the world. The dynamic and interwoven story of how science has progressed over time is represented by the ever-changing landscape of the scientific community, which itself has undergone significant changes, adaptations, and progressions. In the course of this investigation, we will travel through the annals of scientific history, following the winding road of scientific progress and contemplating the factors that have led us to the position we are in right now.

The Beginnings of Science: Some of the First Explorers

The beginning of human civilization may be traced all the way back to when science first got its start. Our forefathers kindled the fire of curiosity that eventually led to the development of science by contemplating the constellations in the night sky, following the orbits of the planets, and observing the workings of nature. Ancient civilizations such as the Babylonians, Greeks, and Egyptians contributed their astronomical knowledge and mathematical discoveries, which paved the way for empirical investigation and set the foundation for modern science.

During the Hellenistic period, philosophers such as Aristotle and Ptolemy were responsible for the development of methodical approaches to the observation, classification, and interpretation of natural phenomena. The natural philosophy of Aristotle, which places a strong focus on empiricism and logical reasoning, constituted a significant change toward a more structured scientific approach at the time it was written. This ancient knowledge spread throughout the world and had an impact on the Islamic Golden Age. During this time period, scientists like Al-Razi and Ibn Sina (also known as Avicenna) perfected scientific methodology and advanced subjects such as medicine and optics.

Both the Renaissance and the Scientific Revolution took place during this time.

The fields of science, art, and culture all experienced a revival of interest during the Renaissance period.

People like Leonardo da Vinci personified the spirit of interdisciplinary exploration, which united the fields of art and science. However, the greatest strides in scientific progress were made during the period known as the Scientific Revolution.

The astronomical observations made by Galileo Galilei with the use of the telescope disproved the geocentric orthodoxy and confirmed the heliocentric model that was developed by Nicolaus Copernicus. The laws of motion and the theory of universal gravitation developed by Sir Isaac Newton fundamentally altered our understanding of the physical universe. The adherence to the Scientific Method, which places a strong focus on empirical observation, the testing of hypotheses, and the reporting of findings, has become the gold standard for scientific investigation.

The beginning of modern science coincided with the Age of Enlightenment.

During the 17th and 18th centuries, a period of history known as the Age of Enlightenment was characterized by the proliferation of rationalism and a dedication to empirical, evidence-based research. "Cogito, ergo sum" (which translates to "I think, therefore I am") was a phrase coined by the French philosopher René Descartes and is considered to be a cornerstone of contemporary philosophy and science. Reason, tolerance, and secularism were all causes that were championed by philosophers like Voltaire.

Through the promotion of reason as the supreme judge of truth, the Enlightenment was instrumental in laying the framework for modern science. Carl Linnaeus was responsible for the categorization of species during this time period. Benjamin Franklin and Antoine Lavoisier made important contributions to the field of chemistry during this same time period. It was also an age of exploration, with naturalists such as Charles Darwin setting sail on expeditions to study biodiversity and provide the groundwork for the idea of evolution. This era lasted from the 16th to the 19th centuries.

The beginning of specialized fields of study along with the beginning of the industrial revolution

The 19th century was a time of rapid expansion for several subfields within the scientific community. Mathematics, physics, and the other three branches of the natural sciences—chemistry and biology—emerged as their own separate fields of study, each with their own unique ideas, theories, and practices. The scientific community was thrown into a loop in 1859 when Charles Darwin's book "On the Origin of Species" was released. This book introduced the concept of evolution through the process of natural selection.

Concurrently, societies all across the world were undergoing profound change as a result of the Industrial Revolution. Industry as well as day-to-day living were completely disrupted by developments in metallurgy, transportation, and steam engines.

The convergence of scientific research and industrial design resulted in the invention of ground-breaking technologies such as the telegraph and the locomotive, both of which influenced the development of human history.

Quantum mechanics, general relativity, and other scientific breakthroughs of the 20th century

The 20th century represented the beginning of a new era of scientific inquiry, one that was characterized by significant shifts in our comprehension of the cosmos. The theory of relativity proposed by Albert Einstein fundamentally altered how we conceive of space and time. The strange and counterintuitive world of subatomic particles was unveiled by the theory of quantum mechanics, which was developed by such eminent scientists as Max Planck and Niels Bohr.

This century also saw a number of significant breakthroughs in the medical profession, including the identification of antibiotics, the production of vaccinations, and the creation of new surgical procedures. The development of computing technologies, which was initially sparked by Alan Turing's groundbreaking work on codebreaking during World War II, ultimately resulted in the invention of the modern computer as well as the beginning of the information technology industry.

The beginning of the age of big data science and the digital revolution

The latter part of the 20th century and the beginning of the 21st century were watershed moments in history as they signified the transition into the Digital Age and the beginning of the exponential expansion of big data. The development of personal computing, the internet, and the World Wide Web have all had a significant impact on the way in which scientific research is carried out.

The advent of the digital revolution has ushered in a new era of big data science, which sees the production of enormous datasets across a variety of disciplines. Petabytes of data are a challenge in many fields, including genomics, astronomy, climate science, and high-energy physics, to name just a few. Because of this transformation, the creation of digital infrastructure, which includes high-performance computing, data storage solutions, and data analytics tools, has become necessary.

Collaborating across professional boundaries and addressing global issues

In the past few years, there has been a growing awareness of the significance of multidisciplinary collaboration in the scientific community. The knowledge of researchers from a wide variety of professions is required in order to effectively address complex issues like climate change, pandemic preparedness, and comprehending the human brain.

The proliferation of collaborative research centers, programs that cut across academic disciplines, and open scientific platforms has made it possible for scientists to pool both their knowledge and their resources.

At this point in time, the most important focus of scientific pursuits is on resolving global problems. These problems include sustainability, the energy transition, and access to healthcare. Research in the field of environmental science focuses on mitigating the effects of climate change and reducing the loss of biodiversity, whereas research in the field of healthcare investigates ways to diagnose, cure, and prevent new diseases. The utilization of data-driven insights and the facilitation of worldwide cooperation are both made significantly easier by the presence of digital infrastructure.

Taking Into Account Ethical and Social Factors

The constantly shifting terrain of scientific inquiry has likewise brought to the foreground concerns pertaining to ethics and society. The ethical considerations that are raised by the proper application of developing technologies, such as artificial intelligence, gene editing, and biotechnology, call for the establishment of severe norms. To manage these problems successfully, science needs to maintain a sharp focus on equity, transparency, and the well-being of humanity.

A Glance Into the Future: What Does It Hold for Science?

As we move forward into the future, the terrain of scientific inquiry will undoubtedly continue to develop. New technologies, such as quantum computing, gene editing, and improved materials, present possibilities for the advancement of scientific knowledge that have never been seen before. The quest of a sustainable and equitable future is still an important objective, and the role of science in finding solutions to global problems is becoming increasingly important.

1.1 Historical perspective on scientific research

Research in the scientific realm is an essential component of human development, a demonstration of our natural inquisitiveness, and a potent driver of both innovation and discovery. The beginnings of scientific investigation may be found far back in the chronicles of history. Having a historical perspective on scientific investigation enables us to appreciate the development of this virtuous undertaking. This voyage might be described as a narrative of intellectual courage, communal knowledge, and concepts that have the power to revolutionize the way we think about the world and the universe.

Ancient Foundations: Considerations, Suggestions, and Hypotheses

Research that is now considered to be scientific can be traced back to some of the oldest human civilizations. Ancient peoples from all over the world, such as the Chinese, the Egyptians, and the Babylonians, carried out observations of the natural world in a methodical manner. For example, astronomy was one of the earliest disciplines. Ancient sky watchers tracked celestial phenomena and mapped the heavens, which led to the development of astronomy.

The ancient Greeks, especially in particular the thinkers Thales and Pythagoras, made significant contributions to the early development of scientific thought. Many people consider Thales to be the first philosopher who was also interested in science because of his emphasis on the significance of natural explanations for occurrences. Pythagoras, who is best renowned for his contributions to mathematics, was also instrumental in laying the framework for quantitative analysis in the scientific community.

Mathematics and empirical inquiry characterize the classical era of antiquity.

In classical antiquity, particularly within the Hellenistic realm, there was an uptick in interest in the scientific tradition. Aristotle's natural philosophy was the first to employ a methodical strategy for observing and classifying natural phenomena. His writings covered a wide variety of topics, such as biology, physics, and ethics, amongst others.

Euclid and Archimedes are credited for expanding the instruments available for scientific investigation through the creation of geometry and mathematical principles. In particular, Archimedes made significant contributions to the fields of mathematics and physics by articulating ideas that continue to have an impact on modern research.

The Golden Age of Islam: Preserving Tradition While Making Progress

Scholars from around the Islamic world made major contributions to a variety of scientific fields during the Islamic Golden Age, which lasted from the 8th to the 13th centuries and was also known as the Golden Age of Islam. They maintained, translated, and enhanced scientific knowledge by drawing on ancient knowledge from Greece, India, and Persia.

Al-Razi and Ibn Sina, often known as Avicenna, were two prominent figures who made significant contributions to the early stages of the development of medicine and pharmacology. Their medical treatises, which were founded on practical observation and experience, eventually came to be regarded as basic works in the field of medical history.

Al-Biruni made substantial contributions to the subject of geography, while Alhazen's pioneering work in optics established the basis for the contemporary scientific understanding of light and vision.

A shift in paradigm brought on by the Renaissance and the Scientific Revolution

An interest in the natural world, art, and knowledge had a renaissance during the Renaissance, a cultural and intellectual movement that lasted from the 14th to the 17th centuries and spanned those centuries. The interdisciplinarity that was characteristic of the time period is shown by Leonardo da Vinci's groundbreaking research in the fields of anatomy, engineering, and botany.

The beginning of the Scientific Revolution, on the other hand, is generally regarded as the defining moment in the development of scientific inquiry. The geocentric model of the cosmos was challenged by pioneering luminaries such as Nicolaus Copernicus, Galileo Galilei, and Johannes Kepler, who all contributed to the development of the heliocentric model, which transformed the field of astronomy. The use of the telescope by Galileo to make observations in astronomy that shattered long-held assumptions and served as an example of empirical inquiry.

The laws of motion and the theory of universal gravitation that Sir Isaac Newton developed provided the groundwork for classical mechanics. His work established the study of natural phenomena in accordance with a method that was both methodical and quantitative, so contributing to the consolidation of the Scientific Method as the gold standard for scientific investigation.

Empiricism and skepticism came to the fore during the Enlightenment and Age of Reason

During the 17th and 18th centuries, a period known as the Age of Enlightenment promoted the values of reason, empiricism, and the acquisition of information via the application of critical thought. René Descartes, whose famous saying "cogito, ergo sum" (I think, therefore I am) was a symbol of the movement in philosophy toward individual inquiry, was one of the thinkers who helped bring about this shift.

The scientific method, which places an emphasis on empirical evidence as a foundation for truth, was another concept that was actively promoted throughout the Enlightenment. The conceptual roots of modern science were laid by philosophers-scientists like Voltaire, who championed reason, tolerance, and secularism in addition to contributing to the development of modern science.

The Age of Enlightenment was a time of extensive natural history research, and it was during this time that Carl Linnaeus classified the many species.Naturalists like Charles Darwin set out on expeditions to gather evidence of the diversity of life on Earth, an essential step in the development of his theory that evolution occurs through the process of natural selection.

The Nineteenth Century: The Birth of Specialized Disciplines and the Development of Industry

The 19th century was a time that saw an explosion in the number of specialized scientific specialties. The four disciplines of physics, chemistry, biology, and mathematics evolved into separate fields, each having their own fundamental ideas, theoretical frameworks, and practical applications. The systematic arrangement of scientific knowledge provided a platform upon which in-depth research could be carried out.

The time period was distinguished by a number of significant discoveries and innovations. The contemporary understanding of electricity and magnetism can be credited to the contributions that Michael Faraday made to the fields of electromagnetic and thermodynamics. The ground-breaking investigations conducted by Louis Pasteur led to the establishment of the germ hypothesis of disease, which in turn revolutionized medicine and public health.

Concurrently, societies all across the world were being disrupted by the Industrial Revolution. Industry as well as day-to-day living were completely disrupted by developments in metallurgy, transportation, and steam engines. The collaboration of scientists and engineers resulted in the development of ground-breaking technologies that redirected the path of human history.

Quantum mechanics and relativity became prominent in the 20th century.

The ground-breaking theories of Albert Einstein caused a seismic upheaval in our knowledge of the cosmos during the 20th century. This shift is mostly credited to the century. The world's understanding of space and time underwent a sea change as a result of his groundbreaking theory of relativity. Understanding the behavior of things travelling at high speeds required the formulation of the theory of special relativity in 1905, which set the framework for this understanding. The theory of general relativity, which was developed in 1915, completely changed the way we saw gravity.

Simultaneously, quantum mechanics arose as a sophisticated and paradoxical theory to describe the behavior of subatomic particles. This theory was developed to explain how subatomic particles behave. Max Planck, Niels Bohr, and Erwin Schrodinger were among the pioneering physicists who presented the peculiar characteristics of quantum physics to the rest of the world. The breakthroughs in quantum physics have paved the way for a revolution in technology and have reshaped our understanding of the atomic and subatomic realms.

The Information Age and the Science of Big Data

The transition from the Analog Age to the Digital Age may be traced back to the second part of the 20th century and the beginning of the 21st century. The introduction of personal computing, the internet, and the World Wide Web has brought about a sea change in the manner in which scientific research is carried out. Both the sharing of information and the working together of people are now conducted on a worldwide scale.

The creation of big data science is one of the most important advances that has taken place in this period. Research in a variety of domains, including genetics, astronomy, climate science, and high-energy physics, today frequently works with enormous datasets, which are frequently measured in petabytes. In order to effectively handle and analyze such large amounts of data, digital infrastructure, which typically consists of high-performance computing, various data storage systems, and various tools for data analytics, has emerged as an essential component of scientific research.

Collaborating across professional boundaries and addressing global issues

In recent years, there has been a growing awareness of how important it is to collaborate across disciplinary lines. The knowledge of researchers from a wide variety of professions is required in order to effectively address complex global concerns such as the mitigation of climate change, the preparation for pandemics, and the comprehension of the human brain. The proliferation of collaborative research centers, programs that cut across academic disciplines, and open scientific platforms has made it possible for scientists to pool both their knowledge and their resources.

It has become increasingly important for the scientific enterprise to focus on finding solutions to global problems such as sustainability, energy transition, and access to healthcare. The goal of research in environmental science is to combat climate change, biodiversity loss, and the degradation of ecosystems, whereas research in healthcare focuses on the creation of therapies and vaccines for newly emerging diseases. In these global endeavors, the role that digital infrastructure plays in fostering international collaborations, harnessing the power of data-driven insights, and making headway toward finding answers is critical.

Taking Into Account Ethical and Social Factors

The constantly shifting terrain of scientific inquiry has thrust questions of ethics and social responsibility into the front. The ethical considerations that are raised by the proper application of developing technologies, such as artificial intelligence, gene editing, and biotechnology, call for the establishment of severe norms. The relationship between science and society is complex, and it is essential to engage in responsible scientific activity in order to solve issues that are both ethical and societal in nature.

A Look Ahead: What the Future Holds for Scientific Investigation

The exponential rise of information, the development of emergent technologies, and the quest of global answers to pressing concerns will all have an impact on the future of scientific research. In the future decades, emerging technologies such as quantum computing, gene editing, and improved materials will offer chances for scientific innovation that have never been seen before.

Science plays a pivotal part in finding solutions to the world's most intractable problems, and achieving a transition to a future that is both sustainable and egalitarian is a goal that we all share. Research on renewable energy sources, attempts to counteract climate change, and other sustainability-related topics are expected to take the lead in scientific inquiry in the near future. The ethical use of emerging technologies as well as its incorporation into everyday life will continue to be at the center of the progression of scientific knowledge.

The Coming to Terms with Human Curiosity and the Advancement of Technology

The historical perspective on scientific study serves as a tribute to human inquisitiveness, intellectual discovery, and the never-ending pursuit of knowledge. Following in the footsteps of ancient thinkers and astronomers all the way up to the quantum physicists and genetic scientists of today, the path of scientific inquiry is a representation of the progression of humankind.

Our comprehension of both the natural world and the cosmos owes a debt of gratitude to the scientific revolution, which broke down barriers of culture, geography, and even time. It has given rise to groundbreaking technology, fundamentally altered entire industries, and made significant strides in medical care. When we look to the future, the collaborative and interdisciplinary nature of modern research holds the potential of finding solutions to some of humanity's most pressing problems, such as access to healthcare and the preservation of the environment.

The progression of scientific inquiry across time serves as a useful reminder that, in our quest for knowledge and advancement, we literally stand on the shoulders of intellectual giants, and that the potential for new discoveries is virtually limitless. It is evidence of the ever-present human spirit of inquiry, investigation, and the never-ending pursuit of comprehension, and it is a monument to this character.

1.2 The digital revolution's impact on science

The digital revolution, which is frequently referred to as the third industrial revolution, has had a significant and game-changing impact on practically every facet of human existence. The rapid development of digital technology has had a tremendous impact on science, which is both one of the most important and dynamic domains of human activity, and has generated significant forward movement in the subject. A new era of scientific discovery, collaboration, and invention has begun as a direct result of the convergence of digital infrastructure, high-performance computing, data analytics, and global connection. In the course of this investigation, we will look into the myriad of ways in which the digital revolution has permanently altered the terrain of scientific study.

1. **Science that is Driven by Data in This Age of Big Data**
   As a result of the digital revolution, scientists now have access to a vast treasury of data, which they can use for the purposes of research and analysis. The era of big data research has begun as a direct result of the widespread availability of sensors, satellites, and other technologies that are able to generate massive volumes of data. Data sets with sizes measured in petabytes and exabytes are being produced in a variety of scientific disciplines, including astronomy, particle physics, climate research, and genomics.
   Scientists are now able to store, organize, and access these enormous datasets thanks to advancements in data storage and retrieval technology. The use of high-performance computers, in conjunction with parallel processing and sophisticated algorithms, makes it easier to analyze large amounts of data and get valuable insights from them. This methodology, which is driven by data, has revolutionized research in a wide variety of sectors, including economics, environmental science, and healthcare.
2. **The Speeding Up of Research Using Computer Simulation**
   Experimentation is a common part of scientific study, and the digital revolution brought about significant changes to the way in which experiments are carried out. Researchers are able to model their theories and test them using sophisticated computer simulations, eliminating the need for time-consuming and

resource-intensive actual tests. This is especially clear in areas of study such as the study of materials, the discovery of new drugs, and the modeling of climate.

Through the use of simulations, scientists have been able to investigate scenarios that could not be carried out in real life or that would violate ethical standards. For instance, in the field of pharmaceutical research, potential medication candidates can now undergo virtual efficacy and safety testing before undergoing time-consuming and expensive clinical studies.

3. **High-Performance Computing: A Propelling Force in the Scientific Community**

   The development of high-performance computing, sometimes known as HPC, is one of the most significant aspects of the influence that the digital revolution has had on the scientific community. The field of computational science has entered a new age with the advent of technologies such as supercomputers, clusters of processors, and cloud computing resources. High-performance computing offers previously inconceivable levels of complexity in modeling, data analysis, and simulations.

   High-Performance Computing (HPC) is utilized in disciplines such as Astrophysics to mimic the birth and development of the universe. High-performance computing is essential to climate modeling, which uses it to forecast global weather patterns and evaluate the effects of climate change. Computational chemistry is used in the discovery of new drugs in order to search through millions of molecules for possible therapeutic candidates.

4. **The Revolution in DNA Sequencing and Genomics**

   The sequencing of the human genome and the subsequent development of genomics are two significant achievements that can be attributed to the information technology revolution. The sequencing of DNA used to be a tedious and time-consuming procedure, but recent developments in high-throughput sequencing technologies have completely changed the landscape of the field.

Researchers now have the ability to sequence complete genomes in a relatively short amount of time at a reasonable cost, which paves the way for customized therapy, genetic disease analyses, and research of evolutionary biology. The Human Genome Project was a historic endeavor that showcased the synergy between technology and biology. It was made feasible by the use of high-performance computing and intensive data analysis.

5. **The advancement of artificial intelligence and machine learning**

   In recent years, artificial intelligence (AI) and machine learning (ML) have emerged as crucial instruments in the realm of scientific investigation. Data analysis, pattern recognition, predictive modeling, and even autonomous testing are all possible thanks to the tools available today.

   AI has many applications in the medical field, including disease diagnosis, the determination of therapy alternatives, and the examination of medical pictures. In the field of astronomy, ML algorithms can be used to identify celestial objects, and in the field of ecology, they can examine massive datasets in order to gain a better understanding of species distributions and biodiversity.

6. **Participation Via Distant Means and the Use of Virtual Laboratories**

   Not only has the digital revolution had an impact on how research is carried out, but it has also modified the ways in which scientists work together. The elimination of geographical constraints and the introduction of internet technologies for collaborative working have paved the way for more international collaboration.

   The ability to remotely access experiments, share data, and conduct collaborative research in real time is available to scientists. This transition has been especially significant in the wake of global issues such as the COVID-19 pandemic, where experts from all over the world collaborated to gain a better understanding of the virus, produce vaccinations, and communicate vital information with one another.

7. **Open-Source Research and Free Public Access**

    The open scientific movement, which places an emphasis on transparency, data sharing, and unrestricted access to research findings, was also spawned as a direct result of the rise of digital technologies. Scientists are now able to freely cooperate, publish their work, and share datasets because to the availability of online platforms and repositories.

    Open access publishing has made it possible for more people to have access to scientific research, which has resulted in more people being able to benefit from scientific knowledge. This method of conducting open science encourages the rapid sharing of findings, studies that replicate those findings, and global collaboration.

8. **Methods of Communicating and Visualizing Scientific Data**

    Not only has the application of digital technology improved the practice of science, but it has also improved the communication of scientific concepts. The use of scientific visualization technologies gives researchers the ability to communicate complicated data and ideas not just to their colleagues but also to the general public.

    These tools make science more approachable and interesting to a wider audience, and they range from interactive visualizations of climate change to 3D models of the structures of proteins. They are extremely important in the dissemination of scientific information, the education of the general public, and the raising of public awareness of scientific issues.

9. **Concerns Regarding Ethical Behavior and Cybersecurity**

    Concerns regarding data ethics and the integrity of digital systems have been brought to the forefront in light of our growing reliance on digital technologies.

    The conduct of scientific research results in the production of huge quantities of confidential data, such as patient records in the medical field and proprietary technology in the engineering field. Securing this data and making certain that it is used in an ethical manner have become of the utmost importance. Researchers and institutions have a responsibility to develop stringent cybersecurity measures and adhere to ethical norms in order to strike a healthy balance between the advancement of science and the protection of personal data.

10. **The Confluence of Different Fields**

The boundaries between conventional scientific fields have also become more porous as a result of the digital revolution. As an illustration, the area of bioinformatics has recently arisen as a multidisciplinary one that incorporates aspects of biology, computer science, and data analysis. Geoinformatics, on the other hand, combines geography, geology, and computer science in order to evaluate spatial data.

These intersections of multidisciplinary research are reshaping the way we tackle difficult scientific topics by shifting our attention to comprehensive solutions that draw from a variety of specialized areas.

The Coming of the Digital Age in the Scientific Community

The influence of the digital revolution on the scientific community has ushered in a new era of investigation and discovery. The limits of what is feasible in scientific investigation have been pushed further out thanks to advances in technology that make it possible to analyse massive volumes of data, simulate complicated systems, and work together across the globe.

The rate at which scientific progress is made accelerates, and new frontiers are opened up as we continue to harness the power of digital technology. A digital renaissance in science has been sparked by the digital revolution. This can be seen in many different areas, such as the revolution in genomics, which has led to the creation of AI-driven drug discovery, the study of the cosmos with supercomputers, and the development of sustainable technologies. It is a monument to human ingenuity, teamwork, and the persistent pursuit of knowledge in this age of digital technology.

1.3 The current state of scientific infrastructure

The scientific infrastructure consists of the instruments, technology, and resources that are essential for the advancement of scientific knowledge. It is the foundation upon which research and innovation are built. Experimentation, data analysis, and the transmission of knowledge are some of the activities that are supported by this system, which incorporates both digital and physical components. When we investigate the current state of the scientific infrastructure, we discover that it is a dynamic landscape that is defined by both great accomplishments and critical concerns. This investigation sheds light on the infrastructure that supports the contemporary scientific endeavor, illuminating everything from cutting-edge computing resources to ultra-modern laboratory facilities.

1. **State-of-the-Art Laboratories and Equipment**

    The quality of laboratories and the capabilities they offer have a direct bearing on the breadth and depth of scientific inquiries; laboratories are the beating heart of scientific discovery. Significant technological and instrumental breakthroughs have led to the current state of laboratory infrastructure, which is characterized by those advancements. Researchers are able to investigate phenomena at the atomic and molecular levels, unravel complicated biological processes, and study the mysteries of the universe thanks to high-tech equipment such as mass spectrometers, electron microscopes, and gene sequencers.

    In areas of study such as biotechnology, materials science, and environmental science, laboratories are outfitted with the most up-to-date instruments for activities such as DNA sequencing, the synthesis of nanomaterials, and the monitoring of environmental conditions. These facilities give scientists the ability to push the limits of what is known and find practical applications, such as therapies for medical conditions and solutions for renewable energy problems.

2. **Facilities for High-Performance Computing (often abbreviated HPC)**
   The availability of high-performance computing facilities is essential to the advancement of
   scientific knowledge, particularly in those subfields of study that call for extensive amounts of computational simulation and data processing. The current state of high-performance computing infrastructure is characterized by exponential development in both the amount of computing power and the capabilities to handle data. Researchers are now able to tackle difficult issues because to the development of supercomputers and clusters of processors that are capable of completing quadrillions of computations per second.
   In fields such as climate modeling, astrophysics, and drug discovery, which require enormous amounts of computational power due to the complexity of their models and the huge datasets they use, these facilities are essential.
   The convergence of high-performance computing and artificial intelligence is bringing about a sea change in scientific computing, elevating data analysis, and hastening the pace of research in fields such as genomics and machine learning.

3. **Solutions for Data Storage and Centers for Processing**
   The deluge of data that is produced by scientific research makes it necessary to develop reliable solutions for data storage and management. The current status of the data infrastructure consists of high-capacity data centers that have the ability to store information on the petabyte and exabyte scales. The critical research data stored in these data centers are protected by multiple layers of redundancy as well as other security measures.
   In the field of genomics, for example, the storing of huge datasets containing DNA sequencing information is a herculean

undertaking. It is absolutely necessary to have data centers that are equipped with effective data retrieval and backup technologies in order to store all of this genetic information. In addition, there has been a rise in the use of cloud-based storage solutions, which provide researchers all over the world with flexibility and accessibility.

4. **Online Communities For Collaborative Research**

The current status of the scientific infrastructure lays a large focus on research collaboration platforms, which is especially important when taking into consideration global concerns and multidisciplinary research. Real-time collaboration among scientists located in different parts of the world is made easier by the use of virtual laboratories, online collaboration tools, and shared resources.

These systems make it possible to participate in experiments remotely, share data, and conduct collaborative analyses. They have proved particularly helpful in addressing global concerns, such as pandemics and climate change, among other such challenges. Researchers now have the ability to pool their knowledge and resources, which enables them to tackle difficult issues on a scale and with an efficiency that was previously impossible.

5. **Facilities Capable of Providing Advanced Imaging and Visualization**

Our comprehension of the natural world has improved as a direct result of the incorporation of highly developed imaging and visualization technologies into the infrastructure of the scientific community. Cryo-electron microscopy, functional magnetic resonance imaging (fMRI), and confocal microscopy are some of the techniques that have provided previously unattainable insights into the structure and function of biological systems, as well as materials and nanoscale structures.

Researchers are given the ability to engage with complicated datasets by using scientific visualization facilities, which are frequently outfitted with immersive technology such as virtual reality. The capacity to visualize and comprehend complex procedures has been significantly improved as a result of the development of new tools in disciplines such as structural biology, neuroscience, and materials science.

6. **Infrastructure that is both sustainable and friendly to the environment**

   Making scientific infrastructure more sustainable and environmentally friendly is becoming more and more importance as the world works toward achieving its sustainability goals. Standards for environmentally responsible construction are being implemented in research facilities and laboratories, and renewable energy sources and energy-saving technologies are also being developed. This movement demonstrates a dedication to lessening the impact that scientific study has on the surrounding environment.

   Green chemistry, which encourages the development of chemical processes that are less harmful to the environment, is a good example of a project that demonstrates sustainable infrastructure practices. In order to decrease waste and lessen the influence that research has on the surrounding environment, more and more laboratories are adopting the concepts of green chemistry.

7. **Initiatives to Open Up Science and Access to the Internet**

The contemporary state of the infrastructure supporting scientific research is also characterized

by a drive toward open science and open access initiatives. Platforms and repositories that are accessible online make it easier for researchers to openly share their discoveries, datasets, and publications. Publishing that is open to anybody with internet connection has grown increasingly common, which has increased the public's and researchers' access to the body of scientific information.

These programs foster openness, collaboration, and the speedy distribution of acquired knowledge. They are especially helpful in addressing global difficulties, where the free interchange of information speeds up research and innovation. This is one of the areas in which they shine.

Concerns and Things to Take Into Account

Sustainability: Despite efforts to make infrastructure more sustainable, there are still hurdles to be overcome in lowering the environmental impact of scientific research, especially in sectors that require a significant amount of energy.

When working with large datasets, it is necessary to implement strong data security and privacy procedures in order to protect any sensitive information that may be there.

Equity and Accessibility: Ensuring that all researchers, irrespective of where they are located geographically or the resources they have at their disposal economically, have access to cutting-edge infrastructure is a challenge that calls for international collaboration.

Collaborative Interdisciplinary study: Although interdisciplinary study is encouraged, it might be difficult to bridge the gap between scientific fields that have historically been considered separate.

Ethical Considerations New technologies, such as gene editing and artificial intelligence, necessitate the development of ethical principles and frameworks in order to resolve potential ethical conundrums.

The situation that scientific infrastructure is in right now is reflective of an exciting era of growth and innovation. A new era of scientific discovery and cross-disciplinary investigation has begun as a direct result of the proliferation of cutting-edge research facilities, high-performance computing, data management technologies, and worldwide collaboration platforms.

Sustainability, data security, accessibility, and ethical considerations are all issues that need to be addressed by researchers as the landscape of scientific infrastructure continues to be reshaped by the ongoing digital revolution. As the scientific community strives to harness the full potential of technology and information for the welfare of humanity and a deeper understanding of the world, the continual growth of scientific infrastructure is a monument to the scientific community's resilience and adaptability.

1.4 The challenges and opportunities presented by digitalization

The process of utilizing digital technologies to modify many elements of society has resulted in a wave of changes that have presented both challenges and opportunities. This process is referred to as digitalization. As we make our way through this digital revolution, it is imperative that we acknowledge and take into account the challenges and opportunities that come along with it. This investigation digs into the complex terrain of digitization, illuminating both the difficulties it creates and the countless opportunities it opens up.

The Obstacles:

1. **The divide caused by digital technology:**
   The "digital divide," which refers to the gap between individuals and communities that have access to digital technologies and those that do not, is one of the most urgent concerns that digitalization presents. Because of this difference, people may not have equal access to information, educational opportunities, or economic prospects. The closing of the digital divide is a pressing issue for modern society, and concerted efforts need to be made in this direction to ensure that people from all walks of life may reap the benefits of technological progress.

2. **Protecting the Privacy and Safety of Data:**
   The advent of digitalization has resulted in the gathering, storage, and transmission of enormous volumes of private and confidential data. A rising concern is making the safeguarding of this data against data breaches and the protection of user privacy. The increasing frequency of cyberattacks and data breaches highlights the significance of stringent data security measures, legislation, and cybersecurity policies for the purpose of protecting digital ecosystems.

3. **Being Fired From Your Job:**
   Concerns regarding the potential loss of jobs due to job displacement have been expressed as a result of the automation and digitization of numerous processes and tasks. While digitalization has the potential to improve efficiency and production, it also has the risk of making some types of occupations obsolete. To overcome this obstacle, the workforce will need to undergo retraining and further education in order to adapt to the ever-shifting requirements of various jobs, and there will also need to be an emphasis placed on the transition to new employment opportunities in the digital era.
4. **An Excessive Amount of Information:**
   There is a risk of experiencing information overload as a result of the rapid growth of digital content and information. It can be very challenging to sift through massive amounts of data in order to locate information that is precise and pertinent. This problem necessitates the development of efficient information retrieval, organizing, and curation approaches in order to assist individuals and organizations in effectively navigating the digital landscape.
5. **Dangers posed by Cybersecurity:**

The threat posed by cyberattacks has become more significant as a result of the increasing digitalization of vital infrastructure, financial institutions, and communication networks.

The integrity of digital systems can be compromised, important services can be disrupted, and sensitive data can be stolen by malicious actors. The difficulty lies in continuously improving cybersecurity procedures in order to protect against ever-evolving attacks and weaknesses.

Occasions to seize:

1. **Increased Availability of Information and Educational Opportunities:**
   The advent of digital technology has made information as well

as educational opportunities more accessible to more people. Knowledge is made more accessible to individuals all over the world thanks to the proliferation of online resources, e-learning platforms, and digital libraries. Because of this possibility, educational inequities may be narrowed and people may be given the means to learn new skills and expand their existing knowledge base.

2. **Improved Methods of Communication and Collaborative Effort:**
The ways in which individuals interact with one another and work together have been revolutionized by digitalization. These technologies, which range from video conferencing and instant messaging to tools for virtual collaboration, have made it simpler for individuals and groups to collaborate across geographic borders. This potential fosters international cooperation, quickens the pace of invention, and makes it easier for people to share information in real time.

3. **Efficiency and automation in relation to:**
The widespread adoption of automation and digitalization has resulted in increased levels of both efficiency and production. Organizations are able to cut their operational expenses while simultaneously delivering products and services of a higher quality if they streamline their processes, automate their regular tasks, and make use of data analytics.

4. **Personalization and the Experience of the Customer:**
The advent of digitalization has made it possible for businesses to tailor their wares and services to the specific requirements of individual clients. Companies are able to better satisfy their customers and earn their loyalty when they conduct research on customer data and preferences and then modify their product and service offerings accordingly. For example, in e-commerce, recommendation engines are used to make product suggestions to customers based on their previous purchases.

5. **Creativity and the Development of New Business Models:**
   The advent of digitalization makes it easier to investigate novel concepts and business models by furnishing individuals with the instruments and resources necessary to do so. Particularly startups have a unique opportunity to take advantage of digital platforms and cloud computing in order to develop innovative goods and services. The rise of the sharing economy, fintech, and the app economy are all prime examples of the opportunities that digitization has made available.
6. **Sustainability in Relation to the Environment:**
   The ability of digitalization to enable more intelligent resource management is one way it can help the environment become more sustainable. For instance, smart grids improve the efficiency with which electricity is distributed, while Internet of Things devices may monitor and cut down on water usage. In addition, the digital transformation of sectors may lead to a reduction in physical waste and the adoption of methods that are friendlier to the environment.
7. **Telemedicine and the Increasing Availability of Healthcare:**

The advent of digital technology has significantly increased accessibility to various medical treatments, most notably telemedicine. Patients are able to receive medical consultations and access healthcare information online, which helps to bridge geographical boundaries and improves access to healthcare, particularly in locations that are underserved or distant.

The advent of digital technology has fundamentally altered the ways in which people live their lives, conduct their careers, and engage with the wider world. It also brings great opportunities for growth, as well as complicated difficulties that require thoughtful consideration and action in response to them. It is essential, in order to effectively navigate this disruptive era, to find a way to strike a balance between seizing the benefits that digitization presents and meeting the obstacles that it poses.

It is vital to make efforts to bridge the digital divide, preserve data privacy, and improve cybersecurity in order to guarantee that the benefits of digitalization are shared by all. In addition, initiatives aimed at reskilling and upskilling workers can assist individuals in adapting to the shifting requirements of their jobs, hence lowering the risk of job displacement.

As the process of digitalization continues to advance, society must maintain its capacity for adaptability and proactivity in order to keep pace with the latest technical advances and make the most of the opportunities these advancements present. The advent of the digital age has presented humanity with a once-in-a-generation chance to mold the future, propel innovation, and construct a world that is more inclusive, efficient, and sustainable.

Chapter 2

Foundations of Digital Infrastructure

The digital infrastructure that exists now serves as the support system for modern society in the 21st century. The unseen network of technologies, systems, and processes that ensures the smooth operation of our day-to-day lives, from communication and transportation to healthcare and education, is what we refer to as the "Internet of Things." In a world that is becoming more linked, having a fundamental understanding of digital infrastructure is absolutely necessary since it affects how we live, work, and communicate with one another.

This investigation takes us on an in-depth dive into the fundamentals of digital infrastructure, including its historical development, important components, problems, and the revolutionary impact it has on a variety of different industries.

1. **A Brief Introductory Discussion on Digital Infrastructure The Concept and Its Significance**

    The term "digital infrastructure" refers to the technologies and systems that lie beneath the surface and make possible digital communication, data storage, and processing. It forms the basis upon which the digital age is built, influencing the ways in which we conduct business, engage with one another, and gain access to services. The Internet of Things (IoT), cloud computing, and smart cities are all examples of recent technical advancements that have been made possible by the development of digital infrastructure.

The fact that it is so pervasive in our everyday lives—as seen by the electronics we employ, the computer systems we depend on, and the data we produce—highlights the significance of the phenomenon. The historical development of digital infrastructure is important to comprehend since it sheds light on its current significance as well as its promise for the future.

Development across Time

The evolution of digital infrastructure over the past few decades has been nothing short of astounding. The fundamental components of digital infrastructure have undergone significant development at an accelerated rate ever since the invention of the transistor in the middle of the 20th century and the establishment of the World Wide Web in the 1990s.

The development of the Internet, the introduction of personal computers, and the trend toward mobile devices are all significant steps along the way. The way in which we connect with one another, conduct business, and gain access to information has been fundamentally transformed as a result of developments in technology. The examination of the underlying components of digital infrastructure begins with a look back at the historical development of digital infrastructure.

2. **Components Crucial to the Operation of the Digital Infrastructure**

The digital services that we rely on are provided by a combination of several fundamental components that work together to form what is known as the "digital infrastructure." To fully comprehend the nuances of digital infrastructure, it is necessary to have a solid understanding of these component parts.

Toys and Games

The physical components of the digital infrastructure, such as servers, routers, switches, and data storage devices, are the essential elements of this infrastructure. The provision of the computational power, data processing capabilities, and storage capacity essential to the operation of digital services is made possible by these tangible devices, which serve as the structural pillars of digital systems.

pc programing

Users and various components of hardware are able to interact with one another thanks to various kinds of software, ranging from operating systems to application software. This software layer contains the code that enables web applications, mobile applications, and other types of digital services to function. The software component plays an essential role in the management of data, the execution of tasks, and the provision of a seamless experience for users.

The power of networking

Connecting devices and systems is accomplished through the use of a networking infrastructure, which includes routers, switches, and protocols. This makes it possible to transmit data. Networking technologies, such as the Transmission Control Protocol/Internet Protocol (TCP/IP), are essential to the operation of digital communication on a worldwide scale. The Internet is itself a massive network that is made up of other networks.

The phrase "data centers"

Data centers are the nerve centers of the internet's underlying infrastructure. They house the servers and storage devices that are responsible for storing and managing data. They play an essential part in ensuring that data is both available and accessible to users. The proliferation of cloud computing has brought into sharper focus the critical role that data centers play in the contemporary digital infrastructure.

Protection against cyberattacks

Cybersecurity is a crucial component that protects digital infrastructure from dangers such as attacks, data breaches, and other breaches in security. It incorporates a wide range of precautions, including as firewalls and encryption, as well as intrusion detection systems and security rules. In a world that is becoming more linked, the protection of digital infrastructure from cyber threats is of the utmost importance.

Computing in the Cloud

Cloud computing, which is sometimes thought of as a service for digital infrastructure, enables on-demand access to a variety of computing resources, including data storage and application software. It provides scalability and flexibility, hence minimizing the requirement for significant infrastructure located on-premises. Cloud services, such as Infrastructure as a Service (IaaS) and Software as a Service (SaaS), play a vital role in the ecosystem of digital infrastructure.

3. **The infrastructure of the Internet and other forms of communication**

   The Beginnings of the World Wide Web

   One of the most essential aspects of today's digital infrastructure is the Internet, which is comprised of a worldwide network of computers that are linked together. Its origins may be traced all the way back to ARPANET, which was a U.S. A project that was started by the Department of Defense in the late 1960s. The Advanced Research Projects Agency Network (ARPANET) was a precursor to the Internet that connected four major institutions.

   The Internet began as a tool for conducting research but has now developed into a platform for public discussion. Tim Berners-Lee's invention of the World Wide Web in 1989 was a watershed moment in the evolution of how people access and exchange information. Since that time, the Internet has experienced phenomenal expansion, which has enabled it to link billions of users and provide a platform for a wide range of digital services.

Providers of Internet Service (also known as ISPs)

Internet Service Providers, sometimes known as ISPs, are an essential component of the landscape of digital infrastructure. They are accountable for ensuring that end users have access to the Internet, regardless of whether or not the connection is wired or wireless. The highly competitive market for Internet service providers has prompted improvements in connectivity, such as the rollout of fiber-optic networks and broadband internet access.

Satellites and Cables Beneath the Sea

The Internet's ability to function on a global scale is dependent on an intricate network of communication satellites and undersea cables. Subsea cables, which are strung down the bottom of the ocean, link the continents and allow for the transfer of data on a global scale. Internet access can be provided to locations that are geographically isolated or underserved via the use of satellites that are positioned in geostationary or low Earth orbit.

The Rise of the 5G Revolution

The introduction of 5G technology marks a significant new step forward in the development of communication infrastructure. 5G is going to revolutionize the way we connect to one another and communicate since it will have quicker speeds, lower latency, and higher capacity. It has the potential to power gadgets for the Internet of Things, driverless vehicles, and applications for augmented reality.

4. **Infrastructure for transportation and technologically advanced cities**

    The abbreviation ITS stands for "intelligent transportation systems"

    The development of digital infrastructure has become an increasingly important component of today's transportation networks due to its ability to improve both safety and efficiency. Intelligent Transportation Systems (ITS) are systems that make use of technology to improve highway safety, traffic flow management, and traffic congestion management. ITS is comprised of various components, some of which include traffic management systems, intelligent traffic signals, and connected vehicles.

The Function of the Internet of Things in Smart Cities
The development of digital infrastructure has prompted a paradigm change in urban design, which has given rise to the concept of smart cities. The Internet of Things (IoT) makes it possible for cities to collect data in real time on a variety of topics, ranging from the state of the environment to the amount of energy used. The decisions that are made in cities as a result of this data make cities more sustainable, efficient, and livable.

Vehicles that Drive Themselves
The advancement of self-driving vehicles is strongly reliant on the development of digital infrastructure. Autonomous automobiles and trucks rely on sensors, connection, and artificial intelligence algorithms to navigate and make judgments as they drive themselves. It is possible that in the future of transportation, autonomous vehicles may help minimize the number of accidents that occur in traffic and boost the efficiency of transportation.

The Obstacles and the Future of Sustainability
As the infrastructure of transportation becomes increasingly digital, it will also confront increased issues in terms of sustainability. At the convergence of transportation and digital infrastructure, there are many factors to take into consideration, including the amount of energy that data centers use, the effect that electric vehicle batteries have on the environment, and the requirement for safe communication networks.

5. **Infrastructure for Healthcare and Telemedicine Services**
   The abbreviation for "Electronic Health Records" (EHR)
   The introduction of electronic health records (also known as

EHR) is one of the ways that digital infrastructure is disrupting the healthcare industry. EHR systems allow for centralized, digital access to the health records of patients, which results in an improvement in patient care, a reduction in medical errors, and an increase in the use of telemedicine.

The Combined Use of Telehealth and Telemedicine

Utilizing digital infrastructure, telehealth and telemedicine allow for the delivery of healthcare treatments to remote patients. Without having to physically visit a doctor's office, patients can communicate with their healthcare providers for the purposes of consultations, diagnoses, and even treatment. Because it allows for care to be provided while limiting the need for direct physical contact, telemedicine has shown to be particularly useful during times of public health crisis.

Devices for Your Body That You Can Wear

Another component of the digital healthcare infrastructure is the growth of wearable devices such as smartwatches and fitness trackers. Individuals are given the ability to take a more proactive role in the management of their health through the use of these devices, which monitor vital signs, physical activity, and health metrics.

Concerns Regarding Personal Information and Safety

Significant issues relating to patients' right to privacy and data protection must be addressed by the infrastructure supporting digital healthcare. It is of the utmost importance to protect patient data from being exposed to breaches and to guarantee the privacy of telemedicine sessions. In order to do this, effective cybersecurity measures and compliance with healthcare standards are required.

6. Institutional Support for Education

Platforms for Electronic Learning

E-learning systems, made possible by advances in digital infrastructure, have fundamentally changed the educational landscape. Learners are provided with a versatile and easily accessible method of acquiring knowledge through the use of these platforms, which provide online courses, interactive materials, and virtual classrooms.

The Gap Between Education and Technology
The digital gap is one of the most urgent problems that must be solved in the educational infrastructure. Because not all students have access to the essential gadgets and high-speed Internet, this can make it more difficult for them to succeed in their academic pursuits. Overcoming this difference is necessary in order to provide equal access to educational opportunities.

Technology in Education and Online Resources
The digital infrastructure that supports educational technology (EdTech) has resulted in an abundance of online resources being made available to users. These materials enrich the educational experience and encourage students to continue their education throughout their lives. Some examples of these resources are digital textbooks, interactive simulations, and video lectures.

The Prospects for the Field of Education
Learning will look very different in the future as a result of the intersection of digital infrastructure and education. One of the most anticipated developments in the field of immersive education is the growing use of virtual reality (VR) and augmented reality (AR). In addition, unique educational experiences may be adjusted to the needs of each individual student thanks to AI-driven learning pathways.

7. **Infrastructure of the Financial Sector and Financial Technology**
Systems of Electronic Transactions
Transactions involving money have become much simpler because to the proliferation of digital payment methods like mobile wallets and contactless payments. The proliferation of online payment methods has repercussions for both the conventional

banking system and the way individual people handle their financial affairs.

Blockchain technology and virtual currency

The underlying technology of cryptocurrencies like Bitcoin, known as blockchain, is credited with revolutionizing the financial architecture of the world. Its distributed and secure ledger technology has the potential to revolutionize a variety of industries, including supply chains, financial transactions, and more.

The Growth of New Financial Technology Businesses

Startups in the financial technology industry (often known as "fintech") are using digital infrastructure to develop new types of financial services. These start-up companies provide answers for a wide range of problems, including peer-to-peer lending, robo-advisors, and digital insurance platform providers.

Problems Associated with Regulations

There will be issues for regulators brought on by the incorporation of fintech into the traditional financial system. In this rapidly changing environment, governments and financial institutions will need to make adjustments in order to maintain consumer protection, cybersecurity, and financial stability.

8. Infrastructure Relating to Energy and the Environment

Management of energy and intelligent grids

Through the use of smart grids, digital infrastructure plays an essential part in the management of energy. These grids make it possible to distribute energy more effectively, with real-time monitoring and modifications to maximize efficiency in terms of energy usage. Consumers are also given the ability to monitor and control their own energy consumption by energy management systems.

Internet of Things and Environmental Monitoring

Monitoring of air quality, water quality, and meteorological conditions are all facilitated by environmental infrastructure that makes use of IoT devices. These data are used to inform environmental legislation, disaster response activities, and initiatives to promote sustainability.

Integration of Renewable Energy Sources

The integration of renewable energy sources into the grid is facilitated by the presence of digital infrastructure. Digital technologies are essential to the management of renewable energy sources like solar, wind, and hydropower in order to maintain a reliable and sustainable energy supply.

Methods That Are Ecologically Sound

Initiatives aimed at promoting sustainability are an essential component of today's energy and environmental infrastructure. Measures to increase the efficiency of data centers and requirements for environmentally friendly buildings are among the ways that digital infrastructure is evolving to lessen its impact on the environment.

Problems with the Existing Digital Infrastructure

Dangers posed by Cyberspace

The ever-present risk of cyberattacks is one of the most critical issues posed by digital infrastructure. Constant attempts are being made by malicious actors to break into digital systems, steal data, or disrupt services. In order to protect against these dangers, you will need solid cybersecurity measures as well as a quick response to incidents.

Concerns About the Privacy of Data

There are issues raised over data privacy due to the gathering and use of personal data by the components of digital infrastructure. The maintenance of a healthy equilibrium between the usefulness of data and the preservation of individual privacy is a continuous concern that has led to the creation of data protection rules such as the General Data preservation Regulation (GDPR) of the European Union.

Resilience of the Infrastructure

The digital infrastructure needs to be able to withstand disruptions brought on by things like natural catastrophes, technical problems, or cyberattacks. It is a difficult issue to ensure that key services will continue to operate normally in the face of disruptions of this kind.

Inclusion in the Digital Age

The digital gap is still a big problem, as evidenced by the fact that many people do not have access to the digital infrastructure that is necessary for participation in the digital era. In order to address the issue of digital inclusion, access must be provided, devices must be made accessible, and digital literacy initiatives must be established in underserved regions.

The Prospects for the Digital Infrastructure of the Future
New and Upcoming Technologies

Emerging technologies such as quantum computing, 6G wireless networks, and edge computing are set to transform the landscape and are contributing to the ongoing evolution of digital infrastructure. This progress is on a continual trajectory. The advent of quantum computing may usher in a new era of data processing and cryptography, while the advent of 6G networks may usher in an era of connectivity that is both much quicker and more dependable.

Infrastructure for Developing Countries and Emerging Markets

Emerging markets are experiencing a period of fast expansion of their digital infrastructure, which has the potential to revolutionize economies and enhance living standards. The proliferation of mobile connectivity and digital payment systems are helping to make financial inclusion more feasible, and developments in telemedicine and e-learning are making it possible to receive quality healthcare and education from the comfort of one's own home.

Taking Into Account Ethical and Legal Implications

Ethical and legal issues need to be addressed as the digital infrastructure that supports our lives becomes more embedded in our daily routines. Concerns regarding digital privacy, data ownership, algorithmic prejudice, and the ethical application of developing technologies are included in this category of concerns. In order to safeguard persons and sustain ethical norms, the construction of comprehensive legal frameworks is absolutely necessary.

The underpinnings of today's digital infrastructure are intricately entwined with the structure of contemporary civilization. To successfully navigate the intricate, linked, and continuously changing digital world, it is essential to have a solid understanding of these fundamentals. The Internet, transportation, healthcare, education, finance, and energy are just a few examples of how digital infrastructure influences how we work, live, and interact with one another.

When we think about the future, it is clear that the digital infrastructure will continue to advance, which will result in the emergence of both new problems and new opportunities.

The growth of ethical and regulatory frameworks, the incorporation of developing technology, and the extension of digital services to emerging markets will all play significant roles in the formation of the digital infrastructure of the future. In this age of digital technology, the key to realizing the full potential of our linked world lies in our capacity to adapt to existing systems and to innovate within those systems.

2.1 Defining digital infrastructure in the context of science

In the field of science, digital infrastructure refers to the key technological framework that enables research, experimentation, data analysis, and the distribution of information. It also supports and enables these activities. It is made up of the integrated systems, hardware, software, and networks that give researchers the ability to carry out investigations, work together with colleagues all over the world, and publish their findings. It is necessary to define digital infrastructure within the context of science since doing so creates the groundwork for comprehending the crucial function that it plays in the progression of scientific research.

Components Crucial to the Digital Infrastructure of the Scientific Community

High-Performance Computing (HPC): High-performance computing clusters, supercomputers, and cloud-based resources provide the computational power essential for conducting complicated simulations, data analysis, and modeling across a variety of scientific fields. Research in domains such as astrophysics, genetics, and climate modeling is sped up using high-performance computing (HPC).

Data Management and Storage: The exponential rise of data in the scientific community needs the development of innovative solutions for data management and storage. For the purpose of maintaining and gaining access to enormous datasets, it is essential to have data centers, cloud-based storage, and high-capacity storage systems. This is true whether the field of study in question is genomics, particle physics, or environmental monitoring.

Platforms for Collaborative Research Digital infrastructure makes it possible for scientists all around the world to work together. Researchers are able to pool their skills, share resources, and collectively solve difficult challenges thanks to virtual laboratories, online collaboration tools, and data-sharing platforms. This is possible independent of the researchers' physical locations.

Tools for Scientific Visualization: These tools make it easier to create interactive visualizations, 3D models, and images to express difficult scientific data and ideas. The improved comprehension and communication of research findings that result from the use of scientific visualization makes these findings available to a larger audience.

In the context of the scientific community, the term "cybersecurity" refers to the protection of the confidentiality and authenticity of sensitive research data, in addition to vital infrastructure. It is absolutely necessary, in order to keep the reliability of scientific research intact, to take precautions against cyberattacks and to make certain that ethical standards are followed when handling data.

Open Science Platforms: Open Science is a set of principles that are supported by digital infrastructure in the form of platforms. These principles emphasize transparency, collaboration, and open access to research findings and datasets. Scientists are now able to openly publish their work thanks to online platforms and repositories, which has resulted in a more rapid spread of information and increased international cooperation.

The Importance of the Digital Infrastructure to the Advancement of Science

Research that is Led by the Data Digital infrastructure enables researchers to harness the power of large amounts of data. The ability to process and analyze huge information is essential to uncovering patterns, correlations, and insights that drive scientific advancement. This is true across a wide range of scientific disciplines, from genomics to climate research.

Simulation and Modeling: The conduct of scientific research frequently necessitates the execution of intricate simulations and models. Scientists are able to model physical systems, test ideas, and explore possibilities that may not be practical in the physical world thanks to the high-performance computer resources that are available to them. These simulations quicken the pace of discovery in a variety of domains, including the study of materials, the modeling of climate, and the creation of drugs.

Global Collaboration The widespread availability of digital infrastructure enables academics to work together without interruption regardless of location. This global collaboration is essential, particularly in addressing severe global concerns such as the COVID-19 pandemic, in which scientists from all around the world worked together to gain a better understanding of the virus, produce vaccinations, and share key data.

Accessibility and Open Science: The development of digital infrastructure helps to make it possible for more people to have access to scientific information. Open scientific platforms and open access publication eliminate obstacles that prevent people from accessing the results of research, which in turn encourages more inclusivity and teamwork.

Scientific Communication: The development of digital infrastructure has led to improvements in the dissemination of findings from scientific research.

Researchers may make research more interesting and accessible to a wider audience by efficiently presenting their findings to their colleagues as well as to the general public through the use of visualization tools and multimedia.

Interdisciplinary research is made possible by the fact that digital infrastructure facilitates the junction of many scientific fields. Traditional boundaries are blurred in disciplines such as bioinformatics, geoinformatics, and computational chemistry, resulting in the development of an all-encompassing strategy for the solution of difficult scientific problems.

Concerns and Things to Take Into Account

Concerns Raise Themselves Regarding Cybersecurity And The Ethical Handling Of Sensitive Research Data As Society Becomes More Reliant On Digital Technology, There Has Been An Increased Focus On Data Privacy And Cybersecurity. It is imperative to have stringent ethical norms and security precautions in place.

Resilience of the Infrastructure: The scientific infrastructure needs to be able to withstand disturbances of any kind, whether they come from natural catastrophes or cyberattacks. It is of the utmost importance to ensure that key services continue to operate normally.

Inclusion in the Digital Age: It is essential for digital infrastructure to ensure that all researchers, irrespective of their geographic location or financial means, have access to the essential tools and platforms for conducting scientific research.

Emerging technologies, such as artificial intelligence and gene editing, provide new ethical and legal challenges. Considerations in this area are important. To strike a healthy balance between the advancement of science and adherence to ethical principles, researchers and institutions need to master these intricacies.

In the context of the scientific enterprise, digital infrastructure serves as the central pillar around which modern scientific investigation and advancement are built. It incorporates a vast assortment of parts, ranging from open research platforms and high-performance computers to data management and administration of large amounts of data. This infrastructure helps to speed up the process of scientific discovery, improves opportunities for worldwide collaboration, and makes research more accessible.

The continuous development of digital infrastructure is sure to have a significant impact on the course that scientific inquiry will take in the years to come.

When it comes to defining the role of the digital infrastructure in expanding scientific knowledge and tackling global difficulties, the incorporation of new technologies, the modification of existing infrastructure to accommodate emerging markets, and the examination of ethical and legal issues will play a vital role.

2.2 Hardware and software components

It is essential for there to be a mutually beneficial relationship between the many pieces of hardware and software that make up a digital infrastructure. These two pillars provide the foundation upon which digital services and applications are created, and together they make up the backbone of modern computer systems and networks. In the context of digital infrastructure, having a solid understanding of the functions and relationships played by both software and hardware is absolutely necessary.

Components of the Hardware

Servers are incredibly powerful computers that are specifically built to respond to requests and deliver resources to other devices that are connected to the same network. They are vital for the provision of digital services that call for the processing and storage of data since they play a crucial part in the hosting of websites, applications, and databases.

Devices for Storing Data It is essential to have data storage devices, such as hard disk drives (HDDs) and solid-state drives (SSDs), in order to keep huge volumes of digital data. These devices guarantee that data may be accessed, retrieved, and reliably preserved in a secure manner.

Equipment for Networking The infrastructure that permits the transmission of data from one device to another is formed by the equipment for networking, which includes routers, switches, and network cables. It does this by establishing the connectivity that is necessary for devices to communicate both within a network and with resources located outside of the network.

Computers and Workstations: Personal computers and workstations are the primary interfaces that allow people to engage with digital infrastructure. They serve as the principal interfaces since they are the most widespread. They are necessary for activities such as the examination of data, the production of content, and the development of software.

Clusters of High-Performance Computing (HPC): High-performance computing clusters consist of many computers, also known as nodes, that are connected to one another and work together to give remarkable computational capability. They are especially important for scientific research, simulations, and the in-depth study of complex data.

Data centers are enormous facilities that host a wide variety of computers, storage systems, and networking equipment. Data centers are also referred to as "server farms." They perform the function of acting as a centralized site for the processing, storage, and management of data.

Sensors and other Devices linked to the Internet of Things: When discussing the IoT (Internet of Things), various sensors and other linked devices are referred to as hardware components. These devices capture data in real time from the physical environment and transfer it to other digital systems so that the data may be analyzed and decisions can be made based on it.

Components of the Software

Operating Systems: Operating systems, which include Microsoft Windows, macOS, and Linux, are responsible for managing the available hardware resources and laying the groundwork for the execution of software programs. They assure the stability and security of computing systems, in addition to facilitating communication between hardware components.

Application Software: Application software encompasses a vast variety of different programs, each of which is developed to carry out a particular activity or purpose. This category includes anything from word processors and spreadsheets to web browsers, multimedia players, and scientific modeling software. It also includes software that can create diagrams.

The word "middleware" refers to a layer of software that performs the function of an intermediary layer, connecting and enabling communication between various software components. In the context of digital infrastructure, it plays a crucial part in the integration of a wide variety of systems, databases, and applications.

Database Management Systems (DBMS) are software programs that handle the storing, retrieving, and organizing of data in databases. DBMS stands for "database management system." It offers a method that is organized as well as effective for storing, accessing, and manipulating data.

Web Servers and Web Application Frameworks: Web servers and application frameworks play an essential role in the context of web-based services. They make it easier to host websites, web applications, and online services, and they also execute those services.

Firmware is a type of software that is built into physical devices, such as microcontrollers and other Internet of Things (IoT) gadgets. It supplies the low-level instructions necessary for the operation and functionality of the device.

Software for Virtualization Virtualization software facilitates the development of virtual machines (VMs), which are capable of simultaneously running a number of operating systems despite being hosted on a single physical server. This technology is vital for maximizing the efficiency with which resources are used and ensuring flexibility in the operation of data centers.

The dynamic relationship between computer hardware and software

Management of Hardware Resources Both operating systems and software designed for virtualization play a key part in the process of managing and assigning hardware resources. They manage things like the use of the central processing unit (CPU), memory allocation, and access to peripheral devices in order to guarantee that different software applications operate smoothly and without interference from one another.

Compatibility is essential, as software must be compatible with the computer hardware on which it is installed. When building software applications, developers need to take into account the hardware setups and specifications to ensure that the apps run without any hiccups.

Scalability is a feature that digital infrastructure typically has to have, as it is frequently required to accommodate rising demand. When this occurs, the available resources of the hardware can be increased, and the software can be developed to adapt to changes in the configuration of the hardware in a seamless manner.

When it comes to protecting the safety of digital infrastructure, both the hardware and the software play equally important roles. Together with security software, hardware components such as firewalls, intrusion detection systems, and encryption modules provide a layer of defense against potential cybersecurity vulnerabilities.

Performance Optimization: Both the software and the hardware components work together to achieve optimal performance for the system. This entails fine-tuning software applications in order to make effective use of the resources that are available on the hardware.

User Experience The quality of the user experience is directly related to the degree to which the hardware and software are able to work together efficiently.

This comprises user interfaces that are responsive, data processing that is seamless, and data retrieval that is effective, all of which are dependent on the synergy between the two.

2.3 Data storage and management

In this day and age, when practically everything is done digitally, data is the most important resource for both our personal and professional lives. It is impossible to exaggerate how important it is to have effective data storage and management across all levels of business, from individual consumers to big businesses. The exponential increase of data, which is being fuelled by the internet, devices connected to the internet of things (IoT), and the ever-expanding digital environment, has made both the opportunities and the difficulties that exist in this area more substantial than they have ever been.

The Storage of Data

Devices for Storage: Traditional hard drives, also known as HDDs, and solid-state drives, sometimes known as SSDs, are the two types of storage devices that are most frequently used by people and small organizations. They are available in a wide range of storage capacity and physical configurations. In addition, cloud storage services provide off-site storage, which ensures that data may be accessed from any location in the world.

Scalability is a feature of storage solutions that is becoming increasingly important as data continues to accumulate at an unprecedented rate. To achieve this kind of scalability, you may need to upgrade your hardware, implement distributed storage solutions, or make use of cloud-based storage, which can easily expand in response to growing space requirements.

Protecting data from unwanted access, breaches, and corruption is of the utmost importance in terms of data security. The protection of sensitive data requires a number of different safeguards, including encryption, authorization controls, and routine backups.

It is important to back up your data and have a plan in place for recovering it in the event of unforeseen calamities, malfunctioning hardware, or human error. It is absolutely necessary to have robust backup and disaster recovery procedures in place in order to reduce the likelihood of these hazards and maintain the integrity of the data.

Administration of Data

Classification and Organization of Data: Data should be classified and arranged based on the type of data, how sensitive the data is, and how important the data is. The effective tagging and categorization of metadata makes it much simpler to retrieve and examine the material.

Governance of Data: Governance of data covers policies, methods, and roles that determine how data should be managed and how it should be managed. It assures compliance with statutory and regulatory obligations, as well as the quality and accuracy of the data.

Integration of Data: Many companies have data that is scattered over a wide variety of computer systems and online platforms. The process of integrating data entails harmonizing and unifying the data that comes from a variety of sources, which enables a comprehensive view and analysis.

Data analytics is a strong asset since it allows one to gain useful insights from large amounts of data. The use of various tools and methods for data analytics allows for more informed decision-making, the identification of patterns, and the forecasting of future events.

Privacy of User Data and Compliance with legislation Because of legislation such as GDPR and CCPA, data privacy and compliance with regulations are key issues. It is not just good practice but also a legal responsibility to manage data in compliance with the requirements of the applicable laws.

Concerns Regarding the Management and Storage of Data

Data Volume The sheer volume of data that is generated each day has the potential to exceed storage limits and make data management more complicated.

Data Security: There has been an increase in the number of data breaches and cybersecurity threats in recent years, which poses an ongoing threat to the data's integrity and confidentiality.

Quality of the Data: Incorrect conclusions and choices can be made as a result of inadequate data quality. The problem of ensuring that data is accurate and consistent throughout the organization is an ongoing one.

Increasing the capacity of storage infrastructure, putting in place robust data management systems, and keeping up with compliance requirements may all be costly endeavors.

The fragmentation of data across departments or systems can create data silos, which makes data access and integration more difficult.

The Prospects for the Long-Term Storage and Administration of Data

Dominance of the Cloud: Because of the cloud's scale and flexibility, cloud-based storage and management solutions are projected to become even more widespread in the near future.

A.I. and Automation: Artificial intelligence will play a big role in the management of data, automating a variety of processes like data classification, governance, and analytics.

Edge computing: As the number of Internet of Things (IoT) devices continues to grow, an increasing amount of data processing will take place at the edge, which will require new strategies for data storage and management.

Computing on the Quantum Level While quantum computing has the potential to revolutionize data processing and analytics, it also brings significant hurdles in terms of maintaining data security.

2.4 Network connectivity and communication

As a result of the advent of the digital age, network connectivity and communication have evolved into fundamental aspects of our day-to-day lives, dictating how we communicate with one another, run our businesses, and exchange information. Communication comprises the means and methods by which this data is transferred and received, whereas the concept of network connection refers to the ability of various devices and systems to create linkages and exchange data. This ability is referred to as the ability to exchange data. This dynamic partnership is essential to understanding the development of the modern world.

The interconnection of networks serves as the base upon which our increasingly interconnected world is built. It enables devices like smartphones, computers, and other gadgets that are part of the Internet of Things (IoT) to connect to the internet and communicate with one another. This communication is achieved through a variety of methods, including both wired and wireless technological platforms. Wireless technologies such as Wi-Fi, Bluetooth, and cellular networks give the flexibility of mobility, in contrast to wired technologies such as Ethernet cables and fiber optics, which enable high-speed and dependable wired connections.

The internet provides the clearest illustration possible of the need of maintaining network connectivity. The internet is an enormous, worldwide network that connects millions of different devices all over the world. People are able to obtain information, connect with others through social media, engage in e-commerce, and complete a myriad of other jobs because of this capability. Connectivity through networks is the unseen force that drives everything forward and makes it all possible.

The Internet of Things (IoT) is one of the fundamental ideas that are central to the concept of network connectivity. The Internet of Things (IoT) refers to the practice of connecting commonplace things and equipment to the internet in order to provide them the ability to collect and exchange data. The Internet of Things ecosystem can include everything from refrigerators to wearable fitness trackers and even smart thermostats. This interconnection not only makes life more convenient, but it also has important repercussions for a variety of sectors, including the medical field, the manufacturing sector, and the transportation sector.

However, there are other factors to consider besides only network connectivity. The ability to communicate clearly and effectively is essential to making the most of these connections. Between different machines and computer networks, the passing of information in the form of text, voice, or multimedia is referred to as communication. There are many different modes of communication, all of which have developed over the course of history.

Data transmission is by far the most common method of communication that takes place through networks. The data is divided up into packets before being transmitted through the network to the appropriate location. This procedure depends on communication protocols, such as the Internet Protocol (IP), to ensure that data is delivered to the person or organization to which it is addressed. Error correction and data routing are both taken care of by these protocols, which further ensures that the communication is trustworthy.

With the development of Voice over Internet Protocol (VoIP) technology, voice communication has also gone through a period of significant change. Applications such as Skype, WhatsApp, and Zoom have fundamentally altered the way in which we connect with one another across great distances. Because VoIP enables the transmission of voice data over IP networks, it has made international phone conversations more economical and more readily available.

In recent years, progress has been made not just in data and voice communication, but also in multimedia communication. The distribution of high-definition content to users located all over the world via video streaming services such as YouTube and Netflix is dependent on the utilization of fast network connections. In a similar vein, social media platforms allow users to exchange images, videos, and other forms of multimedia content in real time, thereby linking people and cultures all over the world.

The significance of being connected to a network and having clear lines of communication extends far beyond one's own needs. These technologies are essential for the efficient operation of businesses and organizations, which allows them to better serve their clients.

Enterprises utilize various forms of network connectivity and communication, such as cloud computing and virtual private networks (VPNs), in order to manage their data, cooperate with distributed staff, and keep an online presence.

When it comes to the connectivity and communication of networks, security and privacy are of the utmost importance. As the number of cyberattacks and data breaches continues to climb, it is imperative that sensitive information be protected by using strong encryption techniques, secure connections, and authentication processes. In addition, regulatory authorities all over the world have developed guidelines to protect the data of users and the users' right to privacy. One example of these guidelines is the General Data Protection Regulation (GDPR) in Europe.

Chapter 3

Data Management and Sharing

In the data-driven world of today, efficient data management and sharing are absolutely necessary for the success of companies, organizations, and research institutions. Data is frequently said to as the "lifeblood" of modern society because it is the driving force behind various decision-making processes, research activities, and technological developments. Nonetheless, in order to make the most of the opportunities presented by data, it is necessary to put in place reliable data management procedures and to devise effective platforms for the exchange of data. This in-depth investigation will delve into the complexities of data management and sharing, exploring their significance, the issues they face, the best practices that exist, and the changing environment of data in the 21st century.

1. **The Value of Effectively Managing Your Data**
   1.1 The Importance of Data as an Asset
   Data is a valuable asset that can provide insights, promote innovation, and assist informed decision-making. Data is more than simply a collection of numbers and letters; it is a valuable asset

that can provide these benefits and more. When applied to a commercial setting, effective data management can result in strengthened relationships with customers, streamlined operations, and a competitive advantage.

1.2 Improved Capacity for Making Decisions

An organization's capacity to effectively store, organize, and access its data is directly correlated to the quality of its data management. When decision-makers have access to information that is accurate, current, and pertinent to the situation at hand, they are better able to make choices that are likely to result in favorable results.

1.3 Observance of All Regulations

There are stringent standards that govern data management in many different fields of business, such as the Health Insurance Portability and Accountability Act (HIPAA) in the healthcare industry and the General Data Protection Regulation (GDPR) in the European Union. Maintaining compliance with these standards is absolutely necessary in order to stay out of legal and financial hot water.

1.4 The Protection of Data

The appropriate management of data is inextricably linked to the protection of data. It is essential for a business to preserve both its reputation and the interests of its stakeholders by keeping sensitive and secret information secure. Data breaches can result in serious damage to both a company's finances and its reputation.

1.5 Effectiveness and output per unit of effort

Effective management of data can help operations run more smoothly by cutting down on the amount of time spent looking for information and performing tasks twice. This results in an improvement in productivity as well as savings in costs.

2. Procedures for the Management of Data

2.1 Data Collecting and Information Acquiring

The gathering and accumulation of data is the first step in the process of data management. It is essential to guarantee that the data gathered are correct, applicable, and obtained in an ethical manner. For the purpose of information collection, many techniques, including polls, sensors, and data scraping, are utilized.

2.2 The Storing of Data

When storing data, it is necessary to select suitable storage solutions, which can either be located on-premises or on the cloud. Data volume, accessibility, and safety are all important aspects to take into consideration. The data management and collaboration capabilities of an organization might be considerably impacted by the storage solution that is ultimately selected.

2.3 The Organization of the Data

The data should be arranged in a way that is both structured and easily accessible. Depending on the type of data being processed, this frequently requires the utilization of databases, data warehouses, or data lakes. When data are properly organized, they are much simpler to locate and retrieve when they are required.

2.4 Assurance of the Quality of the Data

The quality of the data is critical. It is necessary for businesses to establish quality control processes such as data cleansing, validation, and verification in order to guarantee the accuracy and dependability of their data. The upkeep of data quality helps avoid erroneous decisions from being made based on inaccurate information.

2.5 Governance of the Data

Within an organization, the management of data policies, data standards, and data procedures is referred to as "data governance." It contributes to the maintenance of data integrity as well as security and compliance with legislation. A data governance structure that is clearly established is absolutely necessary for efficient data management.

3. Obstacles Confronted When Managing Data

3.1 An Overabundance of Data

Data is being produced at a rate that has never been seen before in this era of digital technology. This flood of data can be overwhelming for enterprises, making it difficult to recognize useful insights and properly handle large amounts of information.

3.2 Data Walls and Silos

When various departments or teams within an organization do not share data with one another, this can lead to the formation of data silos. This can be a barrier to collaboration and may result in efforts being repeated.

3.3 Concerns Regarding the Privacy and Safety of Data

When data increases in value, it also increases in value as a target for malicious cyberattacks. In order to prevent data breaches and protect sensitive information, companies and other organizations need to make ongoing investments in data security.

3.4 Ensuring Completion of Required Procedures

It is possible for compliance with data protection requirements to be difficult and expensive. Failure to comply may result in monetary fines as well as damage to one's reputation.

3.5 Systems Inherent to the Past

A large number of companies are still dependent on older computer systems and software, which may not be optimal for meeting the requirements of current data management. The process of upgrading or moving these systems is frequently one that is difficult and resource-intensive.

4. **Cooperation and the Exchange of Information**

   4.1 Sharing of Data Through Collaborative Efforts

   The sharing of data is not restricted to the requirements of an organization's internal operations; rather, it encompasses the working relationships with third parties, such as business partners, customers, and suppliers. Sharing information in a collaborative manner enables businesses to operate more effectively together.

   4.2 Initiatives Regarding Open Data

   Initiatives that use open data involve making particular datasets accessible to the general population. Because of this, innovation, research, and the development of apps driven by data are all spurred on. Open data has been particularly embraced by governments as a means of fostering both openness and economic expansion.

4.3 The Sharing of Information Regarding Research

The scientific community is dependent on the sharing of data in order to hasten the process of discovery and develop knowledge. Sharing datasets, methodology, and findings is a common method of collaboration among researchers. The sharing of research data is guided by the FAIR principles, which stand for findable, accessible, interoperable, and reusable.

4.4 Obstacles Facing the Sharing of Data

Sharing data is crucial, but it does not come without problems. These challenges include concerns about data privacy, rights to intellectual property, and the requirement for standardized data formats and metadata. Finding solutions to these problems is absolutely necessary for the proper sharing of data.

5. Exemplary Methods of Information Administration and Collaboration

5.1 Policies for the Management of Data

Policies for comprehensive data management should be established by organizations, and these policies should outline procedures, responsibilities, and best practices. The acquisition, storage, accessibility, and protection of data ought to all be addressed by these policies.

5.2 Governance of the Data

Data consistency and regulatory compliance can be ensured through the deployment of a powerful data governance system.

For the purpose of making educated decisions on the management and sharing of data, this framework should incorporate stakeholders from a variety of departments.

5.3 Assurance of the Quality of the Data

Maintaining the integrity of the data requires regular auditing and cleaning. In the long term, it may be more cost-effective and efficient to make an investment in data quality assurance tools and techniques.

5.4 Protecting the Data

Protecting data requires the implementation of encryption, access controls, and intrusion detection systems. It is necessary to conduct regular security audits as well as personnel training in order to reduce risks.

5.5 Protocols for the Sharing of Data

Establishing clear norms and guidelines for the exchange of data is important for both internal and external cooperation. These protocols should establish who is permitted to access the data, under what circumstances, and for what purposes.

5.6 Normalization and Utilization of Metadata

To make data easier to access and analyze, standardize the formats in which they are stored and make use of descriptive information. Data sources, collecting methods, and any transformations should all be included in the information that is included in the metadata.

6. New Developments in the Administration and Exchange of Data

6.1 Artificial intelligence and machine learning

A number of data management functions, including data classification, anomaly detection, and predictive analytics, are increasingly benefiting from the application of AI and ML. The quality of the data can be improved using these technologies, and certain data management operations can be automated.

6.2 The Technology Behind Blockchain

The distributed and encrypted ledger that blockchain technology offers has the potential to completely change the way people share and access data. It is gaining acceptance in fields where data integrity is crucial, such as supply chain management and healthcare, and it is expected to have a significant impact on these industries in the near future.

6.3 Computing on the Edge

Through the use of edge computing, data processing can take place closer to the data source, hence reducing both latency and bandwidth consumption. This is of utmost significance for applications such as IoT, which require real-time data analysis in order to function properly.

6.4 The Commercialization of Data

Some companies are investigating the possibility of generating new sources of revenue by

commercializing their data. They are able to generate cash while still adhering to privacy and security standards when they share data that has been aggregated and anonymized with third parties.

6.5 Ethics of Data Collection and Methods to Reduce Bias

The usage of artificial intelligence (AI) and large amounts of data is on the rise, and with it comes a greater emphasis on the ethical implications of data management and the elimination of prejudice. It is of the utmost importance to make certain that data are utilized in a just and accountable manner.

In today's data-driven environment, efficient data management and sharing are two of the most important factors. The potential of data can be more effectively harnessed by organizations that make investments in data management methods, address issues, and embrace best practices. The constantly shifting nature of the data landscape, along with the emergence of new technologies and trends, continues to have an impact on the ways in which data is handled, shared, and utilized to foster creativity, efficiency, and cooperation.

As we move forward, it is essential that we continue to make appropriate and ethical use of the data we collect. The difficulty of achieving the delicate balance between making decisions based on data and protecting the privacy and security of individuals' data is one that businesses and other organizations must continually face. If they do so, they will be able to unleash the full potential of data to promote growth and transformation in our society, which is rapidly transforming.

3.1 Importance of data in scientific research

Data are the essential ingredient that keep scientific research alive. It plays the role of the base upon which hypotheses are constructed, experiments are carried out, and conclusions are formed. It is impossible to emphasize the significance of data in scientific study in this day and age, which is defined by an onslaught of information. This article investigates the fundamental role that data plays in scientific investigation, shedding light on its relevance, the numerous sorts of data, and the transformative impact it has on the advancement of human knowledge.

1. ### The Role of Data in the Construction of Scientific Knowledge
   #### 1.1 Research That Is Grounded In Evidence
   The empirical evidence that is required to support or refute scientific ideas can be provided via data. Researchers gather data to support their hypotheses and then conduct in-depth analyses of that data. This process ensures that scientific knowledge is constructed on a solid foundation of evidence.

   #### 1.2 Hypotheses That Can Be Tested
   On the basis of previously acquired information or observations, hypotheses are developed. After then, the data will be used to test these hypotheses. The hypotheses that were initially proposed are either validated or refuted by the findings of these tests, which are recorded as data.

   #### 1.3 Ongoing and Constant Improvement
   Understanding in the scientific community is not static; rather, it continuously develops. Research that is driven by data gives scientists the ability to adjust and improve upon previously held hypotheses in order to account for newly discovered information as it emerges.

   #### 1.4 Advances Made Through Interdisciplinarity
   The collection and analysis of data cuts across disciplinary lines.

The implications that might be drawn from data gathered in one area of study sometimes extend to other disciplines. The exchange of data and collaboration between specialists from other fields are key drivers of innovation and the solving of difficult challenges.

2. **The Many Different Types of Information Used in Scientific Research**

   2.1 The Quantitative Information

   Because it can be reduced to a number and can be measured, quantitative data is very useful for statistical analysis. It takes into consideration things like temperature, weight, amount of time, and count, which enables researchers to arrive at accurate conclusions.

   2.2 Data of a Qualitative Nature

   Insights into the qualities, traits, or aspects of a phenomenon can be gained through the use of qualitative data, which is frequently text-based or descriptive. In order to grasp difficult and context-heavy topics, it is utilized in academic disciplines such as anthropology, sociology, and the humanities.

   2.3 The Results of Experiments

   The controlled experiments that produce the data for the experiments are called experiments. In order to study the relationships between factors, researchers will modify the variables and record the results.

   2.4 Data Derived From Observations

   The gathering of observational data involves keeping a neutral stance while witnessing natural occurrences. It is of the utmost importance in subjects such as astronomy, ecology, and ethnography, where doing direct experiments may be difficult or against ethical standards.

   2.5 The Big Data

   Both the quantity of data and its complexity have significantly grown as a result of the advent of the digital age. Big data refers to big datasets, which necessitate the utilization of sophisticated computational tools and methods for the purposes of storing, analyzing, and interpreting the data. It is particularly relevant in domains such as genomics, climate science, and research on social media.

3. Scientific Progress Motivated by Data

3.1 Recent Developments in Medicine

In the field of medicine, research that is driven by data has resulted in a number of ground-breaking discoveries, as well as individualized treatments and improved patient outcomes. The creation of precision medicine and innovative treatments is made possible by the outcomes of clinical trials, the data from genomic sequencing, and electronic health records.

3.2 Research Concerning the Environment

In order to gain a better understanding of climate change, biodiversity, and ecosystems, environmental scientists rely on comprehensive databases. Understanding environmental patterns and trends is made much easier because to advancements in remote sensing technology, satellite data, and climate models.

3.3 The Study of Astrophysics and the Exploration of Space

Our view of the cosmos has been fundamentally altered thanks to the information gathered by space observatories and robotic trips to other heavenly bodies. Data is the tool that astronomers use to find exoplanets, investigate black holes, and investigate how the cosmos came into being.

3.4 Studies in the Social Sciences

Data is a crucial tool in the study of human behavior, as well as economic and political patterns, within the social sciences. Researchers are able to evaluate societal patterns and develop policies using data collected from surveys, censuses, and social media platforms.

3.5 Years' Worth of Technological Progress

Research that is driven by data has been responsible for a number of notable technical achievements. Massive datasets are essential to the research and development of cutting-edge technologies in fields such as artificial intelligence, machine learning, and robotics.

4. **Obstacles Facing Science That Is Driven By Data**

   4.1 The Quality of the Data

   The importance of the data's quality cannot be overstated. Conclusions that are erroneous can be drawn from data that is inaccurate or incomplete. Researchers have a responsibility to implement quality control procedures and assure the integrity of the data.

   4.2 Methods of Data Management and Storage

   Managing massive datasets, especially in this age of big data, calls for storage solutions that are reliable and data management procedures that are as effective as possible.

   4.3 Concerns Regarding Privacy and Ethical Issues

   The presence of potentially sensitive information in data frequently gives rise to ethical and privacy concerns. When collecting and using data involving human subjects, researchers are required to follow ethical guidelines and comply with applicable data protection regulations.

   4.4 Capacity for Cooperation

   The data gathered in one area of science could be applicable in another area of science. It might be difficult to ensure data interoperability across fields, yet doing so is absolutely necessary for collaborative research.

5. **Cooperation and the Exchange of Information**

The growth of science is greatly aided by the exchange of data and the working together of researchers.

   5.1 The ability to reproduce

   The more data that is shared, the more likely it is that other researchers will be able to repeat and verify the results of the tests, so adding to the credibility of the findings.

5.2 The Working Relationship

The sharing of data is essential to the success of scientific collaboration. Researchers from different institutions and countries can collaborate to share knowledge and resources by working together.

5.3 The Quickening of Discoveries

By preventing individuals from performing the same work again, the process of discovery can be sped up through data sharing. It gives others the opportunity to build upon previously conducted research, which in turn encourages innovation.

5.4 A Free and Open Science

The open science movement promotes transparent research as well as open access to both

data and the conclusions of research. This makes scientific knowledge more accessible to a larger audience, hence democratizing its dissemination.

It is impossible to exaggerate the significance of data in the conduct of scientific research. Researchers are able to put their hypotheses to the test, improve their theories, and propel developments in a variety of sectors because to its role as the foundation of evidence-based inquiry. The ability to investigate complicated occurrences is made possible for scientists by the wide variety of data types, including quantitative, qualitative, and big data.

Research that is driven by data has resulted in significant advances in a number of fields, including medicine, the environment, astrophysics, and technology. It has also brought up issues relating to the quality of the data, storage, protecting users' privacy, and interoperability. On the other hand, researchers can take advantage of the opportunity presented by these obstacles to build robust data management methods and ethical standards.

Sharing of data and working together on scientific projects are two of the most important aspects of the scientific enterprise, as they foster reproducibility, innovation, and open science.

The relevance of data in scientific study is certainly deep, and it will continue to do so in an era in which the bounds of knowledge are continually growing. This will have a significant impact on the future of scientific inquiry and discovery.

3.2 Data collection, curation, and preservation

In today's digital age, data is the most important resource for driving innovation, research, and decision-making. The data lifecycle consists of several critical parts, including the processes of data collection, data curation, and data preservation. They make certain that useful information is not only gathered but also arranged, kept up to date, and safeguarded for both immediate and long-term application. The importance of data gathering, curation, and preservation, as well as their interconnectedness and the shifting context in which they function, is investigated in this article.

1. ### The Accumulation of Data
   #### 1.1 The Groundwork of Our Understanding
   The generation of new knowledge starts with the very first stage, which is the collection of data. It entails the methodical collection of data using a variety of channels, such as questionnaires, experiments, observations, and sensors. The usefulness of later research and decision-making processes is profoundly influenced by the quality and relevancy of the data that was acquired during the process.
   #### 1.2 Different Methods for the Collection of Data
   Primary data collection refers to the process of gathering data in its raw form by in-person methods such as surveys, interviews, or experiments. This approach gives users more control and the ability to tailor their experience, but at the cost of more effort and money.
   Secondary data collection refers to the use of already existing data sources, such as public documents, surveys that have been done in the past, or literature reviews. This strategy may reduce

the amount of precise data that is available, but it is very cost-effective.

1.3 Obstacles Encountered During the Collection of Data

Skewed outcomes can be the result of collecting data in a biased manner.

Inaccuracy: If the data collection process is flawed in some way, the results may not be dependable.

Concerns Regarding Privacy Any activity that involves the collection of personal or sensitive information must comply with applicable privacy legislation.

Limitations in Time, Money, and Access to Data The amount of time, money, and access to data that is available can all have an effect on the quality and scope of the data gathering efforts.

2. **The Processing of Data**

    2.1 Organizing and Structuring

    The process of removing inconsistencies, mistakes, and information that is irrelevant from data is referred to as "data cleaning."

    The process of applying a consistent format and structure to data in order to assure compatibility is referred to as data standardization.

    The process of developing descriptive metadata, which functions as a catalog for data and includes information about the data's sources, gathering methods, and variables, is referred to as "metadata creation."

    Version control refers to the process of managing multiple dataset versions to keep track of changes and updates.

    2.2 Assurance of the Quality of the Data

    The quality of the data must be carefully curated, which is an important part of the process. Accurate analysis and significant insights cannot be achieved without data that has been thoroughly cleaned and arranged. Problems like data duplication and loss can be avoided with the help of curation as well.

    2.3 Making Certain There Is Accessibility

The act of curating data assures that it will continue to be available throughout time. It is much simpler for researchers to locate, access, and utilize data, which is critical for fostering collaboration and ensuring the success of research initiatives over time.

3. **The Maintenance of Data**

   3.1 The Obligatory Necessity of Long-Term Preserving

   The process of protecting data for the long term, guaranteeing that information will continue to be accessible, dependable, and usable throughout the course of time is referred to as data preservation. This is especially important in the field of scientific research, where datasets may be referred to and expanded upon for decades at a time.

   3.2 Archiving and Safekeeping of Data

   For data to be preserved, it is necessary to have safe storage and backup solutions. There is a wide variety of options available, ranging from servers located on-site to solutions hosted in the cloud, and the right choice will rely on the requirements of the company, as well as budgetary and financial constraints.

   3.3 Archive and Repository for the Data

   In research institutions, the establishment of data archives and repositories is a frequent practice. These act as safe deposit boxes where data can be kept, cataloged, and made available to users with the appropriate permissions. Examples of this type of institution include academic libraries and digital archives.

   3.4 The Migration of Data

   The forms of data are subject to change when new technologies are developed. It may be necessary to periodically migrate data to new storage systems or formats in order to guarantee its accessibility in the long run. This is absolutely necessary in order to keep historical documents and the results of study.

4. **The interconnected processes of data collection, curation, and preservation**

   4.1 Data Collection Serves as the Source for Data Curation

The successful curation of information begins with the collecting of data of a high quality. When data is clean and well-structured, it is much simpler to curate and its value is better preserved over time.

4.2 The Curation of Data Makes It Easier to Preserve Data

The process of data curation involves ensuring that the data is well-structured, recorded, and free from discrepancies before putting it away for the long term. Without the appropriate curation, preservation can be difficult, and the long-term utility of the material can be jeopardized.

4.3 Protection of Data Ensures the Security of Data Investments

If proper measures are not taken to protect the data, any resources that are invested in its collection and curation would be wasted. The protection of data assures that it will continue to be a useful resource for research and decision-making in the future.

5. The Constantly Changing Terrain

5.1 The Challenges of Big Data

In this digital era, there is an increase in volume, velocity, and variety of data, all of which bring new issues. In order to successfully handle and store large amounts of data, organizations require sophisticated tools and procedures.

5.2 Information Security and Morality

The procedures for collecting data are coming under increased scrutiny. When working with personal or sensitive information, it is especially important to ensure that ethical data collecting and privacy protection measures are in place.

5.3 Participation in International Activities

An increase in global collaboration has led to initiatives for the preservation and exchange of data across international borders. For the sake of data interoperability and security, international standards and agreements are absolutely necessary.

5.4 Recent Developments in Technology

Data preservation techniques are undergoing a sea change as a direct result of developments in technology such as blockchain, distributed ledger technology, and enhanced data storage solutions.

The phases of the data lifecycle known as collection, curation, and preservation are fundamentally important because they guarantee that the data will continue to be relevant and usable for study, innovation, and decision-making.

These processes are intertwined, and their relevance has been amplified in today's digital age, when data is easily accessible and constantly undergoing change at a breakneck pace. To successfully navigate the intricacies of data in the 21st century, effective data management methods and ethical considerations are necessary. This will eventually protect knowledge for the benefit of both present and future generations.

3.3 Open science and data sharing

Open science and the collaborative sharing of data are two game-changing strategies that have been gaining traction in the scientific community over the past several years. These strategies have the overarching goal of making scientific research that is more open, collaborative, and approachable. In this piece, we will investigate the ideas of open science and data sharing, as well as their significance, advantages, disadvantages, and the shifting environment of research in the digital age.

1. ### Open Science as a Shift in the Paradigm
   #### 1.1 Openness and honesty
   The principles of open science place an emphasis on maintaining research integrity. Researchers are generous in sharing their processes, data, and discoveries, making it possible for others to examine and build upon their findings.
   #### 1.2 The Working Relationship
   Open science cannot exist without the participation of others. Researchers collaborate across academic fields and geographic borders, drawing on the experience of the group as a whole to

find solutions to difficult challenges.

1.3 Free and Public Access

Open access publication makes it possible for the general public to read research articles without cost. This removes obstacles that impede access and makes it possible for a greater number of people to benefit from scientific breakthroughs.

2. The Sharing of Data as a Foundational Element of Open Science

2.1 Capability of Being Reproduced

The more data that is shared, the more likely it is that other researchers will be able to duplicate experiments and validate conclusions, so bolstering the credibility of scientific work.

2.2 The Art of Innovating

Open data encourages creativity because it enables scientists to build upon previous research, which speeds up the rate at which new discoveries are made.

2.3 Participation of the Public

The sharing of data encourages public participation in scientific endeavors. The gap between scientists and the public can be bridged by allowing citizens, educators, and students access to scientific research as well as the ability to understand that research.

2.4 Reduction in Expenses

The exchange of data helps to cut down on redundant data collection, which can save money and free up a lot of resources. It maximizes the efficiency of the research efforts.

3. The Advantages of Engaging in Open Science and Sharing Data

3.1 The Quickening Pace of Scientific Advancement

The elimination of redundant work and the facilitation of increased collaboration both contribute to open science's ability to hasten the pace of scientific advancement.

3.2 Increased Openness and Availability

The scientific community gains trust and confidence when there is transparency in the conduct of research. It makes it possible for research techniques and conclusions to be scrutinized, validated, and evaluated critically.

3.3 A Greater Number of Potential Users

Publications with open access and data that are freely shared can be accessed by a wider audience, including researchers working in situations with limited resources, policymakers, and the general public.

3.4 An Increase in the Quality of the Data

Because they are aware that their work will be reviewed by others, researchers who share their data are more likely to keep the data quality and organization standards to a higher standard.

4. Obstacles Faced by Open Science and the Sharing of Data

4.1 Concerns Regarding Privacy and Ethical Behavior

Concerns about privacy and ethics are raised whenever data is shared, but this is especially true whenever it incorporates personal or confidential information. Researchers have a responsibility to ensure that the sharing of data follows all applicable legal and ethical requirements.

4.2 Administration of the Data

The efficient administration of data is absolutely necessary for the sharing of data. The correct organization, documentation, and storage of data requires an investment of both time and resources from the researchers.

4.3 Property of an Intellectual Nature

It can be difficult to strike a balance between the sharing of data and protecting intellectual property rights, particularly in situations involving economic interests or patents.

4.4 The Shifting of Culture

The research community will need to undergo a cultural transition in order to fully embrace open science and data sharing. The promotion of these principles is the responsibility of researchers, institutions, and funding agencies.

5. The Constantly Changing Terrain

5.1 Open Platforms for Scientific Research

Open science platforms like Zenodo and figshare give researchers the infrastructure they need to share and preserve their work, which might include datasets, code, and papers.

5.2 Alterations to the Policies

The adoption of open science policies and the requirement that data be shared as a condition for receiving financial support for research is becoming increasingly common among funding organizations, academic institutions, and government bodies.

5.3 Archival Storage Facilities

There are a variety of scientific sectors that are seeing the emergence of specialized data repositories, which provide safe and accessible storage for research data.

5.4 Data Quality Assurance

Standardizing data formats and metadata not only improves the discoverability and usefulness of shared data but also assures that data can be exchanged between different systems.

The scientific community is undergoing a fundamental shift that is being driven in large part by open science and the sharing of data. In the end, the adoption of these techniques hastens the pace of scientific advancement since they improve research transparency, collaboration, and accessibility. Researchers, institutions, and funding agencies are increasingly recognizing the benefits of open science and data sharing in advancing knowledge and addressing complex global concerns. This is despite the fact that there are hurdles. Open science and data sharing are positioned to become even more important to the scientific process, which will unlock new opportunities for innovation and discovery. As the digital age continues to alter the way research is conducted and communicated, open science and data sharing are poised to become even more central.

3.4 Data ethics and privacy concerns

In this digital age, data is a powerful force that drives innovation, improves services, and informs decisions across a variety of industries. On the other hand, the rapid growth of available data has given rise to significant concerns around data ethics and privacy. It is becoming increasingly important that we find a way to strike a balance between the potential benefits of data-driven technology and the protection of individual rights and privacy as we continue to gather, store, and share an ever-increasing number of personally identifiable information. In this article, the ethical implications of data use and privacy problems are investigated. The essay also highlights the obstacles, regulatory frameworks, and best practices that are involved in ensuring responsible data management.

1. **The Ethical Treatment of Data and the Definition of Responsible Data Use**
   1.1 Openness and honesty
   It is imperative that organizations maintain complete candor on the data gathering and utilization procedures they have in place. Users have a right to know what data is collected, why it is being collected, and how it will be used in the future.
   1.2 The Concept of Informed Consent
   Before collecting any personal information from individuals, it is necessary to obtain their clear and unambiguous agreement beforehand. This is a fundamental ethical obligation. This concept ensures that the people whose information is being collected are aware of what will happen to it and give their consent to it.
   1.3 Equitableness
   The gathering of data and the analysis of it have to be objective and fair. It is essential to steer clear of discriminatory policies and procedures, such as algorithmic prejudice and profiling.
   1.4 Accepting Responsibility
   Data collectors and processors ought to be held accountable for the data they collect and the information they process. This

involves putting in place safety precautions to prevent data from being compromised and checking that the data is accurate.

2. **Concerns Regarding Privacy: Keeping Personal Information Confidential**

   2.1 Violations of Data Privacy

   When unauthorized people or organizations gain access to sensitive information, this is known as a data breach. Data breaches frequently result in victims suffering identity theft and financial losses.

   2.2 Data Profiling and Analysis

   Collecting and analyzing data to construct thorough profiles of individuals, including their preferences, actions, and interests, is what data profiling entails. Data profiling can be done both manually and automatically. The use of profiling can be intrusive and lead to repercussions that are not warranted.

   2.3 Keeping an Eye on Things

   Concerns about one's right to privacy are warranted when government and corporate surveillance are involved. Civil rights and the scope of governmental and corporate authority have come under scrutiny in recent years as a result of widespread surveillance and data collecting.

   2.4 Acceptance and Free Will

   Data collection often occurs without individuals' having provided their informed consent, and individuals may not have a choice in the manner in which their data is used. The loss of autonomy and control over their own personal information results from this.

3. **Obstacles Facing Data Privacy and Ethical Standards**

   3.1 The Quickening Pace of Technological Advancement

   The advancement of technology frequently races ahead of moral and ethical considerations. Emerging technologies, such as artificial intelligence and the internet of things, provide unanticipated ethical challenges that have not been adequately addressed as of yet.

3.2 The Scattered Nature of Regulations

Regulations regarding data protection differ from country to country, which creates discrepancies and adds complexity for businesses that operate in multiple countries.

3.3 The Absence of General Knowledge

There are a lot of people who are ignorant of the amount to which their data is collected, and they might not completely grasp the repercussions this has on their privacy.

3.4 The Commercialization of Data

The commoditization of data has resulted in the creation of financial incentives for companies to gather and trade personal information, which has led to the raising of ethical problems about data-driven business models.

4. Regulatory Frameworks and Industry Standard Operating Procedures

4.1 The General Regulation on the Protection of Data (GDPR)

The General Data Protection Regulation (GDPR), which was put into effect by the European Union, is an all-encompassing framework that gives individuals increased control over their personal data. It mandates that enterprises acquire users' unequivocal consent, tell customers about the data gathering process, and put in place stringent data protection protocols.

4.2 Consumer Protection and Privacy Act of California (CCPA)

The CCPA gives customers in the state of California the right to access their personal data and the ability to request that it be deleted. In addition to this, it puts stringent standards on enterprises regarding data protection and disclosure.

4.3 Reduction of the Amount of Data

Data reduction strategies entail collecting only the minimum amount of information required to accomplish a particular goal. This not only lowers the possibility of data breaches, but it also restricts the quantity of personally identifiable information that companies keep.

4.4 Confidentiality by Design

Privacy by design is a preventative method of data security that integrates privacy considerations into the early stages of product and service creation. This method is also known as "privacy by default."

In today's data-driven world, one of the most persistent challenges is striking a healthy balance between data ethics and privacy concerns, on the one hand, and the potential benefits of data-driven technology, on the other. It is absolutely necessary to ensure that ethical data practices and privacy measures are maintained in light of the fact that data will continue to play an increasingly prominent role in our lives.

Protecting individual rights and creating trust can be accomplished through the responsible use of data by adhering to the values of transparency, informed consent, fairness, and accountability. The General Data Protection Regulation (GDPR) and the California Consumer Privacy Act (CCPA) are two examples of legal frameworks that help hold firms accountable for data protection. Data minimization and privacy by design encourage ethical data practices from the very beginning.

In this constantly shifting environment, it is absolutely necessary to find a happy medium between innovative ideas and precautionary measures. A society can exploit the potential of data while still respecting personal privacy and ethical values if it practices responsible data management. This not only benefits individuals, but it also builds confidence and integrity in the digital economy, which enables the society to benefit from data.

Chapter 4

High-Performance Computing

High-performance computing, also known as HPC, is a subfield of computing that pushes the limits of what is feasible in terms of the amount of data that can be processed, the amount of data that can be handled, and the amount of problem that can be solved. It is a crucial tool for scientific research, engineering, and a range of businesses, since it makes it feasible to execute activities that were long thought to be either impossible or extremely time-consuming in an effective manner. We will go into the history of high-performance computing as well as its applications, technology, obstacles, and future prospects in this all-encompassing investigation of HPC. The goal of this investigation is to shed light on how HPC is revolutionizing our world.

Comprehending the World of High-Performance Computing

The term "high-performance computing" refers to the use of supercomputers and various approaches for parallel processing in order to find solutions to difficult problems that require a great deal of computing power. It is not a single technology or concept, but rather an aggregation of hardware, software, and algorithms designed to operate together in sync to give superior computing capabilities. Specifically, it is referred to as a "cloud." Processing and analyzing data at speeds and scales that are impossible to achieve with standard computing methods is the core objective of high-performance computing, or HPC.

A Concise Overview of the Development of High-Performance Computing

Beginning in the middle of the 20th century, high-performance computing may be traced back to its origins. In the early 1960s, the term "supercomputer" was initially used for the purpose of describing devices such as the Control Data Corporation (CDC) 6600, which is widely regarded as the world's first supercomputer.

The CDC 6600, which had a peak capability of 3 million floating-point operations per second (FLOPS), is credited with laying the groundwork for high-performance computing throughout the 1960s.

In the 1970s, Seymour Cray, who is known as the "father of super-computing," created a series of supercomputers. One of these machines, the Cray-1, was capable of speeds of up to 80 MHz and had a peak performance of 250 MFLOPS.

In the 1980s, parallel computing became an important technology, and vector processors such as the Cray-2 gained popularity. These processors were able to achieve peak capabilities in the gigaflop range.

Massively parallel processing (MPP) devices, such as the Connection Machine and the Cray T3D/T3E, were pioneers in the field of scalable, high-performance computing in the 1990s.

The decade of the 2000s saw the rise of cluster computing and grid computing, both of which enabled academics to tap into the power of distributed systems and the internet.

Accelerated computing, which made use of graphics processing units (GPUs) and field-programmable gate arrays (FPGAs), introduced a new facet to high-performance computing in the 2010s and made it possible to achieve even higher levels of speed.

During the 2020s, quantum computing began to gain traction as a disruptive technology that held the promise of unmatched computational powers.

The search of more computing power has been unrelenting over the course of this history. This goal has been driven by scientific curiosity, engineering problems, and the ever-growing requirements of a variety of applications.

Utilizations and Case Studies of High-Performance Computing

1. **The Advancement of Science**
   High-performance computing is essential to the process of scientific discovery. In disciplines such as astrophysics, climate science, quantum chemistry, and molecular biology, it makes complicated simulations, data analysis, and modeling much easier to accomplish. The accuracy with which researchers are able to model cosmic phenomena, anticipate changes in the climate, or understand the behavior of subatomic particles is astounding.

2. **Modelling of the Weather and Climate**
   High-performance computing is essential to the processes of weather forecasting and climate modeling.
   For these applications to produce accurate forecasts and evaluate long-term climate trends, the processing of enormous volumes of data and the running of complicated simulations is required. The accuracy of these models can have significant repercussions for society, ranging from the prevention of natural disasters to the distribution of resources.

3. **Medical Research and the Pharmaceutical Industry**
   High-Performance Computing is being used in the pharmaceutical industry to speed up the
   processes of drug research and development. The search for promising drug candidates, the prediction of their interactions with biological systems, and the optimization of their properties are all carried out with the assistance of molecular dynamics simulations and bioinformatics analysis. High-Performance Computing (HPC) is useful in the healthcare industry for genetics, personalized medication, and the analysis of medical images.

4. **Engineering in Aerospace and Other Domains**

    In the aerospace and engineering industries, high-performance computing (HPC) is utilized in the process of designing and simulating complex systems. These systems include aircraft, spacecraft, and automobiles. Engineers are able to optimize designs, cut costs, and increase safety with the use of computational fluid dynamics (CFD), finite element analysis (FEA), and structural simulations.

5. **The Investigation and Modeling of Energy Sources**

    For reservoir simulation, seismic imaging, and the optimization of drilling operations, high-performance computing (HPC) is essential to the energy business. These apps make it possible for energy businesses to discover new sources of energy, improve extraction procedures, and lessen their influence on the environment.

6. **Modeling of Financial Situations**

    High-performance computing is used in the banking and finance industry for risk analysis, algorithmic trading, and portfolio optimization. High-performance computing (HPC) is the only technology that can make high-frequency trading, for example, which requires rapid data processing and decision-making, possible.

7. **A.I. and M.L. (Machine Learning and Artificial Intelligence)**

    The construction and training of machine learning and artificial intelligence models rely heavily on high-performance computing (HPC). Because deep learning methods, neural networks, and tasks involving natural language processing all require enormous computer resources, high-performance computing has become a vital instrument for the evolution of artificial intelligence.

8. **The Defense of the Nation and Its Security**

    High-Performance Computing (HPC) is utilized by government agencies and defense groups for activities such as cryptography, cyber warfare, and threat analysis. The decryption of encrypted data, the simulation of military operations, and the analysis of intelligence data are all performed by supercomputers.

9. **Referring to the Arts and the Media**

The depiction of complicated visual effects in movies, the simulation of physical processes in video games, and the improvement of the quality of digital content are all areas in which the entertainment sector can profit from HPC.

The majority of potential applicants are not even being considered here. High-performance computing has an all-pervasive impact on a vast number of sectors, making it possible for advances that have a direct bearing on our everyday lives and the world around us.

High-Performance Computing and the Technologies That Drive It

1. **Computors and Boosting Devices**

   CPUs, or central processing units, have long served as the backbone of high-performance computing (HPC) systems. For accelerated computation, however, modern high-performance computing systems also rely on components such as graphics processing units (GPUs) and field-programmable gate arrays (FPGAs). Simulations in the fields of science and engineering, machine learning, and artificial intelligence have all been significantly advanced thanks to the advent of GPUs, which are specifically built to perform simultaneous operations in an effective manner.

2. **The Rank Order of Memory**

   In order to reduce the amount of time spent accessing data, HPC systems incorporate a complex memory architecture. Caches with a high data transfer rate, multi-channel memories, and non-volatile memory technologies like Intel Optane all contribute to a performance boost and a reduction in the number of data bottlenecks.

3. **Establishes connections**

   It is essential for high-performance computing clusters to have interconnects that are both quick and scalable. This ensures that data can be moved quickly between processing units. The required bandwidth and low-latency connections can be provided by technologies such as InfiniBand and Ethernet, in addition to any unique interconnect solutions that may be implemented.

4. **Stacking of Software**

   The software utilized by high-performance computing environments (HPC) is extremely specialized. It consists of operating systems, compilers, libraries, and parallel programming models. Developers are able to design parallel programs by utilizing technologies such as the Message Passing Interface (MPI) and OpenMP. These technologies allow developers to take advantage of the full capability of HPC computers.

5. **Various Options for Storage**

   When working with massive datasets and needing to support fast I/O operations, high-performance storage systems are absolutely necessary. The storage infrastructure for high-performance computing (HPC) relies heavily on parallel file systems, distributed storage solutions, and ongoing improvements to solid-state drives (SSDs).

6. **Control of the Power Supply and Cooling**

   High-performance computing systems produce a substantial quantity of heat due to the high processing demands they must meet. For the sake of maintaining the dependability of the system, it is vital to use effective cooling solutions, such as liquid cooling and sophisticated air cooling. In addition, the technologies that manage electricity strive to improve performance while simultaneously decreasing the amount of energy that is consumed.

7. **Computing on the Quantum Level**

Despite the fact that it is still in its infancy, quantum computing has the promise of having an order of magnitude higher processing power than traditional computing. Because quantum bits, also known as qubits, are able to concurrently represent several states, classical computers may not be able to solve some problems as quickly as they could using qubits. Quantum computing technology is now being actively developed by businesses such as IBM and Google, as well as by startups like as Rigetti.

High-Performance Computing Faces a Number of Obstacles

While high-performance computing has made significant strides in recent years, the industry still confronts a number of obstacles that must be overcome if it is to maintain its pace of growth and innovation.

1. **Efficient Use of Energy**

   The use of high-performance computing systems can result in a significant amount of energy consumption. The key issue for high-performance computing (HPC) is to achieve more processing capability while simultaneously minimizing the amount of power consumed. This covers developments in power-efficient processors as well as improvements in cooling methods.

2. **Capacity to Grow**

   The task of ensuring that applications can scale efficiently so that they can make use of all of the available resources is an ongoing one as high-performance computing systems continue to grow in size and complexity. There is a constant requirement for innovative algorithmic and programming models that are able to fully leverage the potential of these systems.

3. **Management of the Data**

   In high-performance computing, one of the most common challenges is managing massive volumes of data. In order to prevent bottlenecks and the loss of data, it is essential to implement efficient storage systems and data management methods. This is especially important to keep in mind when dealing with applications such as genomics, climate modeling, and simulations on a big scale.

4. **The Complicated Nature of Software**

   The software used for high-performance computing is extremely specialized and frequently complicated. It takes a lot of skill and resources to create, optimize, and maintain software for high-performance computing (HPC) computers. Both simplifying the process of developing software and making it more user-friendly are continuing aims.

5. **The presence of a heterogeneous mix**

   The addition of accelerators such as GPUs and FPGAs to regular CPUs brings an additional level of complexity to high-performance computing (HPC) systems. The problem that developers and researchers confront is making sure that programs can take advantage of these diverse architectures in the most efficient way possible.

6. **Concerns Regarding Safety**

   Cybercriminals see high-performance computing systems as desirable targets. The protection of these systems and the data contained within them from dangers and openings in security is a continuing worry. In the world of high-performance computing (HPC), high-security standards and practices are an absolute necessity.

7. **The portability of software**

Applications designed for high-performance computing (HPC) are frequently extensively specialized for particular hardware, which makes them less portable. Constant effort is required to improve software portability and make it possible for applications to run on a variety of high-performance computing platforms.

The Prospects for High-Performance Computing in the Future

1. **Computing on an Exascale Scale**
   The next major step forward for high-performance computing will be exascale computing, which will have the capacity to carry out one quintillion computations per second (1018). Exascale systems are being aggressively pursued by nations such as the United States and China. These systems have potential uses in the modeling of climate change, the production of fusion energy, and astronomy.

2. **Computing on the Quantum Level**
   The field of quantum computing is continually advancing, and despite the fact that functional
   quantum computers are not yet ready for use in everyday life, these machines have the potential to change fields such as encryption, materials science, and challenges involving optimization.

3. **Incorporation of AI**
   The fields of high-performance computing and artificial intelligence are getting closer and closer together. AI accelerators are becoming increasingly commonplace in high-performance computing (HPC) systems, and AI algorithms are increasingly being utilized in efforts to improve the efficiency of HPC workflows and overall system performance.

4. **Hybridized Building Structures**
   Future high-performance computing (HPC) systems are likely to include heterogeneous designs that combine conventional CPUs with graphical processing units (GPUs), field-programmable gate arrays (FPGAs), and other types of specialized accelerators. The development of applications that are able to utilize these hybrid systems to their full potential will be the primary focus of research.

5. **Computing at the Edge and in the Cloud**
   Edge computing and cloud-based high-performance computing are gaining pace and increasing high-performance computing's reach beyond traditional data centers. This development makes

high-performance computer resources more accessible and gives users more leeway in how they can use them.
6. **Information Technology and Genomic Research**
High-performance computing (HPC) is positioned to be beneficial to the progress of genomics and bioinformatics.
Researchers are analyzing massive information, simulating biological processes, and speeding up drug discovery efforts with the help of high-performance computing tools.
7. **Environmental Responsibility and Computer Technology**
Taking on the task of improving energy efficiency should be a top priority. It is absolutely necessary to implement sustainable high-performance computing practices in order to lessen the impact that high-performance computing has on the surrounding environment. These practices should include the use of efficient cooling solutions and renewable energy sources.
8. **Participation in International Organizations**

In order to effectively address difficult issues that cut over national boundaries, international cooperation in the field of high-performance computing is required. Both collaboration and the pooling of resources are being encouraged thanks to efforts such as the European High-Performance Computing Joint Undertaking (EuroHPC) and international research alliances.

4.1 The role of supercomputing in scientific breakthroughs

Within the area of scientific investigation, supercomputing has evolved into an instrument that is now essential due to the huge processing capacity and powerful computational capabilities it possesses. Over the course of its existence, it has been an essential factor in the development of a great many ground-breaking discoveries and inventions in a wide range of scientific fields. This article digs into the varied role that supercomputing plays in facilitating scientific advances, demonstrating how it has changed research and broadened the horizons of human knowledge.

DIGITAL INFRASTRUCTURE FOR SCIENCE ADVANCEMENT

The Development of Extremely Powerful Computers

The Concept of Supercomputing First Presented Itself in the 1960s, When Machines Like the CDC 6600 and Cray-1 Led the Way The idea of supercomputing first presented itself in the 1960s, when machines like these led the way. Floating-point operations per second (FLOPS) were well within the capabilities of these early supercomputers.

Vector Processors and Parallel Computing: Both vector processors and parallel computing rose to prominence in the 1970s and 1980s. These technologies were utilized by supercomputers such as the Cray-2 and the Cray X-MP in order to achieve higher levels of performance.

Massive Parallel Processing (MPP): The 1990s saw the advent of massively parallel processing (MPP) systems, such as the Connection Machine and the Cray T3D/T3E, which made it possible to scale up computing power and to disperse it.

Computing in Clusters and Grids: The decade of the 2000s saw significant growth in both cluster computing and grid computing. Researchers were able to access a large pool of computer resources by using these technologies, which permitted distributed computing over networks and the internet.

Accelerated Computing: The 2010s ushered in a new era of supercomputing thanks to the widespread use of field-programmable gate arrays (FPGAs) and graphics processing units (GPUs) for accelerated computing. The performance was able to be increased even more thanks to these hardware accelerators.

Computing on the Quantum Level Although it is still in its infancy, quantum computing holds the potential to bring in a new era of supercomputing. Quantum computers have the potential to address issues that classical supercomputers are unable to solve at the present time.

The importance of supercomputing in scientific research has expanded at an exponential rate alongside the development of related technologies.

The Role of Supercomputers in Scientific Research

1. **Computer simulations of the climate and forecasting of the weather**

   The modeling of climate and the forecasting of weather both need the use of supercomputers. These systems process enormous volumes of meteorological data in order to produce precise weather forecasts and to simulate various climatic scenarios. Researchers rely on supercomputing to gain a better understanding of the climate of the Earth, make accurate predictions of natural disasters, and devise mitigation plans for climate change.

2. **The study of astronomy and the universe**

   Astronomers are now able to model intricate astronomical occurrences thanks to the proliferation of powerful supercomputers. They model the behavior of stars, galaxies, and black holes, which helps shed light on the beginnings of the universe as well as the future of the universe. The hunt for exoplanets and the investigation of dark matter and dark energy both benefit from the utilization of supercomputers.

3. **Medical Research and the Pharmaceutical Industry**

   When it comes to the pharmaceutical business, supercomputing is an essential tool for the research and development of new drugs.

   Researchers are now able to screen enormous libraries of compounds, anticipate how those compounds will interact with biological systems, and build more effective medications thanks to molecular dynamics simulations and computational chemistry. The application of supercomputing in the medical field speeds up research in genetics and customized treatment, as well as the interpretation of medical imaging.

4. **The Science of Materials**

   The behavior of materials, down to the atomic and molecular levels, can be simulated using supercomputing, which is used by materials scientists. These simulations are helpful in the process of developing novel materials that have desirable qualities, such as alloys that are lightweight but strong or superconductors that are stable at high temperatures.

5. **The Physics of High-Energy Particles**

   Experiments in high-energy physics, such as those carried out at particle accelerators like the Large Hadron Collider (LHC), are greatly aided by the utilization of supercomputing technology. It provides assistance in the analysis of massive datasets that are produced as a result of particle collisions, which paves the way for the discovery of new particles and a better comprehension of fundamental physics.

6. **The Exploration of Space**

   The use of supercomputers is indispensable for space agencies such as NASA and the European Space Agency (ESA) when it comes to the planning of missions, the design of spacecraft, and the analysis of data. Simulations of space missions, simulations of the mechanics of orbits, and simulations of the interpretation of data from space telescopes and probes are all made possible by this technology.

7. **Energy from Fusion**

   In the pursuit of clean and abundant energy, supercomputers are being used to mimic the processes involved in nuclear fusion. Researchers are able to better understand the behavior of plasma at severe temperatures and pressures by using these models, which also help researchers improve the design of fusion reactors.

8. **Research on the Most Basic Level**

Supercomputing provides the computational power necessary for lengthy simulations in scientific domains such as quantum chemistry, nuclear physics, and condensed matter physics. It contributes to an improved comprehension of the behavior of matter on microscopic sizes, which in turn leads to the discovery of new findings in fundamental science.

The Contribution of Supercomputing to the Furtherance of Scientific Research

1. **Simulations That Are Complicated**
   regular computing platforms are not equipped to handle the complexity of the simulations that may be run on supercomputers. These simulations would be impossible to execute on regular computing platforms. The behavior of proteins at the atomic level or the interactions of thousands of galaxies in a cosmological model can both be simulated by researchers. Complex processes can also be modeled using computer simulations.
2. **A Study of the Data**
   The amount of data that is produced as a result of many scientific experiments is staggering. Supercomputers provide the computing muscle necessary to analyze, process, and extract useful insights from massive datasets. These databases can be found on the internet. This is especially clear in the field of genomics, which creates enormous amounts of data through the examination of DNA sequences.
3. **The art of optimization**
   Supercomputing is a useful tool for solving optimization issues, since it assists researchers in selecting the most appropriate options from a large pool of potential responses. This is useful in areas such as aerospace engineering, which makes use of supercomputers to improve the aerodynamic design of spacecraft and aircraft.
4. **The Use of Predictive Models**
   The ability to create prediction models, made possible by supercomputing, is extremely important in domains such as epidemiology. Researchers are able to design models to anticipate the spread of diseases, assess the impact of public health initiatives, and come up with solutions to contain diseases.

5. **Modeling on Multiple Scales**
   In several subfields of science, phenomena can be observed on a number of different scales. Researchers are now able to model these processes at multiple scales concurrently thanks to the advent of supercomputers. In the field of neuroscience, for instance, multiscale modeling can contribute to a better understanding of the functioning of the brain, from neuronal networks to cognitive processes.

6. **Collaboration Across Multiple Disciplines**
   The use of supercomputers encourages collaboration amongst researchers working in a variety of subjects. With the assistance of supercomputers, interdisciplinary projects that need for a variety of knowledge as well as computational resources can be completed successfully. Scientists that study climate, oceanography, and ecology all work together, for instance, to model the effects that climate change will have on ecosystems.

7. **Putting Hypotheses to the Test**
   The process of performing virtual experiments and putting hypotheses to the test can be sped up with the use of supercomputing. Saving both time and resources, scientists are able to investigate a diverse variety of possibilities in order to validate or disprove ideas.

8. **Initiatives Regarding Education and Community Engagement**

It is common practice for supercomputing centers to participate in educational and outreach activities, thereby making their resources available for use in educational settings. This contributes to the education of aspiring scientists and researchers of the next generation in cutting-edge computational methods.

The Obstacles That Stand in the Way of Supercomputing's Future

Although supercomputing has unquestionably made significant contributions to the advancement of scientific research, the field still has a ways to go before it can fully realize its potential.

1. **Efficient Use of Energy**

   As the processing capacity of supercomputers continues to increase, the amounts of energy that they require also continue to rise. Taking action to solve this problem is absolutely necessary in order to make supercomputing more environmentally friendly. Ongoing research is being conducted into computing systems and cooling methods that are energy efficient.

2. **Capacity to Grow**

   Since supercomputers are become both more complicated and more huge, it is absolutely necessary to build software and algorithms that are scalable. Researchers have a responsibility to make sure that applications can make effective use of the capabilities offered by these systems.

3. **Management of the Data**

   The management of huge datasets continues to be difficult. It is extremely important for data-intensive scientific domains to have solutions that are efficient in terms of data storage, management, and retrieval in order to avoid bottlenecks and loss of data.

4. **Architectures with Heterogeneous Components**

   The use of heterogeneous designs in supercomputers, which integrate several kinds of processors such as central processing units, graphics processing units, and accelerators, is becoming increasingly common. The continuous challenge for developers is to make sure that programs can take advantage of all the capabilities offered by these systems.

5. **Safekeeping**

   Cybercriminals see supercomputers as valuable targets for their intrusions. Constant attention must be paid to preventing unauthorized access to these systems and the data they store. It is essential to have high-security standards and processes.

6. Computing on the Quantum Level

The field of supercomputing is facing both a challenge and an opportunity in the form of quantum computing. Quantum computers have the potential to significantly increase computing capacity, but there are also concerns about its impact on encryption and data security. Researchers in the field of supercomputing are looking into different ways to use the promise of quantum computing.

The future of supercomputing promises a number of interesting possibilities, including the following:

1. **Computing on an Exascale Scale**
   The era of exascale computing, in which a computer is able to complete one quintillion calculations (1018) every second, is not too far off. Many nations and organizations are currently engaged in the development of exascale systems, which will lead to the discovery of previously inaccessible study territories.

2. **The Incorporation of Quantum Computing**
   The combination of classical supercomputing with quantum computing has the potential to bring about a sea change in the way that scientific inquiry is carried out. The use of hybrid quantum-classical algorithms makes it possible to solve issues that could not be solved before.

3. **Eco-Friendly Computing**
   A rising priority in the field of supercomputing is environmental responsibility. The use of renewable energy sources, effective cooling solutions, and environmentally responsible disposal of electronic waste are some of the ways in which the environmental impact of supercomputing can be mitigated.

4. **Cooperative efforts on a global scale**

It is absolutely necessary for nations and organizations to work together in order to confront the scientific issues that face the entire world. Cooperation and the sharing of resources are encouraged through the implementation of projects such as the European High-Performance Computing Joint Undertaking (EuroHPC) and international research alliances.

4.2 Parallel processing and distributed computing

Both parallel processing and distributed computing are examples of foundational concepts that have significantly influenced the development of the computer sector. These methods make it possible to execute complicated tasks in an effective manner by partitioning them into more manageable subtasks and utilizing various computer resources in parallel. We will go into the definitions of parallel processing and distributed computing, as well as their central principles, applications, advantages, and the ever-evolving landscape of these two types of computing.

The Concept of Parallel Processing, an Essential Ingredient

Processing in parallel, often known as parallel processing, is a type of computing in which numerous processors or cores collaborate to carry out a single operation simultaneously. The primary objective is to hasten the execution of a program or computation by breaking it down into a series of more manageable subtasks that can be worked on simultaneously. There are multiple levels at which parallel processing can be implemented, including instruction-level parallelism, task-level parallelism, and data-level parallelism.

Concepts Foundational to Parallel Processing

Executing many instructions or activities in parallel is the core concept of parallel processing. This allows for a greater throughput while also reducing the amount of time needed to complete a task.

Scalability refers to the ability of a parallel processing system to adjust to varying amounts of work by adding additional processors or cores, which enables the system to meet rising levels of computational demand.

Load balancing is the process of effectively distributing workloads among multiple processors such that some are not overworked while others are not being exploited to their full potential.

Synchronization: In parallel processing, synchronization techniques are used to coordinate the execution of activities. This makes it possible to ensure that the tasks do their job at the appropriate time and in the appropriate order.

Exchange of Data: Parallel processing frequently necessitates the exchange of data among the processors. It is vital to have data protection and consistency procedures in place in order to prevent data corruption and conflicts.

Parallel processing in its various forms

Task parallelism is a technique that involves breaking down a major project into several smaller, self-contained subtasks that can be worked on at the same time. Applications such as rendering, video encoding, and distributed web crawling are typical examples of tasks that benefit from parallel processing.

Parallelism of Data: Parallelism of data refers to the process of performing the same operation on several data pieces at the same time. Image processing, scientific simulations, and data analytics are all examples of applications in which this is a common occurrence.

Instruction-level Parallelism Instruction-level parallelism takes advantage of the fact that a single processor or core can simultaneously carry out the execution of many machine instructions. Pipelining and out-of-order execution are two examples of modern techniques that are used by microprocessors to increase the amount of parallelism at the instruction level.

The term "bit-level parallelism" refers to the processing of several bits of data in parallel, which makes it possible to perform arithmetic and logic operations more quickly. It plays an essential role in both the construction of computers and the processing of data.

The capability of systems to engage in parallel processing, which considerably boosts their computational power, is an essential enabler for high-performance computing (HPC) programs.

Utilizing the Full Potential of Computer Networks (Distributed Computing)

The term "distributed computing" refers to a paradigm in the field of computer science in which tasks or calculations are dispersed across a number of networked computers, sometimes known as "nodes." These nodes collaborate with one another to find solutions to difficult issues, share resources, and participate collectively to the process of carrying out a bigger calculation. Through the use of distributed computing, the capabilities of a single machine can be expanded by leveraging the combined power of a number of other devices.

The Most Important Ideas Behind Distributed Computing

Decentralization: Distributed computing systems are decentralized, which means that there is no single point of failure or central control. This approach offers both scalability and the ability to tolerate errors.

Connectivity: In a distributed computing system, the nodes are connected to one another by a network, which enables them to communicate with one another and share data in an effective manner.

Sharing of Resources: Distributed systems frequently combine their resources, including memory, computing power, and storage space. The pooling of resources inevitably results in a more effective usage of those resources.

Concurrency is the ability of numerous users or programs to interact with a system at the same time. Distributed systems are built to handle multiple jobs at the same time, which enables concurrency.

Data Replication and Distribution: In a distributed system, data may be replicated and distributed among different nodes. This is done to ensure that data is always accessible and to improve the system's ability to tolerate errors.

The Various Forms That Distributed Computing Can Take

Computing in a Cluster: This type of computing involves connecting several computers that are located in close proximity to one another, frequently within the same data center. Application execution and high availability are provided by these clusters thanks to their collaborative effort.

Computing on a Grid: Computing on a grid involves the connectivity of resources that are located in different geographical locations to construct a virtual supercomputer.

This paradigm is frequently employed in the conduct of scientific research, which typically requires a significant amount of processing capacity.

The term "cloud computing" refers to a more recent method of distributed computing that makes use of the internet to provide computing resources whenever and wherever they are needed. Cloud service providers such as Amazon Web Services (AWS), Microsoft Azure, and Google Cloud each offer a comprehensive set of services that make it possible for individuals and enterprises to access scalable and distributed resources.

Computing in the Fog: Fog computing is an extension of cloud computing that takes it to the edge of the network. This brings computer resources closer to the location where the data is being generated. Real-time data processing and Internet of Things applications absolutely require it.

Computing on a Peer-to-Peer (P2P) Basis: P2P computing eliminates the need for centralized servers and makes it possible for peers to communicate and collaborate directly with one another. This methodology is utilized extensively in systems for file-sharing and communication, as well as in applications for blockchain technology.

The Benefits of Utilizing Distributed Computing

Scalability is the ability of a distributed system to quickly expand in order to support a growing workload. This expansion can be accomplished by adding more nodes or resources.

Tolerance for Error Distributed systems, by virtue of their decentralized architecture, are intrinsically tolerant of errors. Even if one of the nodes in the system fails, the system as a whole can continue to function thanks to the remaining nodes.

Sharing resources in distributed systems allows for more effective exploitation of available computational resources, which in turn reduces the amount of unused resources.

High Availability High availability can be provided by distributed systems since they distribute data and services over numerous nodes, which in turn reduces the amount of downtime that occurs.

Geographic Distribution Distributed computing makes it possible to geographically distribute resources, which in turn makes it possible to bring services and data to end users who are physically located closer to those resources.

Problems Associated with Distributed Computing

Maintaining data consistency in distributed systems can be difficult, particularly when there are interruptions in the network connection or multiple users are updating the same data at the same time.

Delay in the Network: The communication over a network in a distributed system can sometimes result in delay, which can negatively affect the performance of real-time applications.

Distributed systems have a responsibility to address security concerns, including those of data privacy, access control, and the integrity of data that is transmitted via networks.

Designing and managing distributed systems can be a hard endeavor, one that calls for specialized knowledge and a set of appropriate tools.

Examples of Where Parallel Processing and Distributed Computing Have Been Put to Use

1. **The Advancement of Science**

    When it comes to scientific simulations and data analysis, parallel processing is absolutely essential. In order to make progress in their study, disciplines like genetics, astrophysics, and climate modeling are dependent on the computational capacity offered by parallel processing.

The field of scientific research also makes extensive use of distributed computing, particularly in the area of high-energy physics experiments and molecular modeling. The search for signs of extraterrestrial life is carried out via distributed computer projects such as SETI@home, which examine radio signals received from space for any indications of extraterrestrial life.

2. **Prediction of the weather**

The use of parallel processing by meteorological agencies enables the running of high-resolution weather models, which contributes to more accurate and fast weather forecasts. Parallel computing on a massive scale is required for running the intricate simulations of weather conditions that are required by these models.

3. **Video Animation and Rendering Services**

Parallel processing is essential to the production of high-quality visual effects in motion pictures and 3D animations, which are used in the entertainment sector. The depiction of complicated scenes in real-time 3D games is accomplished through the use of distributed computing.

4. **High-Performance Computing (often abbreviated as HPC)**

Complex simulations, such as those used in nuclear research, material science, and climate modeling, can be executed by high-performance computing centers (HPCs) through the use of parallel processing. In order to supply enormous amounts of processing power for use in scientific research, several computing platforms, such as grid computing and cluster computing, make use of distributed computing.

5. **Analyses of the Data**

Distributed computing frameworks such as Apache Hadoop and Apache Spark are utilized in the fields of big data and data analytics in order to rapidly handle and analyze massive datasets.

6. **IoT (Internet of Things)**
   In Internet of Things applications, where data is generated from an overwhelming number of
   sensors and devices, parallel processing and distributed computing play an important role. Particularly, fog computing makes it possible to perform data processing and analysis in real time at the periphery of a network.
7. **Computing in the Cloud**
   Distributed computing is the backbone of cloud computing, which allows service providers to provide clients with scalable and reliable offerings. The fact that cloud data centers are dispersed across multiple locations guarantees both high availability and fault tolerance.
8. **The Technology Behind Blockchain**
   Distributed computing is necessary for the operation of blockchain networks, such as those used in cryptocurrencies, because these networks keep a decentralized ledger that records transactions in a secure manner.
9. **Distribution of Content**

Content delivery networks, often known as CDNs, make advantage of distributed computing in order to store and serve web content from servers that are physically located closer to end users. This helps to reduce latency and improve speed.

The Changing Face of the Landscape

1. **The Use of Accelerators for Parallel Processing**
   Graphics computing Units (GPUs) and Field-Programmable Gate Arrays (FPGAs) are two examples of specialized hardware accelerators that are utilized in modern parallel computing. These accelerators improve a system's capacity for parallel computing, making the system suitable for a wider variety of applications, such as machine learning and scientific simulations.

2. **Computing at the Edge**

   The principles of distributed computing are extended to the edge of the network through edge computing, which enables real-time data processing and analysis to take place closer to the data source. This is of utmost significance in applications such as internet of things and industrial automation as well as autonomous cars.

3. **Computing on the Quantum Level**

   Despite the fact that it is still in its infant phases, quantum computing represents a new frontier in the realm of parallel processing. Quantum computers have the ability to tackle issues that classical computers are unable to address at this time and offer exponentially more processing power.

4. **Computing on the Hybrid Cloud and Multiple Clouds**

   The on-premises data centers, private clouds, and public clouds that are utilized in hybrid clouds and multi-cloud architectures are used to do distributed computing. These approaches provide scalability, flexibility, and redundancy for their users.

5. **Technologies based on blockchain and distributed ledgers**

   The blockchain and distributed ledger technologies continue to advance, and its applications are expanding beyond the realm of cryptocurrencies to include areas such as the management of supply chains, the verification of identities, and smart contracts.

6. **Computing without a server**

   Serverless computing is a form of cloud computing that eliminates the need for developers to manage servers by utilizing distributed computing to carry out function execution in response to events. The deployment and scalability of applications are made easier by this architecture.

7. **Quantum-Resistant Encryption**

As quantum computing becomes more advanced, there will be an increased demand for encryption techniques that are not vulnerable to quantum computing in order to protect dispersed networks. Ongoing research and development efforts are being made in this area.

4.3 Cloud computing in scientific research

Cloud computing has emerged as a revolutionary force in the field of scientific research, radically altering the processes by which tests are carried out, data is evaluated, and discoveries are made. Researchers in a wide variety of fields can take advantage of the many benefits made available by this technology, which draws on the processing power of remote servers and the distributed computing resources offered by the internet.

Accessibility and Capacity for Growth

Cloud computing offers a number of advantages to scientific research, one of the most significant of which is the accessibility it provides to high-performance computer resources. Researchers are able to gain access to the necessary processing capacity without having to make costly infrastructure investments. academics may now carry out intricate simulations, data analysis, and modeling thanks to the democratization of computational resources. This opens up opportunities for academics working in both well-funded institutions and surroundings with little resources.

In addition, the scalability of cloud computing is an extremely useful asset for scientific study. The computing resources available to researchers can be simply scaled up or down depending on the requirements of a given project. This adaptability is especially important for scientific efforts that call for a significant amount of computer power, such as studies on genomes, climate modeling, or the discovery of new drugs.

The Storing and Management of Data

The use of cloud computing also provides powerful options for the administration and storage of data. Researchers are able to store big datasets safely, which ensures the data's integrity while also making it accessible and providing a backup. This feature is vital for professions such as astronomy, which require storing and analyzing massive amounts of observational data over extended periods of time.

Coordination and Interconnection Across the World

Computing in the cloud encourages collaboration among scholars all around the world. Cloud-based systems make it possible for several academics to collaborate on the same topic at the same time, regardless of where in the world they are physically located.

This feature of collaboration is especially advantageous for multinational research endeavors, which bring together specialists from a variety of places to work on difficult problems.

Economies of scale

The traditional infrastructure required for high-performance computing can sometimes be too expensive. Researchers only need to pay for the amount of resources they actually use, which results in significant cost savings made possible by cloud computing's pay-as-you-go pricing model. This removes the requirement for substantial amounts of funds and makes it possible for research projects to have greater financial flexibility.

The processing and examination of data

The processing and analysis of data are frequently computationally complex operations that are performed in scientific research. Computing in the cloud provides researchers with on-demand access to massive computational capabilities, which drastically cuts down the amount of time needed for data processing. For instance, researchers working in genomics now have a faster way to study DNA sequences, which should lead to more rapid progress in tailored therapy and our overall understanding of disease.

The processes of Simulation and Modeling

Complex simulations and models are essential to the advancement of several scientific disciplines, including astrophysics, materials science, and climate research. The use of cloud computing gives academics the ability to run these simulations on a scale that was previously inconceivable, which in turn opens up new doors for scientific discovery.

In a nutshell, cloud computing has emerged as an indispensable tool in the field of scientific study due to its accessibility, scalability, and cost-effectiveness, as well as the global collaboration it enables. Cloud computing is set to play an increasingly important part in scientific research as technology continues to improve, which will likely lead to the opening of new doors of opportunity and the quickening of the rate of discovery in a variety of fields.

Chapter 5

The Internet of Things (IoT) in Science

The Internet of Things (IoT) is a game-changing technology paradigm that has had a significant effect on many facets of our life, including smart cities and homes, industrial automation, and medical care. This paradigm shift has been brought about by the Internet of Things. The Internet of Things (IoT) has become a potent force in the field of science, where it is transforming the ways in which investigation is carried out, data is gathered, and discoveries are generated. The Internet of Things (IoT) has a wide range of potential applications and ramifications in the scientific community, which are discussed in this article. Some of these disciplines include environmental monitoring, healthcare, agriculture, and more.

Having a working knowledge of the Internet of Things (IoT)

Understanding the fundamental concepts and principles that underlie this technology paradigm

is necessary before delving into the applications of IoT in the scientific community.

IoT Explanation

The term "Internet of Things" refers to the interconnection of physical objects or "things" that have been embedded with sensors, software, and other technologies for the purpose of collecting and exchanging data over the internet or other communication networks. Devices, equipment, transportation systems, structures, and even living organisms can all be examples of things that can be connected to one another.

IoT's Most Important Parts and Pieces

Actuators and Sensors: Sensors are the "eyes and ears" of the Internet of Things; they collect data from the environment around them. Actuators are the "hands" that move things. Actuators, on the other hand, give Internet of Things devices the ability to operate in response to the data that they collect.

Connectivity is essential to the IoT, which is why data transfer between devices and the cloud is accomplished through the use of communication protocols and networks. Wi-Fi, cellular networks, Bluetooth, and Low-Power Wide-Area Networks (LPWAN) are all included in this category.

Processing and Analysis of Data The information that is gathered by Internet of Things devices is uploaded to the cloud, where it is then processed, analyzed, and converted into useful insights.

User Interface: The Internet of Things frequently incorporates a user interface, such as an online dashboard or mobile app, by means of which users may remotely monitor and operate connected devices.

Applications of IoT in the Scientific Community

Monitoring and Investigation of the Environment

1. **Research on the Climate and the Weather**
   Research on climate and weather has been profoundly impacted by the Internet of Things' sensors and weather stations. These instruments collect data on temperature, humidity, air pressure, wind speed, and precipitation, all of which contribute to more accurate weather forecasts and climate modeling. Researchers can

DIGITAL INFRASTRUCTURE FOR SCIENCE ADVANCEMENT

use this data to do analyses in order to investigate the effects of climate change.

2. **Marine sciences, specifically Oceanography and Biology**

   Data on ocean currents, water temperature, salinity, and marine life is gathered by underwater robots and buoys that are enabled with internet of things technology. Studying ocean ecosystems, tracking the migration patterns of marine animals, and monitoring the effects of climate change on marine settings are all made easier with the use of this information.

3. **Protection of the Natural Environment**

   The Internet of Things is an important tool in the fight to preserve the environment. Sensors are utilized to keep track of endangered species, monitor the movement of wildlife, and ensure the protection of ecosystems. For instance, Internet of Things (IoT) video traps can assist in anti-poaching efforts and monitoring of wildlife populations.

4. **Keeping an Eye on the Air Quality**

IoT sensors are used to assess the quality of the air in metropolitan areas by measuring the concentrations of various pollutants. These pollutants include particulate matter, nitrogen dioxide, sulfur dioxide, and carbon monoxide. This information is essential for determining the state of the air we breathe, resolving concerns about pollution, and formulating plans to enhance public health.

Agriculture as well as Agricultural Precision

1. **Agriculture with Great Accuracy**

   Agriculture is becoming a data-driven industry thanks to the proliferation of IoT devices. On farms, sensors gather information about the conditions of the soil, the health of the crops, the weather, and the amount of water that is used. The use of this information enables precision farming, which improves the efficiency of irrigating, applying fertilizer, and controlling pests.

2. **Keeping an Eye on the Animals**
   Tracking devices that are enabled by the internet of things are used by farmers to monitor the well-being and whereabouts of their animals. This technology makes it easier to manage animal care, ensure that animals receive their immunizations on time, and deter theft.
3. **Observation of the Condition of the Crops**
   The health of crops may be monitored with the assistance of IoT sensors and drones fitted with cameras. This allows for the detection of diseases, deficits in nutrients, and pest infestations. The use of this data gives farmers the ability to protect their crops in a timely manner.
4. **the optimization of the supply chain**

The Internet of Things is used to monitor the status of agricultural products as well as their location all the way through the supply chain, from the farm to the consumer's table. This reduces waste while also ensuring the quality and safety of the food.

Healthcare Provision and the Conduct of Biomedical Research

1. **Monitoring of Patients Via Remote Connection**
   Wearables and other Internet of Things (IoT) devices, such as medical sensors, make it possible to remotely monitor patients. Individuals are able to monitor their own health indicators, and medical professionals have access to data in real time, which ultimately results in improved disease management and preventive care.
2. **The Creation of New Drugs**
   The Internet of Things makes it possible to monitor clinical trials and laboratory research in real time, which makes drug discovery and development significantly easier. Researchers have the ability to remotely collect data on the impact of new pharmaceuticals

on patients as well as data on the interactions between different medications.

3. **Genomic Analysis and Individualized Medical Treatment**
   The Internet of Things is an extremely important component of genomics research because it enables the collecting and analysis of massive genomic datasets. This information is used in customized medicine, which is a form of treatment that is formulated specifically for an individual based on their genetic profile.
4. **Devices used in the IoT for healthcare**

Connected medical equipment, such as smart inhalers, insulin pumps, and pacemakers, improve the quality of care that is provided to patients by providing medical personnel with data in real time. Additionally, these gadgets help in the early diagnosis and prevention of medical conditions.

Science of the Skies: Astronomy and Space Exploration

1. **Radio and Television Telescopes**
   Internet of Things is used by astronomers to control radio telescopes, which are used to collect signals from the universe. The information that was gathered is put to use in the investigation of heavenly bodies such as stars, galaxies, and even black holes.
2. **The Communication Between Satellites and Spacecraft**

The transport of data from space missions to Earth is made easier by satellite and spacecraft communication systems that are enabled by the internet of things. This information consists of photos, measurements, and various other observations from the scientific community.

Planning for Urban Development and High-Tech Cities

1. **Intelligent Transportation Systems**
   The Internet of Things is being utilized in urban transportation systems to facilitate an improvement in traffic flow, to monitor

pollution from vehicles, and to enable real-time changes to public transit. This technique helps lessen environmental impact as well as the impact of traffic congestion.

2. **Efficient Use of Energy**

   The monitoring of energy use, optimization of energy distribution, and reduction of energy waste are all ways that smart grids and Internet of Things sensors in buildings and infrastructure contribute to increased energy efficiency.

3. **The Management of Waste**

   IoT-enabled waste management systems improve the efficiency of trash collection by keeping track of the amount of garbage in each container. Taking this method lowers both operational costs and the impact on the environment.

4. **Protection of the Public**

The Internet of Things enables surveillance cameras, gunshot detection systems, and catastrophe response mechanisms, all of which contribute to increased public safety. These technologies make cities safer and improve reaction times in case of emergencies.

Concerns and Things to Take Into Account

Worries About Data Security and Privacy Are Raised Due to the acquisition of Sensitive Data in Scientific Internet of Things Applications The acquisition of sensitive data in scientific IoT applications generates worries about data security and privacy. Strong encryption, access control, and responsible data governance are all absolutely necessary.

Data Volume and Management The Internet of Things creates enormous volumes of data, and effectively managing this data presents a big challenge. Solutions that are effective in data storage, processing, and analytics are required for researchers.

Interoperability refers to the fact that numerous Internet of Things devices and sensors make use of a variety of communication protocols and data formats. It is absolutely necessary to provide interoperability in order to combine several data sources.

Energy Efficiency Many Internet of Things devices are powered by rechargeable batteries. In order to maintain the longevity and sustainability of a gadget, it is essential to optimize its energy consumption.

Compliance with rules Scientific research that uses data collected by Internet of Things devices may be subject to a variety of rules and compliance requirements, such as laws protecting personal information and ethical norms.

The Prospects for the IoT in the Field of Science

Edge Computing: As a result of edge computing, Internet of Things devices are gaining a higher level of intelligence, which enables real-time data processing and reduces latency.

5G Connectivity: The introduction of 5G networks will increase the speed and reliability of data transmission for the internet of things (IoT), which will lead to the creation of new opportunities for data-intensive applications.

Integration of Artificial Intelligence (AI) Internet of Things devices are gradually becoming capable of integrating AI, which enables more advanced data processing, predictive modeling, and decision-making.

The convergence of quantum computing and the internet of things (IoT) has the potential to transform data encryption, sensor technology, and secure communication. This is referred to as "quantum IoT."

Integration of Blockchain Technology: The Internet of Things (IoT) is being connected with blockchain technology in order to improve data security, data traceability, and trust in data collected from a variety of sources.

Interdisciplinary Collaboration: Researchers from a wide variety of fields are working together to harness data from internet of things devices to get insights and make discoveries across multiple fields.

5.1 IoT applications in scientific research

The Internet of Things (IoT) has become an indispensable tool in the realm of scientific research, offering a multitude of applications that have revolutionized the way data is collected, experiments are conducted, and discoveries are made. From environmental monitoring to healthcare research, IoT has enabled scientists to gather real-time data, conduct precise measurements, and analyze complex phenomena. This article explores the diverse and impactful applications of IoT in the realm of scientific research.

Monitoring and Investigation of the Environment

One of the most significant applications of IoT in scientific research is environmental monitoring. IoT devices have transformed the way researchers collect and analyze data related to the environment, providing insights into various ecological processes and enabling better-informed decision-making.

1. **Climate and Weather Monitoring**

    IoT sensors are extensively used in climate and weather monitoring systems. These sensors collect real-time data on temperature, humidity, air pressure, and other meteorological parameters, enabling meteorologists to make accurate weather forecasts and climate predictions. This data is crucial for understanding climate change and its implications on the planet.

2. **Ecosystem Surveillance**

    In the field of ecology, IoT plays a pivotal role in monitoring ecosystems. From rainforests to marine environments, IoT devices such as camera traps, drones, and underwater sensors provide researchers with valuable insights into biodiversity, species migration patterns, and the impact of human activities on ecosystems. This data aids in the development of effective conservation strategies and the protection of endangered species.

3. **Pollution Tracking**

IoT-enabled pollution tracking systems help monitor air and water quality in real-time. Sensors installed in urban areas and industrial zones measure levels of pollutants such as particulate matter, carbon monoxide, and nitrogen dioxide. This data assists environmental scientists and policymakers in identifying sources of pollution and implementing measures to improve air and water quality.

Agricultural Research and Precision Farming

IoT has transformed the agricultural landscape by facilitating precision farming techniques and enhancing crop management practices. The integration of IoT devices in agriculture has enabled more efficient resource utilization, better crop yield predictions, and improved decision-making for farmers.

1. **Soil and Crop Monitoring**

   IoT sensors deployed in agricultural fields monitor soil moisture, nutrient levels, and crop health. This real-time data enables farmers to optimize irrigation schedules, fertilization practices, and pest control measures, leading to improved crop yields and reduced environmental impact.

2. **Livestock Management**

   IoT devices are used for monitoring livestock health and behavior. Wearable sensors and GPS trackers help farmers track the location and well-being of their livestock, ensuring timely medical intervention and preventing the spread of diseases. This application enhances animal welfare and promotes sustainable farming practices.

3. **Supply Chain Optimization**

In the agricultural sector, IoT plays a crucial role in optimizing the supply chain. From monitoring crop storage conditions to tracking product distribution, IoT devices ensure that agricultural products maintain their quality throughout the supply chain. This enhances food safety, reduces waste, and improves overall efficiency in the agricultural market.

Biomedical Research and Healthcare

IoT has transformed biomedical research and healthcare delivery by enabling remote patient monitoring, personalized treatments, and efficient disease management. Through the integration of IoT devices and health monitoring systems, researchers and healthcare professionals can gather comprehensive data and make data-driven decisions.

1. **Monitoring of Patients Via Remote Connection**
   IoT-enabled medical devices and wearables allow for the remote monitoring of patients' vital signs, medication adherence, and overall health status. This technology is particularly beneficial for individuals with chronic illnesses, enabling healthcare providers to offer timely interventions and personalized care plans.
2. **Personalized Medicine**
   IoT plays a critical role in the advancement of personalized medicine. By collecting and analyzing patient data, including genetic information and lifestyle patterns, researchers can develop tailored treatment plans and targeted therapies for specific patient populations. This approach enhances treatment efficacy and reduces the risk of adverse drug reactions.
3. **Clinical Trials and Drug Development**

In the pharmaceutical industry, IoT facilitates the monitoring of clinical trials and drug development processes. IoT devices track patient responses to new treatments, record medication adherence, and provide real-time data on drug efficacy and safety. This application expedites the drug development lifecycle and improves the overall success rate of clinical trials.

Science of the Skies: Astronomy and Space Exploration

In the field of astronomy and space exploration, IoT technologies enable the collection of vast amounts of data from celestial bodies and space missions. IoT devices play a crucial role in capturing signals from the universe and communicating data from space back to Earth.

1. **Radio and Television Telescopes**
   IoT devices are integrated into radio telescopes to capture signals

from distant galaxies and cosmic phenomena. These devices enable astronomers to study the origins of celestial bodies, analyze cosmic radiation, and explore the mysteries of the universe.

2. **Spacecraft and Satellite Communication**

In space exploration missions, IoT technology facilitates communication between spacecraft and satellites, enabling the transmission of data, images, and scientific observations back to Earth. This technology is essential for monitoring space missions, collecting data from planetary surfaces, and conducting research on extraterrestrial environments.

The applications of IoT in scientific research continue to expand, offering researchers and scientists new opportunities to collect data, conduct experiments, and make groundbreaking discoveries. With the continued advancement of IoT technologies and the integration of artificial intelligence and big data analytics, the future of scientific research is poised to be even more data-driven and transformative.

5.2 Sensor networks and data collection

Sensor networks have ushered in a new era of data collection and information gathering, transforming various industries and scientific fields. These networks consist of interconnected sensors that collect data from the physical world, providing valuable insights for applications ranging from environmental monitoring to healthcare and industrial automation. This article explores the principles, applications, challenges, and future trends of sensor networks and data collection.

Acquiring Knowledge of Sensor Networks
What are Sensor Networks?

Sensor networks are composed of a multitude of sensors, which are small devices designed to capture data from their surroundings. These sensors are interconnected and often communicate with each other and a central data processing unit, such as a computer or a cloud-based platform. This interconnection allows for the collection, transmission, and analysis of data in real-time.

Key Components of Sensor Networks

Sensors: These are the primary data-collecting devices within the network. Sensors come in various types, such as temperature sensors, pressure sensors, motion sensors, and environmental sensors, each designed for specific data capture tasks.

Communication Infrastructure: Sensor networks rely on communication technologies like Wi-Fi, Bluetooth, Zigbee, or LoRa to transmit data from sensors to the central processing unit.

Data Processing Unit: This unit is responsible for receiving, processing, and analyzing the data collected by the sensors. It may be a dedicated computer, a cloud-based platform, or an edge computing device.

Power Supply: Sensors may be powered by batteries, energy harvesting mechanisms, or wired connections, depending on the application and deployment.

Principles of Sensor Networks

Data Collection and Sensing

The core function of sensor networks is data collection. Sensors are designed to sense or measure specific physical properties, such as temperature, humidity, light, or motion. They continually gather data from their environment, creating a stream of information.

Data Transmission and Communication

Once collected, the data is transmitted to the central processing unit using communication protocols. This data transmission can be wireless or wired, and it often employs energy-efficient communication technologies to preserve sensor battery life.

The processing and examination of data

Upon reaching the central processing unit, the data is processed, analyzed, and transformed into meaningful information. This analysis can involve pattern recognition, anomaly detection, statistical analysis, or complex algorithms, depending on the application.

Real-Time Monitoring and Alerts

Sensor networks provide real-time monitoring capabilities. This means that data is continuously updated, and any deviations or specific conditions can trigger alerts or notifications. For instance, in industrial settings, abnormal temperature or pressure readings may trigger immediate alarms to prevent accidents.

Scalability and Flexibility

Sensor networks are designed to be scalable and adaptable. Additional sensors can be added to expand the network's coverage, and the network's configuration can be adjusted to accommodate different data collection requirements.

Applications of Sensor Networks and Data Collection

Sensor networks have a wide range of applications across various industries, enhancing data collection and decision-making processes. Some key areas include:

Environmental Monitoring

Environmental sensor networks are used to track changes in the natural environment. This includes monitoring air and water quality, weather conditions, soil moisture, and the health of ecosystems. Data collected from these networks is essential for climate research, pollution control, and disaster management.

Industrial Automation

In industrial settings, sensor networks are vital for process control and automation. Sensors are deployed to measure variables like temperature, pressure, and flow rates in manufacturing processes. This data is used to optimize operations, improve efficiency, and ensure product quality.

Smart Cities

Smart city initiatives leverage sensor networks to monitor various urban parameters, including traffic flow, energy consumption, air quality, and waste management. These networks improve city planning, enhance public services, and support sustainability efforts.

Healthcare

Healthcare sensor networks play a significant role in remote patient monitoring, allowing healthcare providers to track vital signs and health metrics in real-time. These networks enable timely interventions, personalized treatment plans, and improved healthcare delivery.

Agriculture

Agricultural sensor networks assist farmers in optimizing crop management. Sensors monitor soil conditions, weather patterns, and crop health, providing insights for precision farming practices. This technology improves crop yields and reduces resource wastage.

Home Automation

Smart homes utilize sensor networks to enhance comfort, security, and energy efficiency. Sensors for temperature, lighting, motion, and security enable automation and remote control of home systems.

Wildlife Tracking

Sensor networks, such as radio tags and GPS devices, are used to track wildlife movement and behavior. These networks aid in wildlife conservation, ecological research, and monitoring of endangered species.

Energy Management

Energy sensor networks monitor electricity consumption in homes, commercial buildings, and industrial facilities. Data from these networks enables better energy management, load balancing, and cost savings.

Challenges in Sensor Networks and Data Collection

Data Security and Privacy: Ensuring the security and privacy of data collected by sensors is a significant concern. Unauthorized access or data breaches can compromise sensitive information.

Energy Efficiency: Many sensors are battery-powered, and optimizing energy consumption to extend battery life is essential. Energy harvesting techniques and low-power designs are crucial for sensor networks.

Data Volume and Processing: Sensor networks generate vast amounts of data. Efficient data storage, transmission, and processing methods are required to handle this volume of information.

Interoperability: Sensors from different manufacturers often use various communication protocols and data formats. Ensuring interoperability between sensors is essential to build effective sensor networks.

Calibration and Maintenance: Sensors need regular calibration and maintenance to ensure accurate data collection. This can be resource-intensive, especially in large-scale deployments.

Scalability and Network Management: As sensor networks grow, managing and scaling the network becomes more complex. Effective network management tools and protocols are crucial.

Future Trends in Sensor Networks and Data Collection

Edge Computing: Edge computing enables data processing and analysis to occur closer to the data source. This approach reduces latency and conserves bandwidth in sensor networks.

5G Connectivity: The rollout of 5G networks will provide higher data transmission speeds and lower latency, further enhancing the capabilities of sensor networks.

Artificial Intelligence (AI) Integration: AI and machine learning technologies are being integrated into sensor networks to enable real-time data analysis and pattern recognition.

Quantum Sensors: The development of quantum sensors promises higher precision and sensitivity, enabling the detection of subtle physical phenomena.

Blockchain for Data Security: Blockchain technology is being explored for securing data in sensor networks, ensuring data integrity and traceability.

Distributed Sensor Networks: Decentralized sensor networks are becoming more common, enabling greater redundancy and fault tolerance.

5.3 Real-time monitoring and control

Real-time monitoring and control have emerged as pivotal components in various industries, enabling organizations to collect, analyze, and act upon data with unparalleled immediacy. Whether it's manufacturing, healthcare, transportation, or environmental management, real-time systems offer critical insights and the ability to make timely decisions. In this article, we delve into the principles, applications, challenges, and future trends of real-time monitoring and control.

Understanding Real-Time Monitoring and Control

What is Real-Time Monitoring and Control?

Real-time monitoring and control refer to the continuous and instantaneous tracking of data and processes, coupled with the ability to make immediate decisions or adjustments based on the gathered information. These systems utilize sensors, data streams, and automated processes to provide real-time insights and enable rapid responses to changing conditions.

Key Components of Real-Time Systems

Sensors and Data Streams: These components collect data from the physical world, ranging from temperature and pressure measurements to vital signs and financial transactions. The data streams are sent to a central system for processing.

Data Processing Unit: This unit is responsible for analyzing incoming data in real-time. It applies algorithms, logic, and business rules to determine the significance of the data and make decisions or trigger actions.

User Interface: A user-friendly interface allows human operators to monitor the system, receive alerts, and take control actions as needed. This can be a graphical dashboard or a command-line interface.

Control Mechanisms: Real-time systems often include automated control mechanisms that can initiate actions based on predefined rules or adaptive algorithms. These actions can be as simple as setting off alarms or as complex as adjusting manufacturing processes.

Principles of Real-Time Monitoring and Control

Immediate Data Collection

Real-time systems continuously collect data from sensors and other sources, ensuring that the most current information is available for decision-making.

Rapid Data Processing

Incoming data is processed quickly and efficiently to produce actionable insights. This involves real-time analytics, pattern recognition, and anomaly detection.

Timely Decision-Making

Real-time systems empower organizations to make immediate decisions and initiate control actions based on the processed data. These decisions can be automated or made by human operators.

Feedback Loops

Many real-time systems feature feedback loops that adjust operations in response to changing conditions. This self-regulation ensures that processes remain within desired parameters.

Alerts and Notifications

Real-time monitoring systems generate alerts and notifications to inform operators or decision-makers of critical events or deviations from expected behavior.

Applications of Real-Time Monitoring and Control

Manufacturing and Process Control

In manufacturing, real-time systems monitor production lines, machine performance, and quality control. These systems can make instant adjustments, preventing defects and optimizing production efficiency.

Energy Management

In the energy sector, real-time monitoring tracks electricity generation, distribution, and consumption. This data helps grid operators balance supply and demand, manage peak loads, and reduce energy wastage.

Environmental Monitoring

Real-time environmental monitoring systems collect data on air and water quality, weather conditions, and pollution levels. Immediate insights allow authorities to take corrective actions and safeguard public health.

Healthcare

In healthcare, real-time patient monitoring systems track vital signs, ensuring that healthcare providers can respond swiftly to critical changes in a patient's condition. This technology has been vital in intensive care units and remote patient monitoring.

Transportation and Traffic Management

Real-time systems monitor traffic flow, road conditions, and vehicle movements in urban areas. Data is used to manage traffic signals, optimize public transportation, and inform commuters about traffic incidents.

Financial Services

In the financial sector, high-frequency trading and fraud detection systems rely on real-time data. Algorithms analyze market data to make split-second trading decisions or identify suspicious financial transactions.

Aviation and Aerospace

In aviation and aerospace, real-time monitoring systems oversee aircraft operation, engine performance, and space missions. These systems ensure the safety and efficiency of air travel and space exploration.

Smart Grids

Smart grid technology uses real-time monitoring and control to manage the flow of electricity in an energy grid. This enables utilities to respond to outages, balance loads, and integrate renewable energy sources effectively.

Challenges in Real-Time Monitoring and Control

Data Overload: The high volume of real-time data can overwhelm systems and operators. Efficient data storage, processing, and analysis are crucial.

Data Quality and Accuracy: Real-time data is valuable only when it is accurate. Ensuring data quality and reliability is a significant challenge.

Security Concerns: Real-time systems must be protected against cyber threats and unauthorized access, as a security breach can have immediate and severe consequences.

Latency: Some applications require extremely low latency to operate effectively. Delays in data collection, processing, or control actions can be problematic.

Integration with Legacy Systems: Many organizations have legacy systems that must be integrated with real-time monitoring and control solutions, which can be complex and costly.

Future Trends in Real-Time Monitoring and Control

Edge Computing: Edge computing enables data processing and analysis to occur at or near the data source, reducing latency and bandwidth requirements.

Artificial Intelligence (AI) and Machine Learning: AI-driven algorithms enhance real-time analytics, predictive maintenance, and autonomous decision-making.

5G Connectivity: The deployment of 5G networks will enhance the speed and reliability of data transmission, supporting real-time applications in various industries.

Blockchain for Data Security: Blockchain technology is being explored to secure real-time data, ensuring data integrity and traceability.

IoT Integration: The integration of IoT devices with real-time monitoring and control systems is set to expand, allowing organizations to capture data from a broader range of sources.

Predictive Analytics: Real-time systems are increasingly using predictive analytics to anticipate future events and make proactive decisions.

5.4 Challenges and security considerations

Real-time monitoring and control systems have revolutionized numerous industries, enhancing data-driven decision-making and process optimization. However, as these systems become increasingly integral to critical infrastructure and daily operations, they also face a host of challenges and security considerations that must be addressed. In this article, we will explore the challenges and security considerations associated with real-time monitoring and control.

Challenges in Real-Time Monitoring and Control

1. **Data Overload**

   One of the foremost challenges in real-time monitoring and control is the sheer volume of data generated. In applications like manufacturing, transportation, and healthcare, sensors and devices continuously produce vast amounts of data. Managing, storing, and processing this data can overwhelm systems and operators.

   Solution: Efficient data management strategies, including data compression, filtering, and

   storage solutions, are necessary to handle large datasets in real time.

2. **Data Quality and Accuracy**

   The accuracy and quality of real-time data are paramount. Inaccurate or unreliable data can lead to incorrect decisions, potentially endangering safety and efficiency. Maintaining data quality is especially challenging in environments with sensor degradation, wear and tear, or environmental conditions that affect data accuracy.

   Solution: Regular calibration, maintenance, and sensor redundancy can help ensure data quality. Additionally, data validation and error-checking algorithms should be employed.

3. **Security Concerns**

   Security is a significant concern in real-time monitoring and control systems. Unauthorized access to these systems, data breaches, or cyberattacks can have immediate and severe consequences, particularly in critical infrastructure or healthcare settings.

   Solution: Robust cybersecurity measures, including firewalls, intrusion detection systems, and encryption, are essential to protect real-time systems from cyber threats.

4. **Latency**

   In applications that require rapid decision-making, latency is a significant challenge. Delays in data collection, processing, or control actions can have serious consequences, such as accidents in autonomous vehicles or equipment malfunctions in manufacturing.

Solution: Edge computing, which allows data processing to occur at or near the data source, can reduce latency. High-speed networks, such as 5G, can also help minimize delays.

5. **Integration with Legacy Systems**

   Many organizations rely on legacy systems that must be integrated with real-time monitoring and control solutions. These legacy systems may lack compatibility with modern technologies and may require complex and costly integration efforts.

   Solution: Careful planning and gradual integration strategies can help ease the transition from legacy systems to real-time solutions. API-based integration or middleware can also simplify the process.

6. **Scalability**

Real-time systems must be scalable to accommodate growing data volumes and sensor networks. As organizations expand their operations, ensuring that the monitoring and control systems can handle increased data flows becomes challenging.

Solution: Scalable architectures, such as cloud-based solutions, are often used to meet the growing demands of real-time systems.

Security Considerations in Real-Time Monitoring and Control

1. **Access Control**

   Access control mechanisms must be in place to restrict system access to authorized personnel only. Multi-factor authentication, strong passwords, and role-based access control are common strategies to prevent unauthorized access.

2. **Data Encryption**

   Data encryption is essential to protect data both in transit and at rest. Strong encryption algorithms should be employed to safeguard sensitive information from eavesdropping and tampering.

3. **Intrusion Detection**

   Intrusion detection systems (IDS) and intrusion prevention systems (IPS) should be implemented to monitor network traffic and detect any suspicious or malicious activities. IDS and IPS can trigger alarms and take corrective actions when breaches are identified.

4. **Regular Patching and Updates**

   Real-time systems rely on software and hardware components that may have vulnerabilities. Regular patching and updates of these components are critical to address known security issues.

5. **Monitoring and Logging**

   Comprehensive monitoring and logging are essential for detecting unusual activities and investigating security incidents. Audit trails can provide valuable information about who accessed the system and what actions were taken.

6. **Incident Response Plan**

   Developing an incident response plan is crucial to address security breaches promptly. This plan should outline the steps to be taken when a breach is detected and specify the responsible individuals or teams.

7. **Security Awareness**

   Training and raising security awareness among personnel are essential. Human error is often a significant factor in security incidents, and educated employees can help prevent such errors.

8. **Third-Party Vendors**

   When integrating third-party components or devices, it is critical to assess their security features and ensure that they do not introduce vulnerabilities into the system.

9. **Physical Security**

   Physical security measures should not be overlooked. Unauthorized physical access to equipment can compromise the entire system.

10. **Data Backups**

Regular data backups should be performed to ensure that data can be restored in the event of data loss or a ransomware attack.

Future Trends and Emerging Technologies

1. **Edge Computing**
   Edge computing brings data processing closer to the data source, reducing latency and enabling faster decision-making. This technology is particularly crucial for applications like autonomous vehicles and industrial automation.
2. **Artificial Intelligence and Machine Learning**
   AI and machine learning are increasingly integrated into real-time systems to enhance analytics, predictive maintenance, and autonomous decision-making. These technologies can detect patterns and anomalies in real-time data more effectively.
3. **5G Connectivity**
   The rollout of 5G networks provides higher data transmission speeds and lower latency, which will further enhance the capabilities of real-time monitoring and control systems.
4. **Blockchain for Data Security**
   Blockchain technology is being explored for securing real-time data, ensuring data integrity and traceability. Blockchain can also improve data sharing and trust in multi-party systems.
5. **IoT Integration**

The integration of IoT devices with real-time monitoring and control systems is expanding, allowing organizations to capture data from a broader range of sources. IoT enables the monitoring of various environmental parameters, equipment conditions, and human interactions.

6

Chapter 6

Artificial Intelligence and Machine Learning

In recent years, Artificial Intelligence (AI) and Machine Learning (ML) have emerged as technologies with revolutionary potential. These technologies are redefining industries, generating innovation, and radically transforming the way in which humans engage with technology. This essay, which is 3000 words long, examines the development and influence of AI and ML, beginning with their inception and continuing through their current status, as well as their potential to mold the future.

1. **The Basic Building Blocks of AI and ML**
1. **The Infancy of Things**
    The earliest accounts of artificial intelligence (AI) are found in ancient mythology, in the form of stories about automatons and mechanical men. On the other hand, the current groundwork for AI wasn't established until the middle of the 20th century. Pioneers in the subject of artificial intelligence (AI), such as Alan Turing and John McCarthy, were responsible for the introduction of fundamental ideas, such as the Turing computer and

the Dartmouth Workshop, which are considered to represent the beginning of AI as a field of study.

2. **The Beginning of the Age of Machine Learning**

A subfield of artificial intelligence known as machine learning is the act of giving computers the ability to learn from data without being explicitly programmed. It is possible to date the beginning of machine learning to the work that Arthur Samuel did in the 1950s to train computers how to play checkers. Through his work, he pioneered the idea of "feature extraction," an essential component of machine learning.

II. The AI Apocalypse and its Resurgence

1. **Initial Expectations and Their Fulfillment**
   In the 1950s and 1960s, many had high aspirations for artificial intelligence (AI), but those promises were quickly dashed by the "AI winter." Because of the constraints imposed by the hardware, the algorithms, and the data, progress became more gradual, and enthusiasm level dropped. The first AI systems were rule-based, and they lacked the data-driven approach that machine learning (ML) has today.
2. **The Revival of Interest**

In the 21st century, artificial intelligence (AI) witnessed a renaissance, which can be partly attributed to improvements in computer capacity as well as the development of more advanced machine learning algorithms. The availability of huge data and the rise of deep learning, a subset of machine learning, played an essential part in the resurgence of interest in artificial intelligence (AI).

III. Convolutional Neural Networks and Deep Learning

1. **The Surging Popularity of Deep Learning**
   Deep learning is a subfield of machine learning that processes

and interprets data using artificial neural networks that are modeled after the structure and function of the human brain. Computer vision, natural language processing, and speech recognition have all been significantly impacted by deep learning approaches, in particular Convolutional Neural Networks (CNNs) and Recurrent Neural Networks (RNNs).

2. **Recent Developments in the Field of Image Recognition**
Image identification is one of the applications of deep learning that has received the most attention. At the ImageNet Large Scale Visual Recognition Challenge, the astonishing performance increases made with CNNs were put on display. These networks have achieved an accuracy in picture classification tasks that is superior to that of humans, and their use can be seen in fields such as medical imaging, autonomous cars, and facial recognition.

3. **Processing of natural language (also known as NLP)**

Another area where deep learning has seen substantial progress is natural language processing (NLP). It has been proved that certain models, such as GPT-3 and BERT, have a surprising ability to comprehend and generate writing that is human-like.

Because of this, there have been breakthroughs made in chatbots, translation services, and content generation, all of which have ramifications for a variety of businesses, including customer service and the development of content.

IV. Implementations and Applications of AI and ML

1. **Health Care Services**
AI and ML are having a wide-ranging impact on the healthcare industry. These technologies are strengthening patient care, improving efficiency, and lowering costs. One example of this is the early diagnosis of diseases using medical imaging. Other examples include drug discovery and personalized medicine.

2. **The Finance**
   AI and ML are put to use in the financial sector for the purposes of customer service, algorithmic trading, risk analysis, and the detection of fraudulent activity. These technologies offer a competitive advantage by performing analysis on massive datasets in order to make judgments in real time.
3. **Self-Driving Cars and Trucks**
   Artificial intelligence and machine learning are extremely important to the development of self-driving cars. These technologies give vehicles the ability to perceive and interpret their surroundings, as well as to reason and move in a responsible manner. Businesses such as Tesla, Waymo, and Uber are leading the pack in terms of this type of innovation.
4. **E-commerce (Dot-Com)**
   Artificial intelligence (AI) and machine learning (ML) are being integrated into e-commerce platforms to facilitate tailored product recommendations, dynamic pricing, and fraud detection. These technologies improve the user experience while simultaneously driving increased revenue.
5. **Promotion and Advertising in the Market**
   Because of AI and ML, data is playing an increasingly important role in digital marketing and advertising. Algorithms that assess consumer behavior and preferences are beneficial to ad targeting, content optimization, and A/B testing.
6. **Intelligent Helping Devices**
   Virtual assistants such as Alexa, Google Assistant, and Siri have quickly become indispensable to our day-to-day activities. These systems make use of natural language processing in conjunction with machine learning in order to comprehend user inquiries and provide appropriate responses.
7. **Industrial Production**
   The manufacturing industry is undergoing a sea change as a result of automation and robots powered by AI. Productivity,

quality control, and preventative maintenance are all improved because to these solutions.

8. **Instruction**
   Educational platforms powered by AI can deliver individualized teaching and learning experiences. Adaptive algorithms monitor a student's development and modify the material to meet their specific requirements.

9. **Amusement and Recreation**

Both AI and ML are making their imprint in the entertainment sector, from the production of computer-generated imagery (CGI) in movies to the provision of content recommendations on streaming platforms.

V. Implications for Ethical Considerations and Society

1. **Impartiality and Balance**
   The elimination of bias in computer programs is one of the most difficult problems to solve in the fields of AI and machine learning. Train[ing] models on biased data can perpetuate and amplify already-present prejudices in society, which can lead to discriminatory outcomes. In order to find a solution to this problem, efforts are currently being made to build fairness-aware algorithms and data collection methodologies.

2. **Confidentiality and Safety**
   Concerns concerning privacy and safety are raised as a result of the collection and utilization of massive volumes of data. When it comes to protecting individuals' personal information, it is absolutely necessary to put in place effective data protection methods and encryption strategies.

3. **Unemployment and the Displacement of Workers**
   Concerns about job loss have been sparked by the increased use of artificial intelligence and machine learning. There is a possibility that certain jobs will be automated, which will cause a shift

in the labor market. In order to successfully manage this change, it will be necessary to acquire new skills and improve existing ones.

4. **Accountability and Openness to the Public**

When AI systems get more self-sufficient and intricate, determining who is to blame when anything goes wrong is a task that becomes increasingly difficult. A critical challenge is the need to ensure accountability and openness in decision-making that involves AI and ML.

VI. The Prospects for Machine Learning and AI

1. **Developments in Computers and Other AI Component**
   The development of specialized hardware that is designed for AI and ML workloads, such as Graphics Processing Units (GPUs) and Tensor Processing Units (TPUs), will continue to drive gains in performance.
2. **AI that can be explained**
   There is an increasing demand for interpretability and transparency in artificial intelligence systems as these systems get more complex. Research in the field of explainable artificial intelligence (XAI) strives to make AI systems more intelligible, particularly in crucial fields such as healthcare and finance.
3. **Artificial Intelligence (AGI) that is Generalized**
   Even though current AI is limited to a single field of study, the development of general artificial general intelligence (AGI) that can think in a manner analogous to that of humans in a number of fields is still an important long-term aim. The development of both new hardware and new software would be necessary in order to accomplish AGI.
4. **The Role of Artificial Intelligence in Scientific Research and Climate Change**
   There has been a recent uptick in the application of AI to tackle global problems such as climate change and scientific study. Data

relating to the climate are analyzed using models, and these models can also be used to forecast natural disasters and speed up scientific discoveries.

5. Ethics and Regulations Regarding AI

The future of AI and ML will be significantly influenced by the creation of AI ethics frameworks and legislation. This will be an extremely important factor. Guidelines for the development and deployment of artificial intelligence in a responsible manner are currently being developed by several groups and governments.

The development of artificial intelligence and machine learning have both had a significant and game-changing impact on society as a whole. These technologies have had a profound impact on practically every facet of our lives, beginning with their unassuming beginnings in the middle of the 20th century and continuing on to their current level of innovation and expansion. Despite the fact that AI and ML have the ability to change industries and improve our quality of life, they also come with a host of ethical and societal concerns that will require careful consideration to solve.

AI and ML are continuing to make strides forward as we look to the future, with an emphasis on the establishment of ethical standards, transparency, and their ability to address urgent problems on a global scale. The voyage of artificial intelligence and machine learning is not even close to being finished, and as these technologies continue to advance, they will impact the world in ways that we are not yet able to completely fathom. It is crucial that we continue to be alert, mindful, and responsible in our effort to harness the full potential of these powerful tools while simultaneously ensuring that the advantages they provide are available to everyone.

6.1 Leveraging AI/ML for scientific discovery

The dawn of a new era in scientific research was marked by the development of Artificial Intelligence (AI) and Machine Learning (ML). The way that researchers evaluate data, make predictions, and carry out tests is being revolutionized as a result of these technologies, which is enabling breakthroughs in a variety of scientific domains. In this article of 700 words, we will investigate the various applications of artificial intelligence and machine learning in the field of scientific research.

Increasing the Speed of Data Processing and Analysis

The capability of AI and ML to handle and analyze enormous amounts of data at speeds that were not before feasible is one of the key contributions that AI and ML have made to the advancement of scientific discovery. The amount of data that is produced is staggering in some scientific subfields, such as genetics, climate research, and particle physics. The algorithms that make up AI are able to quickly sort through this data, recognize patterns, and derive insightful conclusions. For instance, AI has considerably sped up the analysis of DNA sequences, making it possible for researchers to find genetic markers for diseases and potential treatment targets. This is thanks to the field of genomics.

Research and Development of New Medicines

The field of pharmaceuticals is undergoing a transformation thanks to AI and ML. Drug discovery is a process that is both time-consuming and expensive; nevertheless, AI-driven algorithms have the ability to screen thousands of chemical compounds in search of prospective drug candidates. They can also make predictions about the biological activity of molecules, which helps speed up the process of developing new medications. This is especially pertinent in the context of fast responding to newly developing diseases, like as the development of COVID-19 vaccines, in which AI played an essential role in discovering vaccine candidates.

The Science of Materials

In the subject of material science, artificial intelligence is being utilized to make predictions about the properties of novel materials. These predictions can have implications in a variety of fields, including electronics, renewable energy, and more. The features of materials already in existence can be analyzed using machine learning models, which then enables scientists to forecast how particular alterations will affect the characteristics of the materials. This power of prediction helps save a large amount of time and resources while searching for innovative materials with particular features.

Research in the Fields of Climate and the Environment

Understanding climate change and other environmental problems requires a variety of methods, and AI and ML are two of the most helpful. AI is used in climate models to more accurately represent the Earth's complex systems so that more accurate predictions may be made. Algorithms that use machine learning may examine satellite photos, climatic data, and other environmental indicators in order to assess biodiversity, monitor deforestation, and forecast natural disasters. These technological advancements have the potential to assist us in reducing the effects of climate change and in safeguarding our planet.

Research in Healthcare and the Medical Profession

The fields of medical research and healthcare have benefited significantly from the application of AI and ML. They are able to examine medical images, such as X-rays and MRIs, in order to identify diseases in their earliest stages. Natural language processing (NLP) facilitates the extraction of useful information from medical records and scientific publications, while predictive models can assist in the identification of patients who may be at risk for particular medical diseases. The application of AI and ML in the medical field has resulted in advancements in the areas of patient care, drug discovery, and diagnostics.

Physics of individual particles and astronomy

Artificial intelligence and machine learning are reshaping data analysis in the fields of particle physics and astrophysics. Experiments carried out at locations such as the Large Hadron Collider (LHC) produce massive datasets that call for intricate analysis.

The application of artificial intelligence tools, such as neural networks, to identify unusual occurrences and discrepancies in the collected data is a significant contributor to the identification of previously unknown particles and fundamental physics principles. Artificial intelligence is being used in the field of astrophysics to evaluate enormous datasets obtained from telescopes. This is assisting scientists in their efforts to detect celestial objects, dark matter, and gravitational waves.

Research in Biology and Genome Sequencing

Artificial intelligence and machine learning have made great strides in the field of biological research and genomics. Researchers can utilize machine learning to conduct analyses of DNA and protein sequences, make predictions about the structures of proteins, and gain a better understanding of the genetic basis of diseases. These technologies play an important part in evolutionary biology as well by tracking the lineage of different species and determining the links between them. Artificial intelligence and machine learning will be essential in releasing the full potential of genomics data as it continues to develop.

Technologies Like Robotics and Automation

The process of scientific discovery frequently involves laborious and uninteresting tasks. Automation and robots driven by artificial intelligence are becoming increasingly commonplace in laboratories, where they are employed to carry out experiments, manage samples, and collect data. This not only lessens the likelihood of mistakes being made by humans, but it also quickens the pace at which scientific research is conducted by enabling researchers to concentrate on the more imaginative and analytical components of their work.

Cooperation Between Different Disciplines

The traditional compartmentalization of scientific research is being dismantled by AI and ML. Researchers from a variety of fields are able to work together and share data in a more efficient manner, which can lead to the development of cross-disciplinary innovations. For example, the methods of artificial intelligence that have been created in the field of computer science can be applied to the analysis of complicated biological data, which can lead to new discoveries at the intersection of these two fields.

Confrontations, as well as Ethical Considerations

While AI and ML present significant opportunities for furthering scientific research, these technologies also raise important moral and legal questions. Data privacy, bias in algorithm design, and the ethical application of artificial intelligence in research are all important considerations. Researchers have a duty to guarantee that AI systems are open to inspection and that they are used in a responsible and ethical manner.

6.2 Data analysis and pattern recognition

In today's information processing, two of the most important skills to have are data analysis and pattern detection. In this essay of 700 words, we are going to delve into the significance of data analysis and pattern recognition by investigating their applications across a variety of areas and highlighting their role in driving innovation and the decision-making process.

Acquiring Knowledge of the Data Analysis Process

The process of examining, cleansing, manipulating, and modeling data in order to get useful

insights is referred to as data analysis. As a result of the exponential growth of data in the digital age that we live in today, doing efficient data analysis has become of the utmost importance. It lets enterprises to recognize trends, obtain a thorough understanding of complicated systems, and make decisions that are based on accurate information.

Applications in the Fields of Economics and Business

In the fields of business and economics, the analysis of data is an extremely important component in the process that drives strategic decision-making. Businesses are able to arrive at well-informed judgments on product development, marketing tactics, and resource allocation when they do in-depth analyses of market trends, consumer behavior, and financial data. Organizations have the potential to acquire a competitive advantage and more effectively adjust to changing market conditions if they can recognize trends in the preferences of consumers and variations in the market.

The Application of Data Analysis in Healthcare

In the field of healthcare, data analysis makes it easier to spot patterns in illness progression, outcomes for patients, and the effectiveness of treatments. Medical personnel are able to increase the accuracy of their diagnoses, create individualized treatment plans for patients, and conduct predictive analysis to better anticipate the occurrence of significant health hazards when they analyze patient data. In addition, data analysis in the healthcare industry makes it possible to recognize trends in public health, which contributes to the development of effective strategies for the management and prevention of diseases.

Learning by Machine, as well as Pattern Recognition

Data analysis is broken down into subfields, one of which is called pattern recognition. Pattern recognition focuses on finding regularities or patterns within datasets. In pattern recognition, one of the most important roles played by machine learning algorithms is that of enabling computers to automatically learn from experience and improve themselves without being expressly designed to do so. The ability to recognize patterns is essential in a wide variety of applications, including as speech and picture recognition, natural language processing, and predictive modeling.

Image and Voice Recognition Technology

In the field of image identification, sophisticated algorithms are able to recognize and categorize things like objects, faces, and sceneries that are contained within digital photographs or movies. This technology has a variety of applications, including security surveillance, driverless vehicles, and medical imaging, to name a few of those disciplines. In a similar vein, when it comes to the process of speech recognition, machine learning algorithms can transform spoken language into text. This opens the door for the creation of virtual assistants and voice-operated devices, which in turn improves the user experience and accessibility.

Processing of natural language (also known as NLP)

The field of natural language processing examines how computers and people communicate with one another via language. NLP stands for natural language processing, and it is the application of several approaches for machine learning that enables computers to comprehend, interpret, and synthesize human language in a manner that is meaningful and contextually relevant. The use of natural language processing in areas as diverse as sentiment analysis and language translation, as well as chatbots and virtual assistants, is radically altering the ways in which people engage with information and technology.

Analysis of the Financial Market

The detection of trends, market fluctuations, and investment possibilities is made possible through the use of pattern recognition and data analysis, both of which play an important role in the analysis of financial markets. Financial analysts are able to make educated decisions regarding investment strategies, risk management, and portfolio diversification by doing an analysis of historical market data and applying predictive models.

Research in the Natural Sciences and Analyses of Data

Data analysis and pattern recognition are two aspects of scientific study that help contribute to a better understanding of complicated occurrences as well as the construction of scientific models. Analysis of data enables researchers to recognize significant patterns and arrive at relevant conclusions on a wide range of topics, including the study of experimental results in physics and chemistry, as well as biological processes and changes in the natural environment. These realizations contribute to the expansion of scientific knowledge as well as the development of novel solutions to difficult issues.

Confrontations, as well as Ethical Considerations

Data analysis and pattern recognition may have transformed many different fields, but they also present problems and ethical implications that must be addressed. Data privacy, algorithmic bias, and the responsible use of data are all key concerns that need careful attention. Other important concerns include the responsible use of data.

In order to keep people's faith and keep the integrity of the applications of these technologies intact, it is vital to ensure that data analysis techniques are used in an ethical and transparent manner.

Prospects for the Continued Development of Data Analysis and Pattern Recognition

The fields of data analysis and pattern recognition both have a bright future ahead of them thanks to the ongoing development of technology. The capabilities of these technologies will continue to improve as a result of developments in artificial intelligence, deep learning, and big data analytics, which will ultimately lead to the development of more sophisticated applications across a variety of industries. In addition, the combination of data analysis and pattern recognition with various other developing technologies will be a driving force behind innovation and will stimulate the development of new opportunities in research, business, and society in general.

6.3 Predictive modeling and simulations

The fields of data science, mathematics, and computer science come together dynamically in predictive modeling and simulations, which offer profound insights into complex systems, aid in decision-making, and drive innovation. In this essay of 1000 words, we will dig into the area of predictive modeling and simulations, investigating their applications, methodology, and the key role they play in comprehending, predicting, and influencing a variety of elements of our life.

1. **A Comprehension of the Predictive Modeling Process**
1. **The Principles and Practices of Predictive Modeling**
   The first step in predictive modeling is always the acquisition of data that is relevant to the problem at hand. This may involve structured data from databases or unstructured data from a variety of sources, such as social media, sensors, or text docu-

ments. Both types of data may be utilized.

Data Preprocessing: In order to guarantee the data's high quality and continued relevance for modeling, the raw data must frequently undergo cleaning, transformation, and feature selection. The management of missing values, the normalization of data, and the selection of the most significant features can all be included in preprocessing.

Model Selection: Various methods of predictive modeling, such as regression, decision trees, neural networks, or support vector machines, may be utilized depending on the nature of the presenting challenge and the available information.

Training and Validation: Models are educated using historical data, with a portion of the data being set aside for later use in the validation process. The validation process helps evaluate the performance of the model so that any necessary adjustments can be made.

Testing and Deployment: After the model has been trained and verified, it can be evaluated for its prediction accuracy by being tested on data that it has not before seen. The applications of the successful models are then taken out into the actual world.

2. **Some Real-World Examples of Predictive Modeling**

The field of finance makes use of predictive modeling for a variety of purposes, including credit risk assessment, the detection of fraud, the prediction of stock price, and algorithmic trading. Financial institutions are able to make educated decisions, effectively manage risks, and make the most of their assets when they do market and historical data analysis.

In the field of healthcare, predictive modeling is extremely important for predicting disease, making diagnoses, and managing patients. It is used, for instance, in the forecasting of disease epidemics, the personalization of medical treatment, and the optimization of hospital resources.

For the purpose of improving their marketing strategy, businesses often utilize predictive modeling. Analyzing the behavior of customers allows businesses to provide more personalized product recommendations, which in turn helps to increase customer retention and makes advertising efforts more effective.

In the manufacturing industry, predictive maintenance involves the use of models to anticipate when pieces of equipment may break down. This helps to cut down on costly downtime. The quality control process can also benefit from predictive modeling, as it can assist in the detection of flaws and the enhancement of manufacturing procedures.

Climate modeling is a branch of environmental science that makes use of predictive models in order to understand climate patterns, forecast natural disasters, and evaluate the impact of changes in the environment.

II. The Effectiveness of Modeling and Simulations

1. **The Theory Behind Computer Simulations**
   Model Construction: The construction of a mathematical model that accurately depicts the system being simulated is the first step in the simulation process. Equations, parameter values, and starting conditions are all included in this model.
   Methods of Numerical Computation In order to come up with an approximation of the solutions to the mathematical model in either time or space, numerical methods such as finite difference, finite element, or Monte Carlo simulations are utilized.
   Data Inputs: In order to perform scenarios, simulations need to have data inputs. These data might consist of boundary conditions, initial values, and model parameters, among other things.
   Execution: Running the mathematical model with the data that was defined as input is what constitutes execution of a simulation. In order to make an accurate prediction of the system's behavior, the model is solved numerically.

Following the completion of the simulation, the findings are examined in order to reach a conclusion regarding the system that is the subject of the study. This can involve analyzing the effects of the various factors, gaining a grasp of the dynamics of the system, or improving the processes.

2. **Real-World Implications of Computer Simulations**

The fields of physics and engineering make substantial use of simulations for a variety of purposes, including but not limited to the following: understanding the behavior of physical systems, inventing and testing new products, and optimizing structures and materials.

Astronomy and Astrophysics: Through the use of simulations, astronomers are able to mimic the behavior of celestial bodies, the generation of stars, and the history of the universe, which helps them throw light on astronomical events.

Simulations enable climate scientists comprehend the Earth's climate system, predict climate change, and evaluate the impact of various environmental policies. This is accomplished through the process of climate modeling.

Simulations are utilized in the fields of traffic management and urban planning in order to model the flow of traffic, improve road networks, and evaluate the impact of new infrastructure.

Simulations are used extensively in the field of epidemiology, and epidemiologists use them to research disease outbreaks, evaluate the success of vaccination efforts, and evaluate public health policy.

III. Synergy Between Predictive Modeling and Simulations

1. **Computer-Aided Fluid Dynamics (also known as CFD)**
   The aerospace and automotive sectors make substantial use of computational fluid dynamics (CFD) simulations, which mimic the behavior of fluids and gasses in complicated systems. In order to build more fuel-efficient automobiles, anticipate airflow patterns, and enhance fuel efficiency, predictive modeling is used

to optimize the parameters inside these simulations. This makes it possible to use predictive modeling to optimize these parameters.

2. **The Art of Drug Inventing**
Predictive modeling is used in the pharmaceutical industry to identify possible medication candidates based on the molecular structures and biological data of the target organism. After candidates have been found, computer simulations are performed to investigate how these medications interact with particular proteins and to speculate about the extent of their usefulness. This speeds up the process of discovering new drugs and cuts both the cost and the amount of time needed for clinical tests.

3. **The Modeling of Climate**

Climate models frequently combine simulations that reproduce the Earth's climate system with predictive modeling in order to comprehend historical climate data and generate forecasts for the future. This allows the models to make more accurate predictions. This method is essential for determining the effects of climate change, gaining a knowledge of extreme weather events, and developing policy pertaining to the environment.

IV. Obstacles and Important Considerations

1. **The Quantity and Quality of the Data**
The accuracy and thoroughness of the data used in predictive modeling are both critically important.
Unreliable models might be the result of using data that is either inaccurate or insufficient. On the other hand, proper initial conditions and parameter settings are essential for simulations.

2. **The Complexity of the Model**
It may be necessary to use intricate models that contain a large number of variables when dealing with complex systems. It can

be difficult to strike a balance between the complexity of a model and its computational viability, given that sophisticated models are often computationally costly.

3. **Considerations of a Moral Nature**
   There are ethical questions that arise from the use of predictive modeling, particularly in sectors such as healthcare and finance. It is possible for decisions to have real-world repercussions when they are based on predictive models, because biases in the data can lead to conclusions that are not fair. Both fairness and transparency are quite important.

4. **Resources for Computational Processing**
   Both predictive modeling and simulations may be very demanding in terms of the amount of computing power they use, thus having access to a significant amount of computing resources is essential. Clusters of high-performance computing or resources hosted in the cloud are frequently required for complicated simulations.

5. **The Processes of Validation and Verification**

In order to ensure that simulations are accurate, it is necessary to validate and verify them against data taken from the real world. When dealing with systems that are difficult to examine firsthand, this procedure may present a number of challenges.

V. Current Predictions for the Future

1. **The Implementation of Artificial Intelligence**
   It is an increasingly common practice to incorporate elements of artificial intelligence (AI) into predictive modeling and simulations. Artificial intelligence has the potential to improve predictive models by automatically selecting and optimizing model features. The use of AI approaches in simulations can help improve numerical approximations and model selection.

2. **Expanded Use in the Healthcare Industry**
   In the field of healthcare, the significance of predictive modeling and simulations will continue to increase.
   The diagnosis and treatment of diseases will be aided by the creation of patient-specific models, such as organ simulations or personalized medicine. These models can be used.
3. **Efforts to Reduce the Impacts of Climate Change**
   The mitigation of climate change will be significantly aided by the use of climate modeling and simulations. Simulations will be used to evaluate the impact of various climate change solutions, including those relating to adaptation, mitigation, and renewable energy.
4. **The Importance of Quantum Computing in Today's World**
   The application of quantum computing could hasten the process of developing predictive models and running simulations. Its capacity to process enormous information and solve complicated equations has the potential to transform various sectors, in particular the drug discovery industry, the materials science industry, and encryption.
5. **Collaboration Between Different Disciplines**

The need for multidisciplinary collaboration amongst data scientists, mathematicians, domain specialists, and computer scientists will only increase as issues get more complicated. Combining the information and experience gained from a variety of fields will result in the development of novel approaches and significant advances.

6.4 Ethical considerations and transparency in AI

The term "artificial intelligence" (AI) refers to a disruptive technology that carries with it a great deal of promise for resolving difficult problems and enhancing many facets of our everyday life. However, in addition to that, it brings up significant ethical considerations that should be addressed. In this essay of 700 words, we will discuss the ethical considerations that are involved in artificial intelligence (AI) as well as the significance of transparency in order to ensure the responsible development and deployment of AI.

1. **Ethical Considerations in Artificial Intelligence**

AI systems, and particularly those that are based on machine learning, are supposed to make judgments, predictions, and recommendations by learning from the data they are provided. Due to the fact that these systems have the ability to have an effect on individuals, societies, and institutions, ethical issues are of the utmost importance.

1. **Impartiality and Balance**
   The existence of bias in computer programs is one of the most fundamental ethical challenges raised by artificial intelligence (AI). AI algorithms that are trained on biased data might contribute to the continuation and amplification of existing prejudices in society.
   It has been established that facial recognition systems display racial and gender prejudice, which can lead to unfair effects such as misidentification and discrimination. One example of this is that facial recognition systems have been shown to exhibit bias. It is necessary to address prejudice in artificial intelligence in order to guarantee equitable results and prevent discrimination.
2. **Confidentiality**
   When it comes to making predictions and suggestions, AI frequently draws on massive volumes of personal data. Significant issues about users' privacy are raised by the collection, storage, and use of these data. It is absolutely necessary to find a happy medium between the advantages of AI and individual rights to privacy. For the purpose of protecting the privacy of individuals and their data, regulations such as the General Data Protection Regulation (GDPR) have been enacted in Europe.

3. **Accountability and Openness to the Public**
   The opaque nature of AI algorithms makes it difficult to ascertain who is to blame when anything goes wrong. It is becoming increasingly challenging to understand the decision-making processes behind AI systems as these systems become more complicated and autonomous. For the sake of ethical considerations, it is essential to ensure that AI decision-making processes are both accountable and transparent.
4. **Consent and Control**
   People should have the right to know when they are dealing with AI systems, and they should have choice over how their data is used. Individuals should have the right to know when they are interacting with AI systems. Consent given voluntarily by a user is essential to the development of ethical AI. Users ought to have a solid understanding of the inner workings of AI systems, including what data is gathered and how it influences decision-making.
5. **Protection**
   Artificial intelligence systems can have far-reaching ramifications, and the deployment of these systems in fields like autonomous vehicles and healthcare requires safety considerations to be taken. It is essential, in order to prevent accidents and harm, to make sure that AI systems are dependable, that they fail in a gracious manner, and that they include built-in safety mechanisms.
6. **Displacement from One's Job**

Concerns regarding job displacement have been raised in response to the increased deployment of AI and automation.

Although artificial intelligence has the potential to boost production and create efficiency, it also has the potential to make certain employment unnecessary. Ethical considerations ought to include steps for upskilling and reskilling the worker in order to lessen the impact on employment opportunities.

II. The Importance of Being Open and Honest

1. **Explanable AI (also known as XAI)**
   Explainable AI is a burgeoning field with the primary goal of increasing the interpretability and transparency of AI algorithms and models. Users will be able to comprehend the logic that behind AI-generated recommendations or actions if this feature achieves its goal of providing insights into the process by which AI systems arrive at their conclusions. Explainable artificial intelligence is especially important in industries like healthcare, where the decisions that are made might have life-changing repercussions.

2. **Documentation of the Model**
   AI developers are obligated to produce documentation that not only outlines the model, but also its training data and how it arrives at its conclusions. This information can assist users and regulators in understanding the operation of the system and evaluating its fairness as well as any potential biases it may include.

3. **Standards and Guidelines Regarding Ethical Conduct**
   Ethical principles and standards for the development and deployment of AI are now being developed by many governments, organizations, and industry agencies. These rules offer a foundation for transparent and responsible artificial intelligence. Examples include the IEEE Global Initiative on Ethics of Autonomous and Intelligent Systems and the Principles for AI created by the European Commission. Both of these initiatives are examples of artificial intelligence ethics.

4. **Public Auditing and Open-Source Software**

Tools for open source AI and public audits of AI systems both have the potential to contribute to greater levels of openness. By making the code and data used in the creation of AI available to the public, it is possible for the system's behavior to be evaluated and validated from an outside perspective.

III. A Responsible Approach to AI Moving Forward

A complete methodology is required for the development and deployment of artificial intelligence systems that take ethical considerations and are transparent.

1. **Teams Comprised of Professionals from Different Disciplines**
   To guarantee that ethical issues are incorporated into each level of the development process of AI systems, the AI development teams should be comprised of persons with a wide range of experiences, including individuals with expertise in ethics.
2. **Ongoing Monitoring and Auditing of Operations**
   Audits and monitoring of AI systems should be performed on a regular basis and should be ongoing in order to detect and rectify possible problems, such as bias and unexpected consequences.
3. **Ethical Principles and Guidelines**
   AI developers should ensure that the systems they construct are in accordance with the values of justice, transparency, and accountability by adhering to existing ethical frameworks and norms and ensuring that their work complies with such standards.
4. **Coordination and Regulatory Measures**
   It is absolutely necessary for governments, businesses, and members of civil society to work together in order to design and enforce legislation that govern AI. These regulations may include ethical AI concepts and standards if the government so chooses.

5. **Education and Conscientization**
   Users, organizations, and developers should be informed about the ethical aspects involved with AI, as well as the significance of transparency, through education and awareness campaigns.
6. **User Agency and Participation**
   Users should be given access to tools and user interfaces that provide them the ability to make educated decisions about how AI systems will utilize their data and what suggestions they will be given.
7. **Analysis of Ethical Considerations in AI**

Before the deployment of AI systems in important areas, there should always be a common practice of doing an ethical assessment of AI. With the use of this assessment, the system's ethical implications, as well as its fairness and transparency, would be evaluated.

Chapter 7

Virtual Labs and Collaborative Platforms

In recent years, virtual labs and collaborative platforms have arisen as strong tools that are altering education and research across a variety of fields. These changes have been brought about by advances in technology. These technologies are making it possible to conduct experiments remotely, are facilitating worldwide collaboration, and are providing chances for hands-on learning that have never been seen before. In this extensive essay of 3000 words, we will investigate the significance of virtual labs and collaborative platforms in the fields of education and research, as well as their history, evolution, applications, difficulties, and potential for the future.

1. **The Opening Statements**
1. **The Development of Virtual Laboratories and Other Platforms for Collaborative Work**
   The limits of traditional laboratory sets and physical collaboration inspired the first conception of the idea of virtual labs and collaborative platforms, which were initially envisioned as a response to these limitations. These technologies make use of the

power of the internet, specialized software, and various communication methods in order to make remote access to laboratories easier and to build virtual environments in which workers may collaborate. The growing need for educational and research solutions that are both accessible and innovative has helped to speed up the development and implementation of these solutions.

2. **The Aims of the Essay as Well as Its Organization**

The purpose of this essay is to present a full grasp of collaborative platforms and virtual labs. The origins of these technologies, the progress of these technologies, their applications across numerous fields, the challenges that they offer, and the possibilities that they represent for the future will all be investigated in depth during this course. We are going to investigate the effect that these technologies have had on education and research, as well as their part in transforming the way that we learn, experiment, and work together.

II. The Development of Virtual Laboratories and Platforms for Collaborative Work

1. **Initial Steps and Developments**
   In the latter half of the 20th century, fields such as computer science and engineering were among the first to make use of the idea of virtual labs and collaborative platforms. In many cases, fundamental simulations and straightforward online collaboration tools were used in these early trials. The capabilities and applications of virtual labs and collaborative platforms have increased in tandem with the progression of technology.
2. **Developments in Newer Technologies**
   The advancement of computer technology, software, and the internet has had a direct impact on the development of virtual labs and collaborative platforms. These technologies have become significantly more approachable and powerful as a direct result

of the proliferation of high-speed internet connections, cloud computing, and advances in visualization methods.

3. **The Expanding Scope of Education**

   Education has seen a considerable uptick in the utilization of virtual labs and collaborative platforms. Students can gain valuable hands-on experience in the fields of science and engineering by participating in experiments and projects using these. These instruments have been used by educational institutions all around the world as a means of overcoming limits imposed by physical labs. These limitations include funding constraints, accessibility difficulties, and safety concerns.

4. **Development Into Research Areas**

   Research is another area that has seen significant application growth for collaborative platforms. They make possible the working together of researchers from all over the world, the sharing of data, and the fluid interchange of ideas. Platforms that facilitate collaborative research have made it simpler for researchers of all academic disciplines to work together, regardless of their locations.

5. **Integration of Interdisciplinary Perspectives**

The development of these technologies has paved the way for the integration of several fields of study. It is possible for researchers, educators, and students working in diverse sectors to work together and benefit from the expertise of each other. This multidisciplinary approach has resulted in the development of creative solutions and the discovery of new information.

III. Applications in Teaching and Learning

1. **Advancing Education in the STEM Disciplines**

   Education in the STEM (science, technology, engineering, and mathematics) fields is being completely transformed via virtual labs. Students are given the opportunity to gain hands-on experience and exposure to scientific processes that are carried out in the real world in these laboratories, which offer an option that is both safe and cost effective. Students have the opportunity to perform experiments and examine results through the use of interactive simulations, which contributes to a more in-depth comprehension of scientific principles.

2. **Availability of Access and Encouragement of Inclusion**
The ease with which virtual labs can be accessed is one of the chief benefits associated with using them. They make educational opportunities available to students who, for a variety of reasons, such as those related to geography, finances, or other factors, may not have access to physical laboratories. Inclusion is fostered and education is made accessible to a larger population thanks to the use of virtual laboratories.

3. **Experiments That Involve No Danger**
Experiments may be hazardous, costly, or difficult to carry out in their usual laboratory settings if they are to be performed in specific fields. Students are able to conduct experiments in virtual labs without the dangers, costs, or resource limits that are typically connected with such activities.

4. **Learning That Is Adaptable**
The level of difficulty of the experiments in virtual laboratories can frequently be altered to correspond with the student's existing level of ability. This type of adaptive learning feature is common in virtual labs. This approach to learning is adaptive, which increases the learning experience while also ensuring that pupils are suitably challenged.

5. **Education That Lasts a Lifetime**
Education can now be obtained outside of the conventional classroom setting thanks to virtual labs. They encourage learning throughout a person's lifetime as well as continual professional development, giving people the opportunity to expand their skill sets and stay current in a variety of fields of study.

6. Learning Through a Blended Method

Blended learning environments, which make use of both online and in-person instructional strategies, usually make use of the incorporation of virtual labs within their overall structure. This strategy allows for the versatility of remote access to labs, while also providing the advantages of in-person education.

IV. Applications in Research

1. Cooperation at the International Level
   Because they make it possible for researchers from different countries to work together, collaborative platforms have fundamentally changed the nature of research. Researchers located in many regions of the world are able to work together on projects, share data, and communicate their thoughts in real time. This global collaboration has resulted in the development of novel solutions and has helped to speed up the advancement of scientific research.
2. Openness in Science and the Exchange of Data
   The sharing of data, which is essential to the ideals behind open science, can be facilitated by collaborative platforms. Transparency, repeatability, and a wider impact of research are all encouraged when there is open access to data, study findings, and methodology.
3. The use of Crowdsourcing and Participatory Science
   Crowdsourcing and other forms of citizen science are now possible thanks to the proliferation of collaborative platforms. Researchers have the ability to involve members of the public in data gathering and analysis, thereby tapping into the intellect of a global community as a whole to address difficult issues.
4. Research Done From a Distance
   Platforms that facilitate collaboration make remote study possible, an ability that is particularly useful in fields such as astronomy

and environmental science. Researchers no longer have to be physically present at each individual research site because they may obtain data and carry out tests remotely from a variety of locations.

5. **Research That Cuts Across Disciplines**

   Interdisciplinary research is encouraged through the use of collaborative platforms, which bring together specialists from a variety of disciplines to handle difficult problems.

   The sharing of information and ideas across academic fields has resulted in significant advancements in a variety of fields, including biotechnology, nanotechnology, and materials science, amongst others.

6. **Research and Collaboration Networking**

Researchers often make use of collaborative platforms as a means of both professional networking and connection development. These platforms make it easier to find potential partners and mentors by facilitating the finding of specialists in specific sectors and so facilitating the process.

V. Obstacles and Causes for Concern

1. **The Assurance of Quality**

   When it comes to education, it can be difficult to ensure that the quality and accuracy of virtual labs. Both the content and the simulations need to be in line with the educational standards that have been established, and they need to be updated on a regular basis to reflect any developments in the relevant field.

2. **An insufficient amount of real-world practice**

   Even though virtual laboratories offer beneficial learning experiences, in many fields, they are not able to completely replace the need for hands-on experimentation. Experimentation in one's physical environment is the only way to develop certain skills and techniques.

3. **Infrastructure and accessibility comes in at number three.**
   Connectivity to the internet and the availability of the appropriate gear are prerequisites for gaining access to virtual labs and collaboration platforms. Opportunities for education and research might be unequally distributed when there is a disparity in access to relevant resources.
4. **Data Security**
   A important worry in the realm of research is the protection of data. It is imperative that collaborative platforms implement stringent security protocols in order to safeguard sensitive research data and intellectual property.
5. **Considerations of a Moral Nature**
   When utilizing collaborative platforms for the sake of data sharing and research, ethical concerns, such as data protection and permission, as well as ethical research techniques, need to be addressed.
6. **Obstacles of a Technical Nature**
   The utilization of virtual labs and collaborative platforms can be disrupted when technical issues such as incompatibility across systems, software defects, and server outages occur. This has the potential to have an impact on educational and research endeavors.
7. **The Gap in Digital Access**

The "digital divide," which describes the disparity in access to digital technologies, is a problem that affects both the educational system and the scientific community. To guarantee that everyone has access to opportunities on an equal footing, bridging this barrier is crucial.

VI. The development of Virtual Laboratories and Online Collaboration Platforms

1. **Increased Lifelikeness of Virtual Laboratories**
   It is anticipated that the future of virtual labs will contain

simulations that are both more realistic and immersive. It is anticipated that cutting-edge technologies such as virtual reality (VR) and augmented reality (AR) would play a big part in the process of developing authentic laboratory experiences.

2. **The Implementation of Artificial Intelligence**
   Artificial intelligence (AI) will be included into virtual labs in order to provide individualized feedback, coaching, and learning experiences that are adaptable to individual needs. AI will make it easier to customize instructional content to the specific requirements of individual students.

3. **Increased Opportunities for Collaboration Across Disciplines**
   Platforms for collaborative work will continue to be helpful in fostering collaboration across disciplines. Researchers from a wide variety of fields will collaborate to address difficult problems on a global scale, which will result in the development of novel solutions.

4. **Progress Made Towards the Collaboration of Data**
   The sharing of data and the proliferation of open science projects will continue to be facilitated by collaborative platforms. Interoperability of data will be given a greater priority, which will make it easier for academics to collaborate smoothly across a variety of datasets and fields of study.

5. **Discussing Equity and Inclusivity in the Workplace**
   It is planned to make an effort to eliminate digital inequalities and make virtual laboratories and collaboration platforms available to individuals and organizations located all over the world. The advancement of inclusion and equity in educational and research settings will be the primary emphasis of the initiatives.

6. **Learning Over the Course of a Lifetime and Continuing Education for Professionals**
   It is anticipated that virtual labs will continue to play an important role as resources for continuing education and professional advancement. People will have access to a vast array of different

courses, tutorials, and simulations so that they can improve their skill sets and progress further in their careers.

7. AI that is both ethical and responsible

Ethical and responsible standards for artificial intelligence will direct the creation of virtual laboratories and collaboration platforms, as well as their use. There will be precautions taken to protect the confidentiality of the data, as well as ensuring transparency, equity, and accountability.

The rapid development of virtual labs and collaborative platforms has resulted in the provision of novel solutions in the fields of education and research. Access has been increased, global collaboration has been encouraged, and multidisciplinary research has been made possible as a result of these tools. Even while difficulties like as ensuring quality, increasing accessibility, and addressing ethical concerns are still present, there is a lot of hope for the future.

These technologies will play a vital role in addressing some of the most important concerns in science, education, and society as they continue to become more immersive and realistic in virtual labs and as collaborative platforms continue to connect researchers and educators across the globe. The key to reaching this potential lies in responsible development, equal access, and a dedication to the cultivation of ethical and inclusive settings for learning and research. reaching this potential will require all of these things. Education and research are about to be revolutionized in ways that have never been seen before because to the continuous development of virtual labs and collaborative platforms. These changes will make it possible for more people to get access to information and new forms of creativity.

7.1 The concept of virtual laboratories

In the realm of education, the groundbreaking notion of virtual laboratories, which are often commonly referred to as "virtual labs," has recently come into existence. They are revolutionizing the way students and learners of all ages interact with courses that fall under the STEM umbrella (science, technology, engineering, and mathematics). In this essay of 700 words, we will discuss the idea of virtual laboratories, as well as their relevance, uses, advantages, and the effect they have on experiential learning.

1. **An Overview of Online Facilities and Equipment**

   As their name suggests, virtual laboratories are digital or online platforms that recreate the conditions and procedures of traditional laboratories. They provide a digital setting in which students and other learners can conduct experiments, investigate scientific concepts, and acquire practical knowledge in a variety of STEM fields. The hands-on experience of working in a physical laboratory may frequently be replicated through the use of interactive simulations, multimedia components, and data analysis tools in virtual labs.

2. **The Importance of Online Laboratories**

1. **Accessibility and inclusivity**

   The ease with which virtual laboratories can be accessed is among the most important benefits associated with using them. They eliminate barriers based on location and finances, making it possible for a greater number of people to obtain a STEM education of a high standard. Students who live in places that are underprivileged or distant, as well as those who do not have access to physical laboratories that are adequately equipped, can now participate in experiential learning.

2. **The Affordability and Reliability of It**

   Experimentation can take place in a setting that is both secure and under control when using virtual labs. They remove the dangers that come with handling harmful substances, chemicals, or valuable pieces of equipment. It is possible for schools and other educational institutions to reduce the amount of money spent on maintaining and equipping physical laboratories, which will result in STEM education being more cost-effective.

3. **Learning Through Doing**
   The provision of a hands-on learning experience is at the heart of the concept of virtual laboratories. Students take an active role in the learning process by engaging with the material, conducting experiments, and analyzing the results, just as they would in a traditional laboratory setting. This hands-on experience helps students develop a more profound comprehension of scientific principles.
4. **Participation and Active Involvement**
   Students are kept engaged through the use of multimedia and interactive components in virtual labs. Active learning can be encouraged through the use of computer simulations, animations, and real-time feedback. This allows students to investigate complicated ideas and experiment with a wide variety of factors.
5. **Instruction Tailored to the Learner**

A wide variety of online laboratories now provide adaptive learning options. They have the ability to change the level of difficulty and provide tailored feedback, making it possible for students to advance at their own speed while still being adequately challenged.

III. The Uses and Benefits of Virtual Laboratories

1. **Education from Kindergarten to Grade 12**
   Students in grades K-12 are exposed to the fields of science and technology through the utilization of virtual labs in today's classrooms. Experiments and interactive lessons designed for children of the right age range are provided in order to pique students' interest and inspire them to pursue careers in STEM fields.
2. **Education at a Higher Level**
   Virtual labs are increasingly becoming a component of undergraduate and graduate STEM programs in educational institutions like colleges and universities. They are useful not only as supplemental tools for theoretical classes, but also for online or

remote learning programs, where their utility cannot be overstated.
3. **Acquiring Experience in One's Field**
Professional development and vocational education often make use of online simulations of working labs. For instance, they are utilized in the training of medical and healthcare professionals, providing a risk-free setting in which the trainees can perform surgical procedures and care for simulated patients.
4. **Research in the Field of Science**

When it comes to scientific investigation, virtual labs provide a one-of-a-kind environment for the testing of hypotheses and the simulation of experiments before actually carrying them out in a real laboratory. Researchers now have the ability to simulate complicated systems using virtual labs and study how those models react to varying environmental factors.

IV. The Benefits Obtained From Online Laboratories

1. **There Are No Constraints Placed on the Resources**
The limitations imposed by physical resources can be circumvented using virtual laboratories. Experiments can be repeated as many as desired without the need to continually purchase new chemicals or replace outdated apparatus. Learners are able to experience a greater variety of possible scenarios as a result of this.
2. **Safety and Risk Reduction Measures**
A big advantage is the absence of any potential physical dangers. Students are able to conduct experiments without having to worry about their safety, which lowers the risk of mishaps and exposure to potentially harmful substances.
3. **Providing Prompt Responses**
The immediate input and analysis of experimental data are both provided by virtual labs. Students are better able to understand

the consequences of their choices as a result of this rapid response, which also stimulates iterative learning.
4. **Applications to the Real World**
The applications and circumstances of the actual world are frequently simulated in a variety of virtual labs. Because of this, the students' educational experiences become more pertinent and practical, better preparing them for their future employment.
5. **Effects on the Environment**

The consumption of consumables, electricity, and water that are often connected with physical laboratories is significantly cut down thanks to the use of virtual laboratories, which contributes to increased environmental sustainability. This is consistent with the tenets of education that is green and friendly to the environment.

V. Obstacles and Things to Take Into Account

1. **Unsatisfactory Levels of Haptic Feedback**
Because virtual laboratories do not provide haptic feedback, students do not have the opportunity to experience the tactile feelings that are associated with conducting real experiments. Because of this constraint, their comprehension of the texture and nuances of lab work in the real world may be impacted.
2. **Complicated Modeling and Simulations**
It can be difficult to create simulations that are realistic and complicated, and that match tests performed in the actual world. In order to create experiences that are meaningful, developers need to make sure that virtual labs are accurate.
3. **Essential Technical Prerequisites**
The availability of computer hardware, appropriate software, and an active internet connection are prerequisites for virtual labs. The digital divide can be made even worse when certain learners do not have access to these tools, which contributes to the problem.

4. **Instructional Staff Development**
   It's possible that teachers need training before they can effectively use virtual labs into their existing instructional strategies. They have the responsibility of directing students through the virtual experiments and assisting them in comprehending both the theoretical and practical components.
5. **Evaluation and Proof of Authenticity**

The evaluation of work performed in a virtual lab can be difficult. It is essential to take measures to prevent plagiarism and data fabrication, as well as to verify the veracity of the data supplied by students.

VI. The Development of Virtual Laboratories and Their Prospects

1. **Compatibility with New Technological Developments**
   Emerging technologies like virtual reality (VR) and augmented reality (AR) will be included into the operation of virtual labs. These technologies will give experiences that are more immersive and realistic, and they will solve the problem of inadequate haptic feedback.
2. **An Increased Level of Interactivity**
   The interactivity of virtual laboratories will be improved as a result of developments in artificial intelligence (AI). The use of AI algorithms makes it possible to deliver individualized instruction, anticipate students' requirements, and change trials in real time.
3. **Greater Flexibility in Movement**
   The proliferation of mobile devices and applications will make virtual labs more accessible on a wider variety of platforms, hence significantly lowering the bar for technological entry.
4. **Advancing Studies in the STEM Fields**
   The scope of virtual labs will be broadened to encompass a greater number of STEM topics, including subfields such as materials science, nanotechnology, and biotechnology.

5. The Combination of Gamification and Teamwork

Students' engagement will be increased, and teamwork will be encouraged, thanks to the addition of gamification features and collaborative functions that will be built into virtual labs.

Experiential education in STEM subjects has been changed by the rise of virtual laboratories. Because of their accessibility, safety, and ability to give experiential learning through hands-on activities, these instruments are useful in education at all levels. Students are encouraged to participate in active learning in these labs, which gives them the opportunity to investigate difficult ideas, carry out experiments, and get a more in-depth understanding of scientific principles.

As the state of the art in technology continues to improve, virtual laboratories will become increasingly complex and immersive, presenting users with an ever-expanding selection of opportunities and activities. Even if obstacles like haptic feedback and technical needs still exist, the future of virtual labs looks optimistic, and it promises that STEM education will be more inclusive, interesting, and effective for students all over the world. It is expected that these digital platforms will continue to revolutionize the landscape of experiential learning, thereby enabling future generations of scientists and innovators.

7.2 Online collaboration tools for researchers

In recent years, there has been a considerable shift in the environment in which research is conducted, and tools for online collaboration have been an essential component of this development. Now, more than ever before, researchers coming from a wide variety of fields, institutions, and parts of the world have the tools necessary to connect with one another, communicate with one another, and collaborate productively. In this essay of 1000 words, we will discuss the significance of online collaboration tools for academics, as well as their uses, benefits, and obstacles, as well as the prospects for their future.

1. **The Opening Statements**
   The field of research has historically been defined by its emphasis on individual efforts and lonely knowledge. Researchers functioned within their own fields, frequently working alone or within small teams based in their immediate geographic areas. These barriers have been broken down thanks to the development of tools for online cooperation, which has ushered in a new era of interconnected research.
   These tools make it easier for researchers to work together, improve researchers' ability to communicate, and quicken the pace of scientific advancement.
2. **The significance of online tools for group work for researchers**
1. **Overcoming Obstacles Presented by Geography**
   Researchers from all over the world are able to work together without interruption because to the elimination of geographical obstacles made possible by online collaboration tools. Nowadays, physical distance is less of a factor in the formation of fruitful scientific cooperation.
2. **Collaboration Between Different Disciplines**
   It is now much simpler for researchers from different fields to work together, which paves the way for the integration of a wider range of knowledge and points of view. Collaboration across disciplinary lines frequently results in novel solutions and groundbreaking advancements.
3. **The Ability to Exchange and Access Data**
   These tools make data exchange and accessibility easier to accomplish. Researchers now have the ability to exchange datasets, methodology, and discoveries in real time, which promotes research that is both transparent and reproducible.
4. **Conferences and Meetings That Take Place Online**
   The use of virtual conferences, webinars, and meetings can all be supported by online collaboration technologies. Researchers are able to take part in international conferences without having to

be physically present, which cuts down on both the costs of travel and the carbon footprints left behind.
5. **Improvements Made to Project Management**

These applications provide functionality for managing projects, such as task assignment, tracking of progress, and document exchange, among other things. This improves the research teams' ability to organize their work and collaborate with one another.

III. **Uses for Online Communication and Coordination Tools**

1. **Collaborative Data Analysis and Collection**
   Collaborating with other researchers on the collection, analysis, and interpretation of data is possible. Sharing data in real time and doing collaborative data analysis is made easier with the use of tools such as Google Sheets, Jupyter Notebook, and RStudio.
2. **Collaboration on Documents and Editing**
   Researchers are able to produce and edit documents together through the use of collaborative
   document editors such as Google Docs. When it comes to creating research papers, proposals, and reports, this is really helpful information to have.
3. **Managing Construction Projects**
   Tools such as Trello and Asana allow academics to more effectively manage projects, organize their work, prioritize their assignments, and monitor their progress. These tools help research teams improve their project organization and their ability to collaborate with one another.
4. **Means of Interaction and Message Transmission**
   Messaging and chat functions are frequently included as part of the tool set for online collaboration. Researchers are able to connect with one another, share updates with one another, and trade information in real time using platforms such as Slack and Microsoft Teams.

5. **Storing and Distributing Digital Files**
   Cloud storage systems such as Dropbox and Google Drive make it possible to store research documents, datasets, and code safely while also facilitating their collaborative use. If researchers have an internet connection, they can access their files from virtually any location.
6. **Virtual Laboratories is the final option.**
   Researchers are able to conduct their tests and investigations within simulated environments made available by virtual lab platforms. These tools are very useful for conducting research and training over the internet.
7. **Communities and Networks for Academic Research**

By providing areas for the sharing of research findings and engaging in discussions, online platforms such as ResearchGate and Academia.edu establish relationships between researchers and promote collaboration among them.

IV. The Advantages of Utilizing Online Collaboration Tools

1. **Effectiveness**
   The use of these tools enables researchers to perform their work in a more effective manner. The research process can be made more efficient with features such as real-time document editing, collaborative data analysis, and project management.
2. **Reductions in Expenses**
   The necessity for research teams and institutions to physically meet and travel is reduced as a result of the use of online cooperation, which results in cost savings.
3. **Adaptability to Change**
   Researchers have the flexibility to cooperate on their own terms, regardless of whether they are working remotely, across time zones, or within interdisciplinary teams. This allows for greater creativity and productivity.

4. **Current and Accurate Information**
   The use of collaboration technologies allows for documents and data to have their versions controlled and updated in real time. This guarantees that every member of the team is working with the most up-to-date information possible.
5. **Sense of inclusion**

The use of tools for online collaboration increases inclusivity by lowering the obstacles that are caused by differences in geographical location and the availability of resources. Participation in joint research initiatives is open to researchers from a wide range of fields and locations.

V. Obstacles and Things to Take Into Account

1. **The Slope of Learning**
   The earliest stages of the research process can be slowed considerably since it takes time for researchers to become accustomed to new tools and platforms.
2. **The Protection of Data**
   It is essential to protect the confidentiality of data. Researchers have a responsibility to safeguard sensitive research data against breaches and illegal access.
3. **An Excessive Amount of Information**
   The consistent flow of text messages, emails, and notifications can result in an excessive amount of information as well as distractions.
4. **Skills in Working Together**
   It is necessary to have strong communication and interpersonal skills for effective teamwork. There is a possibility that researchers will require training in these areas.
5. **Dependence on Technological Means**

Researchers who rely heavily on technology may be more susceptible to interruptions brought on by problems with the device itself or by cyberattacks.

VI. The Outlook for the Future

1. **Compatibility with New Technological Developments**
   The capabilities of online collaboration tools are going to be significantly improved once upcoming technologies like artificial intelligence (AI) and augmented reality (AR) are incorporated into their design. These technologies will create experiences that are both more immersive and intelligent in terms of collaboration.
2. **Initiatives Regarding Open Science**
   The use of online collaboration tools will continue to be an integral part of open science projects because of the positive impact they have on transparency, reproducibility, and the open dissemination of research results.
3. **Improved Analytical Capabilities for Data**
   In order to accommodate the ever-increasing number of data produced by research initiatives, collaborative data analytics systems are going to continue to develop. Researchers will be able to gain more insights from their data with the assistance of analytics driven by AI.
4. **Social Networking in the Academic World**
   The proliferation of academic social networking platforms will provide researchers with an increased number of opportunities to connect with one another, share information, and work together within specialized communities and networks.
5. **Accessibility Via Mobile Devices**

The accessibility of online collaboration tools on mobile devices is going to increase, which will facilitate research when the researcher is on the move and cater to researchers with a variety of preferred methods of working.

Tools for online cooperation have had a transformative effect on research by increasing connectedness and bringing the scientific community one step closer to its goals. The capacity to work together in real time, share data and resources, and communicate across geographic boundaries has opened up new doors for scientific discovery and innovation.

Although there are still obstacles to overcome, such as the steep learning curve, concerns about data security, and an overwhelming amount of information, the potential for these tools to continue molding the research landscape is enormous. Researchers are becoming more connected to one another, and the future of research looks to be more collaborative, inclusive, and productive thanks to the transformative power of online collaboration tools. Researchers are increasingly networked. These tools will continue to be at the vanguard of scientific advancement, allowing researchers to confront complex global concerns and push the boundaries of human knowledge. As technology continues to advance and integration with emerging technologies becomes more common, these tools will remain at the forefront of scientific progress.

7.3 Remote experimentation and simulations

Researchers and students are now able to perform experiments and investigate intricate scenarios from any location because to the emergence of remote experimentation and simulations, which have emerged as revolutionary tools. The areas of science, engineering, and education have all been significantly impacted by these remote capabilities, which have made previously unimaginable prospects for learning and study available.

1. **Experiments Conducted From a Distance**
   Through the use of a computer interface, participants in a remote experiment are able to exercise control over physical equipment or instruments that are situated in a separate geographical location. This strategy has made it possible for researchers to conduct

tests at specialized facilities without the need for their physical presence. As a result, researchers have been able to save costs and shorten the amount of time needed to complete the studies. It has also made it easier for multiple institutions to share expensive or unusual pieces of equipment, which has increased the efficiency with which resources are used and fostered the growth of collaborative research projects.

2. **Modeling and Attempts**

On the other hand, simulations necessitate the development of digital models that act as close approximations of the corresponding real-world processes or systems as possible. Researchers and students are able to investigate theoretical concepts, put forward and test hypotheses, and study the behavior of complicated phenomena in an environment that is under controlled conditions thanks to these virtual environments. Simulations offer a cost-effective and safe alternative to physical testing, particularly in disciplines in which conducting real tests may be impracticable, hazardous, or expensive. Simulations also give the added benefit of being safer than physical experimentation.

The democratization of scientific discovery and learning is thanks in large part to the contributions that simulations and remote experimentation have made. This has made it possible for a wider audience to participate. These technologies have made the educational experience better by enabling students to acquire practical information and skills without the limitations imposed by physical constraints or geographical boundaries. This has improved the quality of education. In addition to this, they have significantly increased their efforts in research and development, which has encouraged creativity and discovery in a variety of fields. It is anticipated that the options for conducting remote experiments and simulations will expand as these technologies continue to progress, which will contribute to further advances in scientific research, engineering practices, and educational practices.

Chapter 8

Cybersecurity and Research Integrity

Cybersecurity is a crucial issue that needs to be addressed in the digital era because it has the potential to compromise not only personal privacy and national security but also the reliability of research and the advancement of scientific knowledge. This essay, which is 3000 words long, dives into the complex web of connections that exist between research integrity and cybersecurity. It investigates the significance of research integrity, the vulnerabilities in the digital research landscape, the impact of cyber threats on research, and the necessary precautions to take in order to protect the integrity of knowledge in a world that is increasingly linked.

1. **The Opening Statements**

   Integrity in research serves as the basis upon which the scientific community constructs new bodies of knowledge. In the conduct of research, it involves adhering to the tenets of honesty, transparency, objectivity, and accountability. The advent of the digital age has allowed for significant progress to be made in the methodology of study, communication, and the exchange of data. However, this has resulted in the introduction of new vulnerabilities and difficulties in maintaining the integrity of research. The integrity of research data, procedures, and findings can be jeopardized by a wide variety of cyber hazards, from data breaches to cyberattacks. This essay explores the essential nexus between research integrity and cybersecurity, underlining the significance of protecting the knowledge that drives the advancement of scientific research.

2. **The Importance of Maintaining Honesty in Research**
1. **Protecting the Core Values of Science**

    The scientific community must always uphold high standards of research integrity in order to keep its credibility and reputation intact. It makes sure that the study is carried out in an ethical manner, without any fabrication, falsification, or plagiarism, and that the results are reported in an accurate and transparent manner. This dedication to conducting research in an ethical manner is necessary in order to earn the trust of other researchers, institutions, and society as a whole.

2. **The Capability of Being Reproduced and Accountable**

    Integrity in research encourages reproducibility, which in turn enables other people to verify and expand upon the findings of previous study. It ensures accountability by making researchers answerable for their work and holding them accountable for their actions. These guiding principles are essential for the development of new information as well as the avoidance of mistakes and unethical behavior.

3. **Accomplishments in Research and Technological Advancement**

    Protecting the honesty of research is absolutely necessary for advancing scientific knowledge and driving innovation. Research that can be relied on provides the foundation for new findings, technological advances, and evidence-based decision making in a variety of sectors, including medicine, engineering, and the social sciences.

4. Responsibility to Uphold Ethical Standards

The upholding of research integrity falls under the ethical responsibilities of researchers. This necessitates a dedication to truthfulness, objectivity, and the ethical execution of research. Not only does the scientific community profit when researchers adhere to ethical standards, but so does the rest of society.

III. Weaknesses in the Current Context of Digital Research Landscape

1. **Cooperative Work and the Use of Digital Data**
   The advent of the digital age has fundamentally altered the nature of research by making it possible to generate, distribute, and evaluate enormous volumes of data. Additionally, it has made it easier for researchers in different parts of the world to collaborate with one another. While these developments are beneficial to research, they also open up new potential weaknesses. Both remote collaboration and the ease with which digital data can be modified pose potential security hazards.

2. **Violations of Data Privacy and Other Concerns**
   Breach of data security poses a substantial risk to the reliability of research. The disclosure of sensitive data, such as personally identifiable information (PII) and the results of confidential research, might result from these breaches. When researchers acquire, retain, and distribute data without proper safeguards, which could possibly violate ethical norms and legislation, privacy problems arise.

3. **Attacks on the Internet and the Theft of Intellectual Property**
   Cyberattacks can be launched against research organizations and institutions, which can result in the loss of intellectual property and data relating to research. It is possible that malicious actors, such as cybercriminals and hackers supported by states, are working toward the goal of gaining a competitive edge or undermining

national security. These kinds of attacks can put a halt to scientific progress and jeopardize the integrity of research.
4. **Misconduct and plagiarism in online environments**
The simplicity of online publishing has contributed to an increase in unethical practices in the academic world, such as data manipulation and plagiarism. It is possible for researchers to be tempted to take short cuts, imitate the work of others, or manipulate data, which would undermine the credibility of their research and violate the criteria for research integrity.
5. **Problems Associated with Digital Forensics and Attribution**

In today's environment of digital research, tracking down the sources of study data and determining who is responsible for unethical behavior can be difficult tasks. For the purposes of upholding the integrity of research and investigating charges of wrongdoing, digital forensics, data authentication, and attribution methods are very necessary.

IV. The Effects of Online Dangers on Scientific Investigation

1. **The erosion of one's credibility and trustworthiness**
If a research organization or researcher is found to have been the victim of a cyber attack, their credibility and trustworthiness may be damaged. Breaches and hacks can undermine confidence among peers and the general public in the researchers' findings by casting doubt on the veracity of their research.
2. **The Compromised State of the Research Data**
The loss of sensitive scientific data due to cyberattacks has the potential to have catastrophic effects. It is possible that irreplaceable datasets could be destroyed, which will expose research initiatives to a substantial setback. In addition, unlawful modification of data might result in inaccurate study conclusions, which puts the credibility of scientific knowledge in jeopardy.
3. **Holdups in the Advancement of Research**
It is possible for research initiatives to experience severe delays as

a result of cyberattacks and data breaches.

Time and resources will need to be redirected so that security vulnerabilities can be resolved, data can be restored, and an investigation can be conducted. These delays can impede the progress of science and have an effect on the opportunities for funding.

4. **Implications for Our Morality and the Law**

When data breaches or misbehavior occur at research organizations, those institutions could be subject to legal and ethical implications. These implications can include inquiries by regulatory agencies, legal action, and harm to the reputation of the organization.

V. **Protecting the Authenticity of Scientific Research in an Electronic Age**

1. **Precautions to Be Taken for Cybersecurity**
   In today's digital world, strong cybersecurity precautions are very necessary in order to protect the integrity of research. Firewalls, intrusion detection systems, encryption, secure access controls, and routine security audits are a few examples of these measures. Protecting research data and networks requires investment from both individual researchers and institutions.
2. **The Administration of Data and Its Governance**
   For the sake of scientific honesty, proper data management and administration are absolutely necessary. Researchers are required to create rules for the protection and preservation of data, which will ensure that data is kept and disseminated in a secure manner. This involves concealing personally identifiable information as well as sensitive data.
3. **Awareness and Instruction in Ethical Conduct**
   It is critical to encourage ethical behavior in research. Training on research integrity and the ethical use of digital tools should be provided by both academic institutions and individual researchers.

Individuals may have a better understanding of the repercussions of their actions by participating in awareness initiatives.
4. **Tools for Secure Collaborative Work**
The adoption of secure collaboration solutions that include end-to-end encryption, two-factor authentication, and secure cloud storage is strongly recommended for researchers. During remote research collaboration and data sharing, these tools safeguard the confidentiality of the study data.
5. **Policies and Procedures for Handling Cybercrime and Incidents**
Policies and procedures for handling cybersecurity incidents ought to be developed by institutions. These strategies assist to minimize the impact on the integrity of the study by outlining the procedures that should be taken in the event that a breach or cyberattack occurs.
6. **Working Together with Highly Qualified Cybersecurity Professionals**
Integrity in research can be improved through collaboration with professionals in fields such as digital forensics and cybersecurity. These professionals are able to detect weaknesses, conduct inquiries into possible unethical behavior, and offer advice regarding the protection of data.
7. **Ethical Considerations in the Planning Stage of Research**

When planning their investigations, researchers must to take into account any ethical repercussions that may result. It is necessary to ensure the protection of data, to obtain informed consent, and to adhere to ethical norms right from the beginning.

VI. The Prospects for Cybersecurity and the Authenticity of Research

Both the progression of technology and the nature of the threats that are already present will have a significant impact on the future of research integrity and cybersecurity. An active, preventative stance towards cybersecurity will become even more important as the scientific community continues to rely more on digital tools and platforms. Researchers, research institutions, and policymakers all need to collaborate in order to successfully address emerging difficulties and devise original approaches to preserving the integrity of research.

1. **New Forms of Technology and Potential Dangers**
   The methods and strategies employed by cyber threats continue to develop with technological advancements. Researchers and institutions have an obligation to stay one step ahead of developing dangers and to continuously upgrade their cybersecurity procedures in order to close any gaps that may have been discovered.
2. **Cooperation on the International Level**
   Threats posed by the internet are not limited by national boundaries. In order to successfully counteract cyberattacks aimed at research institutions and data, international cooperation and the sharing of information will be absolutely necessary.
3. **Governance and Ethical Considerations in Research**
   The creation of guidelines for research ethics and governance will be an essential part of the process of guaranteeing the integrity of research.
   These frameworks need to be adapted to the context of digital research and should tackle the ethical challenges that are offered by evolving technologies.
4. **Collaboration Across Different Fields of Study**

It will be essential for researchers, institutions, people with expertise in cybersecurity, and specialists in digital forensics to work together in order to protect the integrity of research. Methods that draw from other disciplines have the potential to offer a more comprehensive understanding of cybersecurity research.

Cybersecurity and the integrity of research are inextricably interwoven, and the importance of these two concepts has never been higher than it is in today's digital world. The safeguarding of the information that supports scientific advancement is a shared obligation that calls for proactive cybersecurity measures, ethical behavior, and collaboration across disciplinary boundaries. Researchers and academic institutions can ensure that the scientific community will continue to thrive and build knowledge by making the protection of research integrity a top priority in the face of cyber threats. Trust, credibility, and transparency will serve as the foundation of the scientific community.

8.1 The importance of cybersecurity in science

It is impossible to emphasize how important cybersecurity is in this day and age of rapid technological advancement, and this is especially true in the field of research. Because of its heavy reliance on digital technologies, data sharing, and online collaboration, the scientific community is particularly susceptible to the effects of cyberattacks. This essay of 1000 words will investigate the significance of cybersecurity in the scientific community, the potential dangers, and the necessary precautions to take in order to preserve scientific research and data.

1. **The Opening Statements**
   The advent of the digital age has resulted in significant changes being made to the scientific method. For the purposes of data collection, analysis, communication, and collaboration, researchers are becoming increasingly reliant on technology. Even though these technological breakthroughs have made scientific study significantly easier, they have also made it possible for new threats to emerge. It is absolutely necessary to safeguard scientific data as well as the results of research in order to preserve the honesty of research, protect intellectual property, and guarantee that scientific advancement will continue.
2. **The Importance of Cybersecurity in the Scientific Community**
   1. **The Honesty of the Research**
      When it comes to protecting the honesty of research, cyber

security is of the utmost importance. In order to save their data, evaluate it, and communicate it with one another, researchers rely on digital technologies. Any compromise or modification of these data could potentially lead to erroneous research conclusions, which would be detrimental to the integrity of scientific knowledge.

2. **Protection of Confidential Information and Intellectual Property**

   The intellectual property held by members of the scientific community is extremely valuable. Cybersecurity protects scientific discoveries, innovations, and proprietary data from being stolen or accessed in an unauthorized manner, thereby protecting the results of laborious scientific investigation.

3. **Protecting Personal Information**

   The majority of the time, scientists are tasked with handling sensitive data, such as personal information obtained from clinical studies, patient records, or secret formulas. Protecting the privacy of data and ensuring compliance with legal and ethical norms both require the implementation of cybersecurity measures.

4. **The Ongoing Nature of the Research**

   Research activity and project completion can both come to a standstill if cyber risks are present. Protecting against these dangers is crucial to ensuring that research will continue uninterrupted and to avoiding expensive delays.

5. **The importance of one's good name and credibility**

   A data breach or cyberattack has the potential to harm the reputation of research institutes and scientists, as well as their credibility. In this day and age of knowledge, trust is more important than ever for those working in the scientific community.

6. **Trust in the Public Sector**

The public's trust in science is vitally important because it serves the public welfare. Cybersecurity ensures that the conclusions of research are not compromised, thereby protecting the public's confidence in the advancement of scientific knowledge.

III. Potential Dangers to the Cybersecurity of Scientific Organizations

1. **Violations of Privacy**
   Breach of data security might put critical research information in the hands of unauthorized individuals. Because of this, there is a risk of losing intellectual property, having one's privacy violated, and having the validity of study undermined.
2. **Attacks Made Online**
   The term "cyberattack" refers to a wide variety of online attacks, such as distributed denial of service (DDoS) attacks and ransomware attacks. These attacks have the potential to interfere with research efforts and put data security at risk.
3. **Dangers Coming From Within**
   The term "insider threat" refers to those who have allowed access to research data but
   nonetheless have the potential to misuse or steal this material. These dangers could originate from within the walls of research institutions.
4. **Threats from State-Sponsored Spies and Activities**
   In the field of science, espionage and cyber threats sponsored by states can have the goal of stealing scientific findings, intellectual property, and information that is vital to the nation's security.
5. **Phishing and social engineering are both covered here.**

Researchers and staff are the targets of phishing attempts, which take the form of fraudulent emails or communications. Researchers run the risk of exposing important information or providing access to attackers without even realizing it.

IV. Precautions to Be Taken to Ensure the Cybersecurity of the Scientific Community

1. **The Encryption of Data**
   Data should be encrypted not only while in transit but also while it is stored. Encryption assures that the data will remain unreadable to unauthorized users even in the event that there is a breach in security.
2. **Ongoing Maintenance and System Updates**
   It is essential to regularly update all of your software and hardware. Patches to fix known vulnerabilities are frequently included in updates. Cyberattacks are easier to launch against outdated computer systems.
3. **Controls for Gaining Access**
   Install stringent access controls to restrict the amount of people who have access to sensitive data. Increasing access security with the help of a multi-factor authentication system is a beneficial tool.
4. **Instruction of Staff Members**
   Raise the level of awareness on cybersecurity among the workers and researchers. Individuals are better able to identify dangers, resist phishing efforts, and adhere to security rules when they have received training.
5. **Audits of the security system and evaluations of potential risks**
   Audits and risk assessments should be performed on a regular basis so that vulnerabilities and problem areas can be located and addressed. Taking a proactive approach to addressing these challenges improves cybersecurity.
6. **Emergency Procedures and Plans**
   It is crucial to have an incident response strategy that is fully defined and ready to implement in the event of a cyber incident. This plan explains the steps that need to be taken in order to reduce the impact of the incident and recover from it.
7. **Efforts Made in Collaboration**
   Collaborate with people who are knowledgeable about cyber-

security and organizations that focus on scientific cybersecurity. The sharing of information and resources is one way to improve protection against cyberattacks.

8. **Observance of All Regulations**

Make sure you're complying with all of the applicable privacy and data protection rules. Maintaining compliance with these standards helps secure data and keeps legal repercussions at bay.

V. The Prospects for Cybersecurity in the Scientific Community

Both continued technological progress and newly discovered dangers will have a significant impact on the trajectory of scientific cybersecurity in the future. Because the scientific community is becoming more reliant on digital tools and platforms, preventative cybersecurity measures are going to become ever more important. For the purpose of protecting scientific research and data, researchers, institutions, and policymakers all need to collaborate in order to respond effectively to emerging difficulties and devise original approaches.

1. **Developments in Technology and Their Potential Dangers**
   The constantly shifting nature of potential dangers will continue to pose problems for scientific cybersecurity. Researchers and institutions have a responsibility to stay one step ahead of new threats by regularly updating their cybersecurity procedures to close any newly discovered holes.
2. **Ethical Considerations in the Planning Stage of Research**
   When designing their studies, researchers should take into account any ethical implications that may arise, including any necessary precautions regarding cybersecurity. From the very beginning, one of your primary concerns should be the protection of users' privacy and the safety of their data.
3. **Participation in International Efforts**

Because cyber threats are not constrained by national boundaries, it is necessary for countries to work together to combat them. When it comes to scientific cybersecurity, information sharing and the exchange of best practices can help bolster global defenses.

In the realm of science, cybersecurity is of the utmost importance. It is not only important to protect scientific research and data from cyber attacks in order to preserve the quality of research, but also to preserve intellectual property, privacy, and the credibility of the scientific community. Researchers and institutions can ensure that the knowledge gained via scientific investigation is safe, trustworthy, and will continue to serve society provided cybersecurity is prioritized.

8.2 Protecting research data and intellectual property

In this day and age of information and constant digital connectivity, research data and intellectual property (IP) constitute the very essence of innovation and the production of new knowledge. The generation and utilization of these assets requires a large investment of both time and resources on the part of researchers, institutions, and organizations.

It is of the utmost importance to secure research data as well as intellectual property, not only for the purpose of preserving significant work but also for the purpose of upholding ethical standards and facilitating future growth.

1. **The Importance of the Data Collected for Research**
1. **The Engine That Drives Innovation**

    The foundation of scientific and technological advancement is found in the facts gleaned from research. It is the driving force behind new discoveries, makes it possible to produce new products and services, and contributes to breakthroughs in a variety of sectors, ranging from engineering to medical.
2. **Making Choices and Decisions**

    Decision-making that is informed by data has become widespread throughout many businesses today. Research findings that are trustworthy and accurate are essential for informing policy, strategy, and planning. It provides both the public sector and the commercial sector with a roadmap for making informed decisions.

3. **Developments in the Academic and Scientific Communities**

In the world of academia, research data is absolutely necessary for the purposes of knowledge development, validation, and replication. The availability of reliable data that other researchers can examine, provide feedback on, and build upon is essential to the progression of scientific knowledge.

II. The Importance of Intellectual Property in Modern Society

1. **Safeguarding New Developments**
   Protecting innovations is the responsibility of intellectual property rights, which include patents, copyrights, and trademarks. Because of this protection, innovators and artists are encouraged to talk about their work without worrying that it would be taken advantage of.
2. **Incentivizing Capital Formation**
   The protection of intellectual property rights offers a means of luring financial contributions to scientific investigation and innovation. Projects that are legally protected are more likely to receive financial backing from investors.
3. **The Expanding Economy**

The importance of intellectual property to the expansion of a nation's economy cannot be overstated. It encourages business owners to develop and market innovative goods, services, and technologies, which in turn propels the expansion of the economy.

III. Obstacles Faced When Attempting to Protect Intellectual Property and Research Data

1. **Violations of Privacy**
   Research data is exposed to a major risk whenever there is a data breach. It is possible for malicious hackers, hacktivists, or even those working within an organization to get illegal access to sensitive research findings, which puts both the data's integrity and confidentiality at danger.
2. **Attacks Made Online**
   Research operations and the security of data can both be jeopardized by cyberattacks such as ransomware and distributed denial of service (DDoS) assaults. These kinds of attacks have the potential to disrupt projects, put the progress of research in jeopardy, and even result in the loss of research data.
3. **Dangers Coming From Within**
   Both research data and intellectual property are vulnerable to the dangers posed by insider threats. Data and proprietary information are vulnerable to being misused or stolen by disgruntled employees or collaborators.
4. **Plagiarism and other forms of academic dishonesty**

Theft of intellectual property, academic misconduct, and plagiarism are all problems that plague the academic world. There is a risk that researchers will inappropriately use the work of others, which would compromise the integrity of the research.

IV. Securing the Confidentiality of Research Records and Intellectual Property

1. **The Encryption of Data**
   Data should be encrypted not only while in transit but also while it is stored. Encryption assures that the data will remain unreadable to unauthorized users even in the event that there is a breach in security.
2. **Precautions to Be Taken for Cybersecurity**
   Strong cybersecurity measures are required in order to protect

the data collected during research as well as intellectual property. Firewalls, intrusion detection systems, safe access controls, and routine security audits are all components of this.

3. **Controls for Gaining Access**
   Install stringent access controls to restrict the amount of people who have access to sensitive data. Access control is strengthened by using several authentication factors.

4. **Instruction of Staff Members**
   It is vital to increase the level of knowledge among researchers and personnel regarding the security of data and the rights to intellectual property. Training enables individuals to identify potential dangers and adhere to security procedures.

5. **Registration of Rights Regarding Intellectual Property**
   The intellectual property rights of researchers and innovators ought to be registered as quickly as possible. Legal protection can be afforded to creative endeavors and innovations through the use of patents, copyrights, and trademarks.

6. **Working Together With Legal Professionals**
   It is extremely beneficial to work on intellectual property issues in collaboration with attorneys that specialize in this area. They can provide researchers and organizations with guidance on how to protect the discoveries and creative work that they have produced.

7. **Ethical Considerations in the Planning Stage of Research**

When planning their investigations, researchers must to take into account any ethical repercussions that may result. Data privacy, informed consent, and intellectual property rights should all be essential issues right from the beginning of the process.

V. The Prospects for Safeguarding Intellectual Property and the Information Obtained From Research

Protecting research data and intellectual property in the future will continue to go hand in hand with advances in technology and the appearance of new dangers. To preserve the honesty and significance of their work, researchers, institutions, and policymakers must maintain vigilance and be flexible in the face of emerging problems.

1. **New Forms of Technology and Potential Dangers**
   The growth of technology will give rise to a new set of problems as well as opportunities. Researchers and academic institutions have a need to stay one step ahead of new risks by regularly reviewing and revising their protective measures.
2. **Constitutional and Moral Underpinnings**
   In order to protect research data as well as intellectual property, the development of legal and ethical frameworks will be of critical importance. These frameworks need to be able to adjust to the changing environment and solve the ethical concerns that are offered by new technology.
3. **Participation in International Efforts**

When confronting dangers that extend beyond national boundaries, international cooperation is absolutely necessary. A strengthening of global defenses will result from the sharing of information and best practices around data privacy and intellectual property rights.

In this day and age, the safeguarding of research data as well as intellectual property is an absolutely necessary prerequisite. Researchers, institutions, and organizations are required to employ stringent cybersecurity measures and adhere to ethical and legal norms in order to protect the integrity of their work and maintain its secrecy. We can continue to stimulate innovation, increase knowledge, and drive economic progress while retaining the ethical and legal integrity of scientific and artistic efforts if we make protecting research data and intellectual property a top priority.

8.3 Ensuring research integrity in a digital age

The advent of the digital age has significantly altered the landscape of research, making previously unimaginable options available for collaboration, data exchange, and the advancement of scientific knowledge.

Nevertheless, it has also resulted in the introduction of new obstacles and risks to the integrity of research. In this essay of 500 words, we will discuss the significance of maintaining the integrity of research in an era dominated by technology, as well as the potential dangers involved and the methods that can be utilized to do so.

1. **The Significance of Maintaining Honesty in Research**
1. **Reliability and Credibility of Sources**
   Integrity in research is absolutely necessary for the development of confidence and credibility in the scientific community. Conducting research in an ethical manner ensures that the findings are credible, accurate, and transparent, which inspires confidence not only among researchers but also among the general public.
2. **Reproducibility and Openness to Public Inspection**
   Integrity in research is essential to ensuring reproducibility, which is a bedrock of scientific advancement. Other researchers are able to verify and build upon earlier work, which contributes to the advancement of knowledge when researchers follow ethical and transparent research techniques.
3. **Responsibility on an Ethical Level**

The upholding of research integrity falls under the ethical responsibilities of researchers. This necessitates a dedication to truthfulness, objectivity, and the ethical execution of research. Not only does the scientific community profit when researchers adhere to ethical standards, but so does the rest of society.

II. **Obstacles Facing Efforts to Maintain the Integrity of Research in an Electronic Age**

1. **Protection of Personal Information and Data**
   In this day and age, protecting one's data and maintaining one's privacy are of the utmost importance. Researchers have a responsibility to protect sensitive data from being compromised,

stolen, or accessed inappropriately. The unintentional disclosure of sensitive information can occur during collaborative research projects that involve the exchange of data. This leaves the information open to attack by digital criminals.

2. **Plagiarism and other forms of academic dishonesty**
Plagiarism, data manipulation, and other forms of academic misconduct have become much more straightforward because to the proliferation of online tools. The integrity of research and the originality of scientific output are both jeopardized as a result of these unethical activities.

3. **The Dangers of the Internet**
The advent of the digital age has introduced new dangers to the reliability of research, such as data breaches and cyberattacks. It is possible for malicious actors to compromise research data, which can result in fake study conclusions, damage to reputation, and a reduction in confidence.

4. **The Predatory Publishing Company, Inc.**

The development of digital technology has given rise to the problem of predatory publishing. Publishers who lack integrity take advantage of researchers by exploiting them by demanding expensive fees for publishing studies in dubious journals, frequently without conducting rigorous peer review.

III. Methodologies to Guarantee the Authenticity of Research

1. **Methods of Encrypting Data and Other Safety Precautions**
In order to shield their study data from potential cyberattacks, researchers need to implement stringent data encryption and security procedures. This involves making use of secure servers, firewalls, intrusion detection systems, and keeping security measures up to date on a consistent basis.

2. **Ethical Education and Consciousness-Raising**
It is critical to encourage ethical behavior in research. Training

on research integrity and the ethical use of digital tools should be provided by both academic institutions and individual researchers. Individuals may have a better understanding of the repercussions of improper behavior thanks to awareness programs.

3. **Platforms for the Safe Exchange of Data**

   Make use of safe platforms for sharing data, such as those that provide encryption, access controls, and authentication systems. These platforms make certain that data is only distributed to those who have been given permission to access it.

4. **Guidelines and Codes of Conduct Regarding Ethical Considerations**

   It is important for researchers to abide by both the ethical norms and the codes of conduct that have been created. Integrity in research can be ensured by the implementation of lucid rules and standards by research institutions and organizations.

5. **Protocols for the Conduct of Collaborative Research**

   Create protocols for collaborative research that place an emphasis on the ethical treatment of data and data security. Researchers and institutions should come to an agreement regarding the proper handling of data and the security of personal information.

6. **Validation of the Research Conducted by Peers**

   It is absolutely necessary to have rigorous peer review systems in place in order to guarantee the accuracy of study findings. The work that researchers produce should be submitted to conferences and journals of renowned standing that adhere to ethical principles.

7. **Precautions to Be Taken for Cybersecurity**

   In order to protect themselves from potential cyberattacks, institutions and researchers need to employ cybersecurity measures. This includes conducting frequent audits of the system's security, training employees, and developing incident response strategies.

8. **Cooperation on a Global Scale and Regulatory Frameworks**

Given that research occurs beyond national boundaries, international collaboration on research integrity is absolutely necessary. Collaboration between policymakers and organizations should be pursued in order to establish worldwide standards and rules that encourage the ethical conduct of research.

V. The Prospects for Honesty in Scientific Investigation in the Age of Technology

The continual development of new technologies, the emergence of new dangers, and the adaptation of ethical standards to the digital environment will all play a role in determining the course that the integrity of research will take in the future. In order to safeguard the ethical underpinnings of research, researchers, institutions, and policymakers all need to maintain a heightened state of vigilance and collaborate.

1. **Ethical Considerations in the Conduct of Research Concerning New Technologies**
   As new technologies come into existence, such as artificial intelligence and gene editing, ethical rules need to develop in order to handle the specific ethical concerns that these new technologies face.
2. **International Cooperation and Compliance Standards**
   The formation of global ethical norms as well as the importance of international collaboration are both crucial. To ensure that the integrity of research is preserved across international borders, researchers, institutions, and organizations will need to collaborate.
3. **Raising Awareness in the Community and Lobbying**

The degree of public knowledge and advocacy for the honesty of research will play a significant part in determining the course of the future. The general population needs to be educated on the need of doing research in an ethical manner as well as the repercussions of acting unethically.

Integrity in research is essential to the advancement of science and the production of new information. Protecting this integrity is more important than it has ever been in this day and age of digital technology.

In a world that is increasingly linked and digital, researchers, institutions, and politicians need to make ethical research conduct a priority, implement effective security measures, and work together to develop global standards in order to guarantee that the integrity of research will not be compromised. The scientific community may continue to construct knowledge that is reliable, open to scrutiny, and beneficial to society if they uphold the highest ethical standards.

8.4 Ethical dilemmas and the responsible use of technology

The proliferation of ethical conundrums brought on by advances in technology calls for thoughtful deliberation and responsible decision-making on the part of individuals and institutions. Because of the quick pace at which technology is advancing, society is faced with a plethora of ethical dilemmas, all of which require careful consideration for their resolution. The ethical application of technology necessitates overcoming these problems with a focus on maintaining one's honesty and empathy while also prioritizing the health of both persons and communities.

1. **Privacy and the Protection of Personal Information**
   The gathering and utilization of individual data presents one of the most significant challenges to ethics in this age of information technology. To achieve a healthy equilibrium between the benefits of data-driven insights and the protection of individuals' rights to privacy, technology developers and enterprises need to give careful consideration to ethical concerns and relevant regulations.

2. **Bias and Fairness in the Use of Algorithms**
   Concerns regarding unfairness and bias have been raised as a result of the development of algorithms and systems using artificial intelligence. It is essential to the promotion of ethical use of technology that precautions be taken to ensure that these systems

do not engage in behaviors that perpetuate discrimination and that they are created with inclusion and diversity in mind.
3. **The impact of mechanization and computerization on employment**
   The automation of work through the use of technology has given rise to ethical concerns regarding the loss of jobs and the effect this will have on people's ability to make a living. The consideration of the societal ramifications and the execution of measures to reskill and upskill the workforce in order to adapt to changing job needs are both necessary steps in the adoption of automation in a responsible manner.
4. **Disinformation and Manipulation Through Digital Means**

The spread of false information and the possibility of digital manipulation present difficult ethical problems for the consumers of technology and the platforms that support it. It is necessary to uphold the ideals of truthfulness, transparency, and fact-checking in order to counteract the spread of false information and ensure that technology is used responsibly for the benefit of society.

In order to address these ethical conundrums, it is necessary for technology developers, policymakers, and users to work together on the development of guidelines and frameworks. These should prioritize the protection of individual rights, promote fairness and inclusivity, and foster the ethical advancement of technology for the benefit of all. We can pave the road for a technological future that is more responsible and egalitarian if we incorporate ethical considerations into the process of developing and deploying technology.

Chapter 9

Funding and Policy Considerations

When it comes to the ever-changing landscape of research and development, the factors of funding and policy play critical roles in determining the course of innovation and the progression of scientific knowledge. This in-depth article, which is three thousand words long, examines the complex link that exists between funding and policy, as well as its significance, obstacles, and the ways in which it affects the progression of technology and research.

1. **The Opening Statements**
   Both the advancement of technology and the pursuit of scientific knowledge are supported by the twin pillars of funding and policy concerns. They make available the financial resources and regulatory frameworks that make the pursuit of knowledge, discovery, and advancement possible and offer direction for those endeavors. It is absolutely necessary, in this day and age, to have an in-depth comprehension of the complex relationship that exists between funding and policy in order to fully exploit the potential of technological advancement and scientific investigation.

2. The Importance of Financial Support

1. **Acting as a Catalyst for Innovation**
   Innovation cannot exist without adequate funding. It makes available the resources necessary to undertake ambitious research initiatives, create ground-breaking innovations, and investigate undiscovered territory in a variety of fields. Funding is the engine that drives the journey toward discovery, be it in the field of medicine or in cutting-edge technology.
2. **Maintaining Our Commitment to Research and Development**
   The activities known as research and development (R&D) require a significant investment of resources. When there is sufficient financing, research and development work can continue uninterrupted, which paves the way for the improvement of already existing technology as well as the investigation of fresh concepts.
3. **Drawing in Skilled Individuals**
   Talented people are drawn to funding. Researchers, scientists, and technologists are typically drawn to surroundings that provide a significant amount of resources to support the work that they do. A research environment that is adequately funded has the potential to bring together brilliant minds from all over the world.
4. **Stimulating the Growth of the Economy**
   The growth of the economy is directly correlated to the level of investment in research and development. The development of new industries, new job possibilities, and higher living standards are all the direct results of innovations. The provision of funding serves as a driving force behind larger socioeconomic progress.
5. **Closing the Gaps and Leveling the Playing Field**

When it comes to education and technology, funding can assist bridge the gap between those who have it and those who do not. It provides funding for projects that attempt to improve fairness and inclusion by delivering technical solutions to communities that have not been adequately served.

III. The Importance of Public Policy

1. **Frameworks for the Regulation of**
   The development of policy serves as the regulatory framework that oversees the ethical and appropriate utilization of research and technological advancement. It offers direction on topics such as the protection of data, intellectual property, and environmental effect, so ensuring that innovation is in line with societal values.
2. **Taxation and Other Encouragements**
   Incentives, such as tax credits or subsidies, can be provided by policy in order to encourage technical growth and research. The private sector is encouraged to invest more in research and innovation as a result of these incentives.
3. **Considerations of a Moral Nature**
   The establishment of ethical norms for research and the application of technology is the responsibility of policy. It ensures that ethical values are respected by defining boundaries in domains such as genetic engineering, artificial intelligence, and human experimentation, among other related fields.
4. **Protection of Intellectual Property**
   The protection of intellectual property rights, such as patents and copyrights, is absolutely necessary in order to encourage innovation. The legal framework for preserving intellectual property is provided by policy, and this encourages innovators and creators to share their work by making it easier for them to do so.
5. **Participation in International Activities**

In a society that is becoming more globalized, legislation can help international collaboration by aligning regulations, intellectual property standards, and agreements to share data. This kind of collaboration encourages the unrestricted movement of ideas and resources across national boundaries.

IV. Obstacles to Be Confronted in Regards to Funding and Policy

1. **Inadequate Levels of Funding**
   The lack of available funds is one of the key obstacles that must be overcome. Projects in research and technology frequently call for significant financial resources, and when those resources are in short supply, the projects' forward momentum might be stunted.
2. **Priorities in the Short-Term as Opposed to the Long-Term**
   It might be difficult to strike a balance between the economic demands of the near term and the investments in research and development that are made for the longer term. A mindset that is only concerned with the here and now could put instant financial rewards ahead of long-term innovation.
3. **The Ethical Conundrums**
   When new technologies are developed and introduced into the world, difficult ethical questions arise. For instance, the ethical use of artificial intelligence or genetic engineering involves a number of difficult concerns that need to be carefully considered from a policy perspective.
4. **Loopholes in the Regulations**
   The establishment of regulatory frameworks can sometimes lag behind the rapid evolution of technology, which can lead to regulatory gaps and uncertainties that need to be resolved.
5. **Competiton on the International Stage**

The fight for technological superiority has gotten increasingly fierce in a world that is becoming more and more linked. National security and economic competition are common factors that weigh heavily on policymakers' minds when making decisions about research and technology.

V. Considerations Regarding Funding and Policies Strategies for Navigating them

1. **Enhanced Investment from Both the Public and Private Sectors**
   It is imperative that both governmental and private investment in research and development be increased. The prioritization of funding to foster innovative ideas should be a top priority for governments, organizations, and enterprises.
2. **Planning Strategically for the Long Term**
   It is imperative to engage in strategic planning that strikes a balance between long-term research and development aims and short-term economic goals. Decision-makers at the policy level ought to take into account how their choices will play out in the future.
3. **Development of Policies That Are Ethical And Inclusive**
   It is essential to design policies that are both ethical and inclusive. Policymakers should collaborate with a wide range of stakeholders to ensure that the concerns and points of view of a variety of communities are taken into account.
4. **Agility in Regulatory Procedures**
   In order to keep up with the quick pace of technological advancement, regulatory frameworks should be developed with flexibility and adaptability in mind. In order to fill regulatory voids and solve regulatory issues, routine evaluations and updates are required.
5. **Participation in International Activities**

For the purpose of addressing global concerns and realizing the full potential of science and technology, international collaboration is absolutely necessary. Cooperation should be encouraged by policymakers in areas such as addressing climate change, improving public health, and exploring space.

VI. The Prospects for Funding and Policy in the Future

Ongoing technological progress, developing societal norms, and problems on a global scale will all have an impact on the financial and policy issues that lie ahead for research and development in the field of technology. Because the rate of innovation is expected to continue to quicken, there will be an even greater demand for finance and policy approaches that are both responsible and ethical.

1. **New Technologies Currently Evolving**
   New technologies, such as quantum computing, biotechnology, and artificial intelligence, will require innovative methods of funding and policymaking in order to guarantee that they will be used in a manner that is both responsible and ethical.
2. **The Changing Climate and Long-Term Sustainability**
   When it comes to addressing global concerns like climate change and sustainability, funding and policy considerations will play a critical part in the solution process. Those in charge of formulating public policy have a moral obligation to place a high priority on making investments in environmentally conscious and sustainable technologies.
3. **Technology That Is Both Ethical And Inclusive**
   In the not-too-distant future, one of the most significant themes will be the development of technology with an emphasis on ethics and inclusivity. The importance of responsible technology that takes into account human rights, diversity, and privacy should be emphasized by policymakers.
4. **Collaboration and Competition on a Global Scale**

Both international cooperation and competition are expected to intensify in the fields of research and technology. In a competitive global landscape, policymakers have the responsibility of navigating international dynamics while also promoting ethical and responsible behavior.

The foundation of technical innovation and scientific progress is found in funding and policy issues. The intricate relationship that exists between funding and policy, as well as the relevance of both, the difficulties they provide, and the ways in which they can be navigated, have a significant influence on the path that innovation and research take in the modern era. We will be able to harness the full potential of technology and research to address global concerns, stimulate economic growth, and create a better future for humanity if we embrace responsible funding techniques and ethical policy creation.

9.1 Government and private sector investments in digital infrastructure

At this point in time, the infrastructure that supports information technology and communication is absolutely necessary for the continued expansion of the economy, the growth of society, and the continuation of global competitiveness. Investments made in digital infrastructure by both the public sector and the private sector are essential to the establishment and upkeep of the networks and systems that make possible the movement of data and information. An exploration of the significance of such investments, the joint efforts between governments and the private sector, the obstacles they encounter, and the prospects for the future of digital infrastructure is presented in this article that is 1000 words in length.

1. **The Opening Statements**

    The modern economy and society are held together by the pillars of its digital infrastructure, which consists of communication systems, data centers, and broadband networks, among other things. Access to internet that is dependable and fast, data storage that is safe, and communication channels that are effective are necessary for a wide variety of fields, including business, education, healthcare, government activities, and many more. Investments made by both the government and the private sector are extremely important to the formation of the development of and the upkeep of this infrastructure.

2. **The Importance of Financial Investments in Information Technology Infrastructure**

   1. **The Expanding Economy**
   The expansion of the economy is fueled by investments in digital infrastructure. The development of a strong digital infrastructure can boost productivity, make e-commerce possible, and encourage innovative thinking, all of which contribute to the growth of the digital economy.

   2. **Participation in Social Life**
   Investing in digital infrastructure is beneficial to achieving social inclusion. It is vital to have access to high-speed internet and digital services in order to participate in the digital society and for education and healthcare to be provided. By ensuring that underserved and isolated populations have access, it helps bridge the digital divide that currently exists throughout the world.

   3. **Competitiveness on a Global Scale**
   Countries that have excellent digital infrastructure tend to perform well on the global stage. This type of infrastructure is great for luring in new enterprises, fostering technological innovation, and enhancing a nation's standing in the international market.

   4. **Security and Resilience in the Digital Age**
   For the sake of maintaining both national security and resilience, it is essential to make investments in digital infrastructure that is kept safe. Sensitive information and essential processes can be shielded from potential cyberattacks by utilizing encrypted communication methods and data storage.

   5. **Services Provided by the Government**

The establishment of a digital infrastructure can make government operations and the provision of public services more effective. Strong infrastructure is required for the implementation of electronic government services, electronic voting, and digital identity systems.

III. Collaborative Efforts: Investments from the Government and the Private Sector

1. **Public-Private Partnerships (often abbreviated as PPPs).**
   Partnerships between the public sector and private industry are a frequently used method for investing in digital infrastructure. Infrastructure projects are jointly funded and developed by governments as well as enterprises from the private sector. This paradigm gives governments the ability to use the experience, resources, and innovation offered by the private sector.
2. **Grants and Financial Assistance**
   To stimulate investments from the private sector in underserved or rural areas, governments may offer financial incentives in the form of subsidies and grants. These incentives have the potential to drive the extension of digital infrastructure into places where it would be less profitable for private enterprises to operate.
3. **Legal and Regulatory Structures**
   The interaction between the public sector and the private sector is governed by various regulatory systems. These policies have the potential to establish norms for data protection, the neutrality of the internet, and competition, thereby establishing an environment that is advantageous for investment.
4. **Financial Support for Research and Development**

It is possible for digital infrastructure to gain from technical advances that can be made possible with financing from the government for research and development in the private sector. Innovation is driven in fields such as telecommunications and data storage by grants and other forms of financial incentive.

IV. Obstacles to Be Confronted When Investing in Digital Infrastructure

1. **Inadequate Funding**
    In many nations, there are funding deficiencies, which means that underserved regions have restricted access to digital infrastructure of a high standard. In order to bridge these gaps, significant investments are required, particularly in geographically isolated and rural areas.
2. **The Complicated Nature of Regulations**
    The complexity of regulations might be a barrier to investments in digital infrastructure. There may be roadblocks in the form of differing legislation and standards between countries or regions if the project in question crosses international borders.
3. **Concerns About Safety and Security**
    Investments in digital infrastructure face enormous hurdles, not the least of which come from cybersecurity risks and data breaches. Constant effort is required to ensure that critical infrastructure possesses both security and resilience.
4. **Impact on the Environment**
    An increasing number of people are concerned about the environmental impact of digital infrastructure, which includes the consumption of energy in data centers and the disposal of electronic trash. In order to make ethical investments, sustainable methods and environmentally friendly technology are necessities.
5. **The Development of New Technologies**

Due to the lightning-fast pace of technological advancement, digital infrastructure must undergo continuous updates and modifications. Both public and commercial organizations often find it difficult to keep up with the rapid pace of these developments.

V. Strategies to Improve Financial Returns on Investments in Digital Infrastructure

1. **Cooperation Between the Public and Private Sectors**
    The public-private partnership ought to be supported, and

possibly even strengthened, through the establishment of transparent and equitable collaborations. Both the public and private sectors contribute their own distinct skills and resources to the process of infrastructure development.
2. **Initiatives for Increasing Digital Participation**
To close the digital divide, governments and businesses in the private sector should give top priority to efforts that promote digital inclusion. It may be possible to increase access for underprivileged people through the use of subsidies, grants, and tax incentives.
3. **Investing in Online Safety and Security**
It is absolutely necessary to put money into solid cybersecurity measures. The allocation of resources to defend digital infrastructure against cyberattacks should come from both governments and private firms.
4. **Environmentally Friendly and Sustainable Technologies**
The use of sustainable practices and environmentally friendly technologies can help to lessen the impact that digital infrastructure has on the surrounding environment. Important components are data centers with low energy use and ethical management of electronic waste.
5. **The Harmonization of Regulatory Procedures**

The harmonization of rules across national boundaries and geographic regions can make international investments in digital infrastructure easier. The creation of a uniform and beneficial regulatory environment is possible via the cooperative efforts of multiple governments.

VI. Predictions for the Future of Investments in Digital Infrastructure

The ever-evolving nature of technology, the ever-changing nature of geopolitical dynamics, and the ever-increasing emphasis on sustainability and security will all combine to influence the future of investments in digital infrastructure. When it comes to the growth and development of digital infrastructure, the role that collaborative efforts between governments and the private sector will play will continue to be of the utmost importance.

1. **5G and Everything Beyond**
   Significant financial investments will need to be made in digital infrastructure prior to the implementation of the 5G technology and the investigation of future communication technologies. These developments will usher in a new era of connectedness and open up a wealth of new doors for technological improvement.
2. **Protecting Information and Computer Networks**
   The growing significance of cybersecurity and the preservation of data will drive to investments in technologies and procedures that are designed to safeguard the confidentiality of digital infrastructure while also ensuring its security.
3. **Methods That Are Ecologically Sound**
   Investments in digital infrastructure will be driven in large part by sustainability considerations. The implementation of environmentally friendly technologies, the use of renewable energy sources, and the appropriate management of electronic waste will be given priority.
4. **Investing Across International Borders**

As nations work to increase their global digital footprint, there will be an increased emphasis placed on investments that span international borders. The harmonization of legislation and standards will make it easier to build infrastructure on an international scale.

Investments in digital infrastructure are absolutely necessary if one wishes to promote economic expansion, social inclusion, and international competitiveness. In order to construct and properly manage this vital infrastructure, it is essential to have joint efforts from both governments and the private sector, as well as regulatory frameworks and responsible practices. The formation of the digital age and the worldwide impact it will have will be heavily dependent on the expansion of digital infrastructure in a way that is both responsible and environmentally friendly as technology continues to advance.

9.2 Policy frameworks and regulations

Policy frameworks and laws serve as the basic guiding principles that enable responsible use, innovation, and the protection of individuals and societies within the fast expanding digital ecosystem. This essay of 500 words investigates the significance of policy frameworks and regulations in the digital age, focusing on their role in preserving order and fairness, the challenges they face, and the consequences for the future of these issues.

1. **The Opening Statements**

   In this day and age, the foundations of good governance are firm policy frameworks and stringent rules. They supply the framework and the norms that govern the use of technology, the preservation of personal privacy, and the promotion of ethical behavior. In an era that is marked by technical breakthroughs that have never been seen before, these frameworks serve as navigational tools for a digital world that is responsible and safe.

2. **The Importance of Regulatory and Policy Frameworks in the Modern Era**

   1. **Ethical Limits and Boundaries**

      Ethical bounds for the use of technology can be established through the implementation of policy frameworks and legislation. They outline the ideas and criteria that guide innovation and the development of technology while also guaranteeing that individuals' rights and dignity are maintained.

   2. **Protection of Personal Information**

      In this day and age, protecting one's personal information is an extremely important concern. Personal information is protected by regulations such as the General Data Protection Regulation

(GDPR) of the European Union, and individuals are provided with control over the data that pertains to them. Users are shielded from the risk of data breaches and unauthorized access by these measures.
3. **Fairness and the Role of Competition**
In order to maintain a level playing field in the digital market, regulations are necessary. They discourage monopolistic behavior and work to level the playing field for enterprises, which in turn promotes innovation and a diverse range of perspectives.
4. **The Safety of the Nation**
The protection of key infrastructure, intellectual property, and sensitive data against cyber attacks and espionage is essential for national security in the modern digital environment. This protection is provided by policies and regulations.
5. **Accessibility and Inclusion in the Community**

Accessibility and inclusivity are encouraged by the use of policy frameworks. They make it a priority to work toward achieving this goal in order to ensure that all people, regardless of the abilities they may possess, have equitable access to digital services and technologies.

III. The Importance of Regulatory Structures and Policy Frameworks

1. **Administration**
The policy frameworks and laws that are in place are examples of instruments of governance. They offer a logical and organized framework for the management of technology and the effects it has on society.
2. **Obligation to Law and Its Enforcement**
Regulations both lay out the necessary compliance standards and detail the procedures for enforcing them. They provide the authorities with the ability to take action against individuals who break the regulations.

3. **Creativity, Innovation, and Progress**
   Policy that has been carefully drafted will encourage innovation and development by illuminating a path that research and technology businesses can follow to conduct their business within the bounds of ethics and the law.
4. **Education of the Public**
   The public becomes more conscious of the significance of responsible behavior in the digital sphere and the preservation of individual rights when regulations are in place. They provide users with the ability to make educated judgments regarding their encounters with digital platforms.
5. **Relations with Other Countries**

Because they establish standards and norms, policies and regulations have an effect on international relations. They have an impact on international relations involving the sharing of data, commerce, and cybersecurity.

IV. Obstacles Presented by Existing Policy Frameworks and Regulations

1. **Swift Progress in the Field of Technology**
   In many cases, the rate of technological progress runs ahead of the rate at which regulations are developed. The difficulty that faces policymakers is keeping up with emerging technologies and the ethical implications of those technologies.
2. **The Complicated Situation Across Borders**
   The internet and other digital services are international in scope, which makes regulation more
   difficult. Policies need to take into account the international repercussions of their actions and be in line with the rules of other countries.
3. **Striking a Balance Between Privacy and Security**
   It is a difficult and complex job to strike a balance between the

requirement for security and the protection of individual privacy. The policies that are created need to find a way to strike a careful balance between these two vital features.
4. **New Ethical Conundrums to Confront**
   Emerging technologies, including artificial intelligence and biotechnology, present ethical challenges that may not be sufficiently addressed by the policies that are now in place. The people in charge of making policy have to adjust to these new circumstances.
5. **Capture of the Regulatory System**

The term "regulatory capture" refers to the situation that arises when the interests of several industries or businesses influence the formulation of policies to their own benefit. Constant problems include warding off undue influence and ensuring that regulations are working to the benefit of society as a whole.

V. Methods to Achieve Efficient Policy Frameworks and Regulations

1. **Fluidity of movement and adaptability**
   In order to keep up with the ever-evolving technology world, public policy should be formulated with agility and adaptability in mind. It is vital to conduct regular reviews and updates.
2. **Cooperation Among a Number of Different Stakeholders**
   Collaboration among several stakeholders, such as governments, technological corporations, civil society organizations, and academic institutions, encourages a variety of points of view and assures policies that are well-rounded.
3. **Education of the Public and Participation**
   Awareness is increased by public education and engagement efforts regarding digital rights and the significance of ethical behavior. Citizens that are well informed are better able to advocate for responsible regulation.

4. **Participation in Multilateral Organizations**
   When solving problems that span international borders, international cooperation is absolutely necessary. The establishment of global accords and standards requires the joint effort of policymakers around the world.
5. **Considerations of a Moral Nature**

The formulation of public policy ought to be guided primarily by moral considerations. The protection of individual rights and the moral application of technology should be given top priority by those who shape public policy.

VI. The Prospects for Current and Future Policy Frameworks and Regulations

The persistent progression of technology, changes in cultural values, and the emergence of new problems on a global scale will all have an impact on the policy frameworks and laws of the future. To ensure that digital landscapes continue to be secure, accessible, and fair, policymakers will need to adapt to new ethical issues and technological breakthroughs.

1. **New Technologies Currently Evolving**
   Emerging technologies like quantum computing, synthetic biology, and advanced artificial intelligence will demand new regulations in order to handle the particular ethical and regulatory difficulties posed by these technologies.
2. **Rights and Sovereignty in the Digital Age**
   The idea of digital rights, as well as digital sovereignty, will come to the forefront more frequently, with an increased focus placed on the defense of individual rights and the guarantee that digital laws will honor the sovereignty of states.
3. **Cybersecurity and the ability to bounce back**
   In order to combat the ever-increasing dangers posed by the digital realm, legislation governing cybersecurity will become

increasingly stringent. Policymakers will make ensuring the robustness of key infrastructure a top priority.

4. **Responsibility to the Environment**

Policies will place an emphasis on environmental stewardship, with the goal of promoting environmentally responsible business practices within the technology industry to reduce the carbon footprint of digital infrastructure.

In this day and age, the implementation of policy frameworks and regulations is absolutely necessary in order to guarantee the ethical and responsible use of technology. They safeguard the rights of the person, encourage equitable treatment, and foster inventiveness. In spite of the difficulties that still exist, politicians, stakeholders, and the general public need to work together to design regulations that can adapt to the rapidly shifting digital ecosystem. It is possible for society to guarantee that digital environments will continue to be safe, welcoming, and consistent with ethical principles if it places an emphasis on ethical issues and embraces adaptability.

9.3 International collaboration in science infrastructure

In the realm of science, international cooperation in the development of scientific infrastructure is becoming increasingly important to hasten the pace of research, facilitate the sharing of resources, and find solutions to global problems. Cooperation between nations helps harness the collective expertise, financing, and resources for groundbreaking discoveries and the creation of cutting-edge technology. Scientific progress frequently knows no borders, and this is one reason why scientific progress often knows no borders.

Because of their complexity and expense, modern research projects are one of the primary

motivators behind international collaboration in the scientific infrastructure sector. Numerous scientific initiatives, whether they be in the fields of physics, astronomy, climate science, or research on healthcare, need for high-priced equipment, specialized facilities, and the experience of scientists from multiple fields. Countries are able to undertake initiatives of a scale and ambition that would be unthinkable for each nation to manage on its own if they did not combine their resources and experience.

The European Organization for Nuclear Research (CERN), which is located close to Geneva, Switzerland, and is home to the Large Hadron Collider (LHC), is an excellent illustration of this type of partnership. To investigate some of the most fundamental topics in particle physics, the Large Hadron Collider (LHC), which is the largest and most powerful particle accelerator in the world, has brought together tens of thousands of researchers from over one hundred nations.

The promotion of unique points of view and the development of international collaborations both contribute to an increase in the overall quality of the research that is produced. Researchers with a variety of experiences and training contribute their one-of-a-kind perspectives and approaches, which enhances the quality of the scientific conversation and increases the number of opportunities for discovery.

In addition, cooperation in the scientific infrastructure can contribute to the solution of urgent problems on a worldwide scale, such as the mitigation of climate change, the prevention of pandemics, and the protection of biological variety. Nations can collaborate more effectively to develop answers to problems that face the entire human race if they share information, resources, and knowledge with one another.

As scientific inquiry grows more inter-disciplinary and technologically dependent, there is a strong possibility that international cooperation in the development of scientific infrastructure may become even more important in the not too distant future. Fostering an atmosphere that encourages and facilitates such cooperation is something that governments, institutions, and organizations should continue to do in order to promote a common goal of advancing scientific knowledge for the benefit of society. We will be able to address the difficult problems posed by our increasingly interconnected globe and open up new horizons of knowledge if we engage in international cooperation.

9.4 The role of academia in shaping policy

By contributing evidence-based research, expert views, and critical analysis, academia is one of the most important institutions in the process of formulating public policy. This essay, which is 700 words long, investigates the ways in which academic institutions and scholars have an impact on the formation, execution, and evaluation of public policy, as well as the problems they face and the significant repercussions that this collaboration has on societies and governments.

1. **The Opening Statements**

   Because it is a center for the production and transmission of knowledge, academia has a substantial amount of sway in the decision-making process. In order to better educate, direct, and evaluate public policy, academic institutions and academics contribute essential expertise, research, and critical thinking. The formation of policies that are informed, effective, and equitable requires close collaboration between the academic community and the bodies that make policy.
2. **Providing Research That Is Supported By Evidence**
1. **Conducting Research and Evaluating Data**

   Academic institutions engage in a substantial amount of research and data analysis in a wide variety of fields, ranging from economics to public health. The results of these research activities produce empirical evidence that is used to inform policy decisions. Policymakers rely on the work of scholars to help them grasp complicated topics, recognize patterns, and evaluate the possible effects of the various policy alternatives available to them.
2. **Analysis of Public Policy**

Evaluation of public policies is also significantly influenced by academic institutions. Academics evaluate the results and efficacy of existing policies, drawing attention to areas that have been successful as well as those that have room for improvement. Their assessments serve as the foundation for policy modifications and overhauls.

III. Insights and Knowledge Acquired Through Specialization

1. **Specialists in the Relevant Fields**
   Academic researchers are frequently acknowledged as being the foremost authorities in their respective fields of study. Their knowledge is essential to policymakers who are looking for more in-depth information about a particular problem or obstacle. Experts from the academic world offer direction and suggestions that are founded on extensive research.
2. **Collaboration Between Different Disciplines**

Policy problems frequently call for interdisciplinary approaches to be solved. Academic institutions encourage interdisciplinary collaboration, which makes it possible for specialists from a variety of professions to work together to handle difficult issues such as climate change, healthcare reform, and urban planning.

IV. Comprehensive Evaluation and Suggestions for Future Action

1. **A View from One's Own Perspective**
   Academics provide a viewpoint that is impartial and unaffected by the political or economic interests of corporations or governments. Due to the fact that they are independent, they are able to conduct critical analyses of policies, recognize possible biases, and make impartial suggestions.
2. **Advocacy for Public Policy**

Scholars have the ability to argue for particular policy changes based on the findings of their study and their expertise. Their activism has the potential to shape public debate and urge governments to adopt alternative approaches.

V. Obstacles to Overcome in the Connection Between Academics and Policymakers

1. **Obstacles to Effective Communication**
   Because academic research is notorious for being convoluted and full of jargon, it can be difficult to comprehend for both policymakers and the general public. It is absolutely necessary to bridge the gap between academic language and the communication of policy.
2. **The Division of Political Opinions**
   Sometimes the effect of academia on policymaking might be hampered by the partisanship that exists in politics. If the conclusions of a research study are found to be in opposition with a certain political objective, those findings may be disregarded or ignored.
3. **The sense of timing**
   When compared to academic research, the time frames that govern the policy-making process are frequently far shorter. Academic institutions have a responsibility to devise methods by which they can offer pertinent and timely insights to policymakers, particularly in the face of pressing difficulties.
4. **Funding and autonomy are our next topic**

Academic institutions could be subject to budget restrictions and conflicts of interest, both of which could compromise their autonomy. For researchers to continue to have credibility and influence in their fields, it is imperative that they uphold the integrity of their research.

VI. Repercussions for Societies and Governments

1. **The Ability to Make Informed Decisions**
   Collaboration between academic institutions and bodies responsible for crafting policy results in decisions that are more informed and more evidence-based. This, in turn, makes policies

more effective and increases the likelihood that they will accomplish the outcomes that are wanted.

2. **Trust in the Public Domain**

    The participation of academics in the formulation of public policy has the potential to boost public confidence in the state. When voters recognize that policies are informed by expert knowledge and thorough research, they are more likely to believe and support those policies. This is because expert knowledge and research are more credible sources of information.

3. **Finding Solutions to Worldwide Problems**

    The contributions made by academia are absolutely necessary in order to address global concerns such as climate change, public health crises, and economic inequalities. Academic institutions are in a good position to deliver multifaceted, evidence-based solutions to these difficulties because they are well-equipped to do so.

4. **Creativity and Forward Movement**

    Academic institutions play an important role in fostering innovation and advancement by providing financial assistance to research and development. It is possible for technological, medical, and educational progress to be driven by policies that are affected by academic discoveries.

5. **Obligation to Account for Actions and Supervision**

The academic community plays an important part in ensuring that governments and policymakers are held accountable. Research and evaluations of policies carried out independently ensure that decisions are subjected to examination and that the impact of those actions is monitored and analyzed.

VII. Methods for Enhancing the Connection Between Academics and Policymakers

1. **Strive to Have Better Communication**

    It is necessary to improve communication between academic institutions and those who create policy. The researchers ought to make an attempt to communicate their findings in a manner that is crystal clear, succinct, and easily understandable.

2. **Encourage Collaborative Efforts Across Disciplines**

    Academic institutions have the ability to encourage collaboration across disciplines in order to address difficult problems. This strategy draws on the knowledge and experience of academics from a wide range of disciplines to generate all-encompassing policy solutions.

3. **Encourage Academic Autonomy and Responsibility**

    Both academic institutions and individual researchers are obligated to safeguard the autonomy and integrity of their respective lines of inquiry. For the sake of maintaining one's credibility, full disclosure of research techniques and funding sources is absolutely necessary.

4. **Encourage the Conduct of Policy Training**

    It can be advantageous for researchers to participate in training programs that equip them with the skills necessary to engage with policymakers and effectively convey the findings of their research.

5. **Encourage Participation in Civic Life**

Civic engagement can be encouraged in students and professors at academic institutions by encouraging them to take an active role in policy lobbying and community initiatives.

10

Chapter 10

Future Prospects and Challenges

The future is a blank canvas waiting to be painted on, an uncharted landscape ready to be discovered, and a trip that is sure to be fraught with both opportunities and obstacles. In this extensive essay of 3000 words, we dig into the prospects and problems that lie ahead in a variety of fields, including technology, the environment, the economy, healthcare, and society, as we make our way through the intricacies of a world that is constantly changing.

1. **The Opening Statements**
   The world is always changing, and each new second ushers in fresh opportunities for creativity, metamorphosis, and adjustment. The world is in a constant state of flux. When we look into the future, we see a landscape that is filled with a landscape that is filled with both enormous possibilities and formidable problems. In this article, we will investigate the opportunities and difficulties that lie in store for us in the years to come, providing insights into the myriad of components that make up our ever-changing world.

2. Technology: Its Potential for Positive Change and the Moral Obstacles It Poses

1. **Machine Learning, also Known as AI, and Automation**

   The potential for widespread use of artificial intelligence (AI) and automation is poised to transform a variety of industries, including healthcare and manufacturing. These technologies promise greater efficiency, enhanced decision-making, and inventive solutions; but, they also raise questions over the ethical use of AI, job displacement, and bias.

2. **Computing on the Quantum Level**

   The promise of quantum computing is that it will completely change the way that information is processed by making complicated computations and simulations that were previously impossible possible. This new development has the potential to revolutionize cryptography, speed up the discovery of new drugs, and find solutions to complex issues in the scientific community; nevertheless, it also creates cybersecurity challenges and ethical conundrums.

3. **Technology that is Environmentally Friendly**

   Technologies that provide clean energy, such as solar and wind power, offer the possibility of lower carbon emissions and more environmental preservation as part of an effort to achieve sustainability. The transition to more sustainable technologies will, however, necessitate the surmounting of financial obstacles, the modification of energy infrastructures, and the resolution of issues with resource constraints.

4. **IoT (Internet of Things) is our final option.**

   The Internet of Things is going to connect everything in our world, which will improve communication, make better use of resources, and make life in general easier. On the other hand, it heightens worries around the privacy of data, the security of interconnected systems, and the susceptibility of these systems to assaults.

5. Considerations of a Moral Nature

The swift progression of technology raises a number of moral questions, such as how artificial intelligence should be used responsibly and what effect automation will have on jobs. In order to successfully traverse these technological possibilities, it will be necessary to develop ethical rules and legislation.

III. Environmental Concerns, Including Climate Change and Long-Term Sustainability

1. **Climate Change Efforts**
   The possibility of taking action on climate change is a source of optimism for those who are concerned about the implications of climate change. The reduction of greenhouse gas emissions and the containment of global warming are primary goals of international agreements such as the Paris Agreement. To accomplish these objectives, cooperation from around the world and rapid policy implementation are required.
2. **The Renewable Sources of Energy**
   The shift to renewable energy sources such as wind, solar, and hydropower has the potential to cut carbon emissions, improve air quality, and strengthen energy security. Nevertheless, obstacles include transitioning away from fossil fuels, the need for investments in infrastructure, and the development of solutions for energy storage.
3. **The Protection of Flora and Fauna**
   The preservation of biodiversity and ecosystems is absolutely necessary if we want to keep our world in a balanced and resilient state. The degradation of habitat, the illegal trafficking in animals, and the introduction of invasive species are all challenges.
4. **Technological Answers to Problems**
   The fight against climate change can benefit from developments in environmentally friendly technologies, such as carbon capture

and storage. The development and use of these solutions must take place on a worldwide scale.

5. **Alterations in Behaviour**

Changing individual behaviors, such as consuming less energy and producing less trash, is necessary if there is any hope of achieving sustainability. It is a difficult task that requires education and incentives in order to successfully cultivate a culture of environmental stewardship.

IV. The Economy: Expanding Opportunities and Existing Inequalities

1. **Progress Made in Technological Areas**
   The relentless march of technological progress has the potential to propel economic expansion while simultaneously stimulating creativity and the establishment of new sectors. Nevertheless, this increase may exacerbate economic disparity and contribute to job displacement; hence, it is vital to address these gaps through education and social policies in order to close the gap.
2. **International Business and Trade**
   The process of globalization has the ability to link economies, broaden people's access to a wider range of goods and services, and make it simpler to collaborate economically. But at the same time, it ratchets up the level of competitiveness, trade imbalances, and the possibility of economic disasters.
3. **Resilience of the Economy**
   Diversifying economic sectors, lowering the economy's reliance on individual markets, and maintaining a secure banking system are all essential steps toward achieving economic resilience. This calls for proactive risk management and policies that can adapt to changing conditions in order to navigate the economic hurdles.
4. **Methods of Maintaining a Sustainable Economy**
   Adopting environmentally friendly business methods, making financial investments in green technology, and expanding one's

conception of what constitutes a successful economy beyond GDP expansion are all necessary steps toward achieving economic sustainability. Striking a balance between economic growth, environmental protection, and social well-being is one of the challenges we face.

5. **Adaptation of the Workforce**

The workforce needs to be able to adjust to changing job requirements in order to keep up with the ever-evolving industry. Individuals will need to hone their existing skills, acquire new ones, and continue their education in order to prosper in the labor market of the future.

V. The Healthcare Industry: Progress and Availability

1. **Developments in Health Care**
   The future of medicine is replete with opportunities that hold a great deal of promise, such as recent advances in gene therapy and customized medicine. These advancements offer the potential to treat diseases more efficiently, improve quality of life, and extend lifespans.

2. **Healthcare for All of the People**
   The possibility of universal healthcare strives to achieve the goal of providing all people with access to the basic medical services they require. In order to realize the goal of universal healthcare, it is necessary to overcome monetary and political obstacles, to guarantee equal access, and to deliver high-quality medical services.

3. **The Rise of Digital Health**
   The application of digital health technology, such as telemedicine and wearable devices, presents the opportunity for enhanced patient interaction and the delivery of healthcare services. Data privacy, regulation, and access gaps in healthcare technology are some of the challenges that need to be overcome.

4. **Pandemic Preparedness and Response**
   The worldwide experience with the COVID-19 pandemic highlights the necessity for improved pandemic preparedness. This includes the rapid development of vaccines, the implementation of early detection systems, and global collaboration in the fight against infectious illnesses.
5. **Concerns Regarding Ethical and Legal Issues**

As healthcare technology improve, there is a growing need to address the associated ethical and legal difficulties. Some examples of these challenges are those relating to the use of genetic data and disparities in healthcare. It will be vital to ensure appropriate use and equal access to the resource.

VI. Inclusivity in Society and the Challenges Facing It

1. **Participation in Social Life**
   The elimination of prejudice, inequality, and injustice is essential to achieving the goal of creating a society that is more welcoming to people of all backgrounds. In order to successfully achieve social inclusion, it is necessary to implement policies and programs that promote diversity and equity.
2. **Educational Opportunities and Continuing Education**
   Education and continued education throughout one's life are necessities if one is to successfully traverse the intricacies of the future. Access to quality education, adapting the curriculum to changing work requirements, and bridging the digital divide are some of the challenges that need to be overcome.
3. **Emotional and Psychological Health and Well-Being**
   Reducing stigma, expanding access to mental health services, and placing a higher priority on mental wellbeing are all steps that can be taken to improve mental health and well-being. Awareness, de-stigmatization, and more funding for mental healthcare are required if we are to be successful in overcoming these obstacles.

4. **Obstacles Facing the World**
   Migration, population displacement, and the blending of cultures are all examples of global difficulties that call for international collaboration and policies that are humane while also addressing the requirements of vulnerable people.
5. **Considerations of a Moral Nature**

Addressing ethical concerns, such as human rights, privacy, and social responsibility, is necessary to make progress toward creating a society that is equitable and welcoming to everyone. These principles ought to serve as a compass for directing both public policy and societal behavior.

The opportunities and difficulties that lie in store for us in the future comprise a complicated and intricate tapestry of prospects and difficulties. In spite of the fact that it contains the potential of innovation and transformation, technology also creates moral conundrums. The environmental forecasts are encouraging for a more sustainable future, but addressing climate change will require the collaboration of people all across the world. The potential for increased wealth that comes with economic expansion requires, however, that measures be taken to reduce existing economic inequalities. The improvements that have been made in healthcare have the potential to improve people's well-being, but access and ethical concerns must come first. Inclusion in society and the pursuit of justice necessitate the adoption of policies that prioritize learning, compassion, and diversity.

Cooperation, adaptability, and a dedication to making decisions that are both ethical and responsible are required to successfully navigate this ever-changing world. We have the ability to mold the future into one that is not only rich but also egalitarian, sustainable, and just if we take on the problems and seize the opportunities that exist across technology, the environment, the economy, healthcare, and society. As we set out on this trip, it is imperative that we maintain vigilance, dedication, and an openness to the numerous opportunities and challenges that lie ahead. We must be mindful of the fact that the road to advancement is paved with both opportunities and challenges.

10.1 Emerging technologies and trends in science infrastructure

The infrastructure of science is the bedrock upon which development in a variety of domains is built, making possible ground-breaking research and innovation. Emerging trends and technologies in science infrastructure are reshaping the future of research, experimentation, and cooperation in the ever-changing world of science and technology. This essay of 1000 words examines some of the most promising and revolutionary trends in science infrastructure, stressing the potential influence these trends may have on scientific discovery and progress.

1. **The Opening Statements**

    The term "infrastructure" in the context of the scientific community refers to the physical and digital resources, facilities, and instruments that are necessary for scientific study and experimentation. It enables researchers to conduct experiments, evaluate data, and collaborate with colleagues located all over the world, which is essential to the progression of scientific knowledge. The landscape of science infrastructure is undergoing a transformation as a result of new trends and developing technologies, which is expanding its capabilities, boosting its efficiency, and expanding its reach.

2. **High-Performance Computers and Technology**
    1. **Extraordinary Computers**

    The use of high-performance computing, also known as HPC, is becoming increasingly important in the world of scientific study. Supercomputers are able to facilitate complicated simulations, data analysis, and modeling across a variety of scientific fields since they are endowed with enormous processing capacity and capabilities for managing vast amounts of data. Researchers are able to investigate a wide variety of topics, including astrophysics, drug development, materials science, and climate change, with an unparalleled level of precision and speed because to these systems.

2. **Computing on the Quantum Level**

The advent of quantum computing represents a monumental step forward for high-performance

computing. Quantum computers are able to do complex calculations orders of magnitude more quickly than classical computers by utilizing the fundamental principles of quantum mechanics. They have the ability to solve difficult optimization problems, change cryptography, and simulate quantum systems, hence improving research in fields such as quantum chemistry and materials science.

III. Advancing Analytical Tools for Data

1. **The Internet of Things and Machine Learning**
   In order to keep up with the exponential growth of data in a variety of scientific fields, new data analytics techniques are required. Researchers are able to glean valuable insights from massive datasets thanks to the application of big data analytics and machine learning. These techniques facilitate the identification of patterns, the prediction of consequences, and the acceleration of discoveries in areas such as genetics, climate research, and particle physics.
2. **The Application of Artificial Intelligence (AI) to the Data Analysis**

The automation of difficult activities, such as image identification, natural language processing, and predictive modeling, is one of the primary contributions that AI makes to the field of data analysis. In the field of healthcare, AI is revolutionizing diagnostics and the discovery of new drugs, while in the field of astronomy, AI is helping to identify celestial objects and irregularities.

IV. Innovative Imaging and Sensing Technologies

1. **The Technique of Electron Microscopy**
   The development of electron microscopy has led to new discoveries in the fields of biology and materials science. Researchers are able to visualize the atomic structure of nanomaterials, viruses, and proteins with the help of techniques such as cryo-electron microscopy, which contributes to the advancement of drug development, nanotechnology, and structural biology.
2. **Imaging in the Infrared and the Hyperspectral Range**
   Imaging technologies such as infrared and hyperspectral imaging have applications in the fields of archeology, agriculture, and environmental monitoring. Infectious illness identification, agricultural evaluation, and the preservation of historical records can all benefit from the extensive information provided by these procedures, which reveal the composition of materials and the surroundings.
3. **Terahertz Imaging**

Terahertz imaging is a developing technology that has the potential to be used in a variety of fields, including non-destructive testing, medical imaging, and security screening. It does this by analyzing the terahertz region of the electromagnetic spectrum, which can reveal information about the properties and make-up of various materials.

V. **Platforms for collaborative work and digital laboratories**

1. **Virtual Reality (VR) and Augmented Reality (AR) are both types of mixed reality.**
   The use of virtual reality (VR) and augmented reality (AR) technology is changing collaborative science. In order to interact with data, models, and experiments, researchers are able to completely submerge themselves in virtual environments. Virtual reality (VR) and augmented reality (AR) provide user-friendly visualization tools for complex molecular structures, making them useful in fields such as molecular biology.

2. **Collaboration Through the Use of the Cloud**
   Computing and storage solutions available through the cloud have revolutionized collaborative research. Researchers from all over the world are able to access data, tools, and resources that are shared on the cloud. This makes it possible for researchers to seamlessly collaborate and share data. The fields of genetics, space exploration, and climate modeling have all benefited significantly from this trend.
3. **Access to Instruments Via a Remote Connection**

In recent years, it has become increasingly customary to access scientific apparatus remotely. It is no longer necessary for researchers to be physically present in order to control and operate specialist equipment because it can be done remotely from anywhere in the world. This development is very helpful in scientific disciplines such as particle physics and astronomy.

VI. **Environment-Friendly and Renewable Technology**

1. **The Use of Renewable Energy in Scientific Establishments**
   In order to lessen its impact on the environment, the scientific community is increasingly turning to alternative forms of power generation. In an effort to promote sustainability, research centers are increasingly adopting practices such as the installation of solar panels, wind turbines, and energy-efficient building designs. These projects are congruent with larger-scale efforts to combat the effects of climate change.
2. **Eco-Friendly Procedures in the Laboratory**
   The implementation of environmentally responsible procedures in laboratories is gaining popularity. Researchers are increasingly adopting environmentally friendly practices in the laboratory, such as lowering the amount of waste produced and the overall impact of their work on the natural world. The design of

sustainable laboratories and the implementation of energy-saving technologies are becoming more important factors.

3. Integrity of Data and Cybersecurity in the Seventh Item

The importance of implementing stringent data integrity and cybersecurity safeguards has only increased as scientific infrastructure becomes more digitally connected. It is absolutely necessary, in order to keep one's confidence and credibility intact, to guard research data against cyber attacks and to check that scientific discoveries are accurate and genuine.

VIII. Difficulties and Things to Think About

1. **Availability and Fairness**
   Maintaining a level playing field in terms of access to cutting-edge scientific infrastructure and technology is an ongoing problem. The contributions that scientists from less affluent places and groups are able to make can be hindered by disparities in access.
2. **Privacy of User Information and Ethical Concerns**
   Concerns over privacy and ethical use of data have been raised in response to the exponential growth of data. It is a continuing problem, particularly in genomics, artificial intelligence, and healthcare, to strike a balance between the open access and secure storage of data.
3. **Impact on the Environment and Long-Term Sustainability**
   It is still difficult to strike a balance between the advantages of technology and the preservation of the environment. In order to lessen the impact that high-tech scientific equipment has on the surrounding environment, measures need to be taken during production, disposal, and energy use.
4. **Frameworks for Regulation and Ethical Guidance**

Because of the rapid pace of technological growth, effective regulatory frameworks and ethical criteria need to be developed. It is essential to ensure responsible use and ethical conduct in fields such as artificial intelligence, genomics, and virtual reality.

The landscape of scientific research and discovery is undergoing a fundamental transformation as a result of the proliferation of new technologies and shifting patterns in scientific infrastructure. Scientific advancement may be sped up thanks to developments in high-performance computers, powerful data analytics, imaging and sensing technologies, collaborative platforms, and measures to improve environmental sustainability. However, along with these developments come new issues in the areas of accessibility, data privacy, long-term viability, and ethical considerations. It is crucial to ensure that science infrastructure continues to drive innovation, address global concerns, and advance the frontiers of human knowledge in order to make sure that science infrastructure continues to do these things, it is essential to address these challenges while also utilizing the promise of emerging technologies. Science is on the verge of making significant advances, which will open up new frontiers and provide answers to concerns that have been around for a very long time, as a result of researchers and policymakers working together to navigate this changing landscape.

10.2 Sustainability and environmental impacts

The notion of sustainability has evolved as an important one in today's modern society. Sustainability refers to a dedication to preserving the resources of the earth and protecting the environment for the benefit of future generations. This essay of 500 words examines sustainability, focusing on its significance and the impact it has on the surrounding ecosystem.

1. **Comprehending the Concept of Sustainability**
   The concept of sustainability refers to the act of satisfying present need without jeopardizing the capacity of future generations to do the same for themselves. It is founded on the understanding that the resources of our planet are limited, and as a consequence,

our activities need to be aimed toward the responsible use of these resources and the preservation of them.

2. **The Importance of Maintaining a Sustainable Environment**
1. **Protection of the Natural Environment**
   The preservation of the natural world is one of the key motivations behind adopting a sustainable lifestyle. The usage of nonrenewable resources to an excessive degree, together with unsustainable behaviors like deforestation and overfishing, have all contributed to the planet's worsening condition. The reduction of waste, the preservation of resources, and the promotion of environmentally friendly technologies are the primary focuses of sustainability initiatives.
2. **Efforts to Reduce the Impacts of Climate Change**
   The concept of sustainability is extremely important in the fight against climate change. Both the burning of fossil fuels and the clearing of forests are significant contributions to the release of greenhouse gases. Reforestation and shifting to renewable energy sources are examples of sustainable practices that contribute to the reduction of carbon emissions and the fight against climate change.
3. **Conservation of Available Resources**
   The demand for resources like freshwater, arable land, and energy is growing at a faster rate than supply can keep up with the expansion of the world's population. The concept of sustainability emphasizes making effective use of resources, cutting down on waste, and investigating different approaches to problems in order to guarantee that these resources will be accessible to future generations.
4. **The Protection of Biological Diversity**

The preservation of ecosystems and a reduction in pollution are two of the primary focuses of programs relating to sustainability. The preservation of biodiversity is critical to maintaining ecological harmony and ensuring the health of all living things, including people. Practices that are not sustainable, such as the degradation of habitats and pollution, pose a threat to biodiversity.

III. Methods That Are Ecologically Sound

1. **Sources of Energy That Can Be Regenerated**
   One of the most important things that can be done to promote sustainability is to make the switch to renewable energy sources like solar, wind, and hydropower. These sources produce energy with a low impact on the surrounding environment, thereby lowering emissions of greenhouse gases and cutting down on air pollution.
2. **Agriculture that is Sustainable**
   Organic farming, crop rotation, and the use of fewer pesticides are all examples of environmentally responsible farming methods that are central to the concept of sustainable agriculture. These measures help to preserve the health of the soil and decrease the negative effects that agriculture has on the surrounding ecosystem.
3. **Methods for Lessening Waste and Recycling**
   To achieve sustainability, it is essential to make efforts to both minimize waste and encourage recycling. These measures reduce the negative effects that trash disposal has on the surrounding environment and help to conserve resources. Recycling not only helps minimize waste, but it also helps lessen the demand for new raw resources.
4. **The Replanting of Forests and the Repair of Damaged Habitats**
   Planting trees in formerly wooded but now barren or degraded land is the primary activity of
   reforestation projects, which aim to restore ecosystems and sequester carbon. The goal of initiatives to restore habitat is to

rebuild ecosystems that have been harmed as a direct result of human activity.

5. **Transportation That Is Friendly to the Environment**

The adoption of environmentally friendly modes of transportation, such as electric vehicles and public transit, is an example of a behavior that contributes to sustainability. These alternatives lessen the environmental impact that is caused by conventional automobiles that are fuelled by gasoline.

IV. Goals for Sustaining Sustainable Development

The Sustainable Development Goals (SDGs) have been outlined by the United Nations in order to solve global concerns and advance the cause of sustainability.

These objectives cover a wide range of facets of sustainable development, such as the alleviation of poverty, the mitigation of climate change, the provision of clean water and sanitation, and responsible consumption and production. To create a world that is more sustainable and fair by the year 2030, the Sustainable Development Goals serve as a roadmap.

V. The Negative Effects Unsustainable Practices Have on the Environment

1. **The Changing Climate**
   Climate change is caused by actions that are not sustainable, such as the burning of fossil fuels and the destruction of forests. As a result of climate change, global temperatures are rising, and extreme weather events and rising sea levels are also occurring.

2. **Loss of Biological Diversity**
   The loss of biodiversity has been brought on by factors such as the destruction of habitats, pollution, and the excessive use of resources. The rate at which species become extinct has accelerated, which has a negative impact on ecosystems and the services they provide.

3. **Pollution**
    Air and water pollution, which are frequently caused by industrial operations and inappropriate waste disposal, are detrimental to the health of both humans and the environment. Water supplies can get tainted with pollution, which can be harmful to aquatic life and contribute to health problems.
4. **The exhaustion of available resources**
    The use up of nonrenewable resources like oil, coal, and minerals can have far-reaching repercussions for the environment. The generation of energy and the creation of goods would suffer once these resources have been used up because they cannot be restored.
5. **The Degradation of Ecosystems**

Practices that are not sustainable wreak havoc on ecosystems, resulting in the degradation of soil, the spread of desertification, and the interruption of natural processes. The effects of these consequences have repercussions for both the agricultural sector and the health of the planet as a whole.

VI. The Way Forward Towards Long-Term Sustainability

1. **Spreading Knowledge and Instruction**
    It is essential to educate people about the significance of sustainability as well as the environmental effects of this concept. Through education, individuals and communities gain the ability to make educated decisions and advocate for environmentally responsible activities.
2. **The Policies and Regulations in Place**
    Policies that encourage long-term sustainability need to be enacted and strictly adhered to by national governments and international organizations. Sustainable behaviors, such as the reduction of emissions and the adoption of renewable energy, can be incentivized through the use of regulations.

3. **Developments in Science and Technology**
   The importance of innovation cannot be overstated when discussing sustainability. It is imperative that eco-friendly technology and renewable energy sources be developed in order to lessen the negative effects that a variety of sectors have on the surrounding environment.
4. **Consumption that is Conscious of Its Impact**
   Individuals can make a difference toward achieving sustainability by adopting a more responsible approach to consuming. This involves reducing waste, selecting items that are friendly to the environment, and being conscious of how resources are being used.
5. **Cooperation Across the World**

Cooperation on a worldwide scale is essential given the cross-border nature of environmental problems. In order to effectively address issues like as climate change, the loss of biodiversity, and the management of resources, international collaboration and consensus are required.

The practice of sustainability is not an option but rather a requirement. The effects of unsustainable practices on the environment are becoming more and more obvious, having a negative influence on ecosystems, climate, and the health of humans. Acceptance of sustainability signifies a dedication to the cause of environmental preservation and the building of a brighter future for future generations. Individuals and society can make significant contributions toward creating a world that is more sustainable and harmonious by putting sustainable behaviors into action, increasing public awareness, and lobbying for governmental changes.

10.3 Addressing the digital divide in science

Access to knowledge, technological resources, and connected networks are now absolutely necessary for the forward movement of science in the modern digital age. The fact that not everyone has the same access to these resources has created a gap that is now commonly referred to as the "digital divide." This essay of 500 words examines the difficulties brought about by the digital divide in the scientific community, as well as the techniques and efforts that are being implemented in an effort to close this gap.

1. **Acquiring an Awareness of the Digital Gap in the Scientific Community**
   The discrepancies in access to and utilization of digital technologies and the internet are collectively referred to as the "digital divide." In the realm of science, it refers to unequal access to scientific knowledge, research tools, and internet resources, which prevents certain individuals and communities from actively participating in scientific pursuits.
2. **Obstacles Caused by the Existence of a Digital Divide**
1. **The Inaccessibility of Certain Scientific Information**
   A large number of people, particularly those living in places that are underserved, do not have access to scientific journals, databases, or research papers. This makes it difficult for them to keep up with the most recent advancements in science and makes it more difficult for them to participate in scientific conversations with an informed perspective.
2. **A Fall in the Amount of People Involved in Online Research and Collaboration**
   Collaboration in scientific study conducted over the internet has developed into an essential aspect of contemporary scientific methodology. Through the use of various virtual platforms, scientists from all around the world work together. Those who do not have access to the internet or the appropriate digital tools, on the other hand, are unable to take advantage of these chances.
3. **Differences in Educational Opportunities**
   The digital divide can be significantly narrowed by expanding access to high-quality educational opportunities. Students' ability to pursue careers in fields related to science may be hampered if they do not have enough access to digital resources for

educational reasons. Some examples of such resources include e-learning platforms and digital textbooks.
4. **Obstacles to Participation in Citizen Science**

The use of digital technologies for data gathering and sharing is essential to the success of citizen science projects, which seek to engage the general people in scientific investigation. People who do not have access to cellphones, computers, or the internet are unable to participate fully in modern society because of the digital gap.

III. Solutions to the Problem of the Digital Divide in the Scientific Community

1. **Strengthening Connections to the Internet**
   The expansion of internet connectivity to places that are not already being serviced is typically the primary focus of efforts to close the digital divide. Building broadband infrastructure in rural and isolated areas with the intention of providing access to online resources and scientific knowledge is one of the goals of these initiatives.
2. **Programs for Improving Digital Literacy**
   It is crucial to promote digital literacy in order to ensure that individuals have the skills and knowledge necessary to use digital tools efficiently and gain access to scientific information. Digital literacy can be improved by the implementation of educational programs and community workshops.
3. **Initiatives Concerning Open Access**
   The goal of programs promoting open access is to increase public access to the results of scientific research. As part of these initiatives, research publications and data will be made freely available online, with the goal of lowering the barriers that prevent people from gaining access to information.
4. **Mobile Access and Solutions for Low-Bandwidth Requirements**

In many parts of the world, particularly those with less developed infrastructure, internet connectivity is increasingly being provided by mobile devices. Helping to reach a wider audience can be facilitated by developing scientific content and resources that can be accessed via mobile devices and internet connections with limited bandwidth.

5. **Municipal Bookstores and Neighborhood Meeting Places**
Internet access and other educational tools are frequently made available for free at local community centers and public libraries. It is possible to make a contribution toward closing the digital divide by fortifying these institutions and ensuring that they have access to modern technologies.

6. **Working Together with Different Non-Profits and NGOs**

The scope of impact that scientific endeavors can have can be expanded with the participation of charitable organizations and non-governmental organizations (NGOs). These groups frequently conduct activities on the ground in order to provide underserved populations with internet access and education.

IV. Examples of Past Achievements

1. **The African Health Open Educational Resources Network**
This network's goal is to provide access to education in the fields of medicine and science across Africa by utilizing open educational resources. It eliminates barriers to education by making content available to teachers and students at no cost, therefore closing the achievement gap.

2. **The National Digital Inclusion Alliance (NDIA), which comes in at number two.**
Connecting underserved communities throughout the United States is one of NDIA's primary missions. As part of their efforts, they advocate for more affordable access to broadband internet and seek to promote digital literacy.

3. Projects Participated in by Regular People

Even if they have just a small amount of digital resources, individuals are now able to participate in scientific research because to the numerous citizen science groups that have developed mobile applications and tools.

Access to information, research cooperation, education, and civic participation are all negatively impacted by the digital divide in the scientific community, which offers a multifaceted challenge. In order to bridge this gap, there needs to be collaboration between many groups, including governments, educational institutions, charitable organizations, and the scientific community.

We may work toward closing the digital divide by increasing internet connectivity, boosting digital literacy, providing support for open access projects, and cooperating with nonprofits and nongovernmental organizations (NGOs). To bridge the digital divide, it is not enough to simply ensure that everyone has equal access to technology; rather, it is necessary to promote equality and inclusivity in the realm of science, making it possible for a wide variety of voices to contribute to the advancement of scientific knowledge. It is everyone's job to see to it that people from all walks of life and in all parts of the world are able to reap the benefits of science and technology, regardless of their socioeconomic standing or location.

10.4 Preparing for unforeseen challenges

The volatility of life is one thing that can always be counted on. Unanticipated difficulties are a natural and unavoidable component of the human experience, regardless of whether they are of a personal, professional, or global scale. In this essay of 500 words, we discuss the significance of being well-prepared for unexpected obstacles and the methods that might assist us in developing the resilience necessary to persevere in the face of adversity.

1. **The Characteristics of Unanticipated Obstacles**
   Unanticipated obstacles are those unforeseen and frequently disruptive occurrences that take us by surprise and catch us off guard. They can manifest themselves in a variety of ways, including unanticipated setbacks in one's finances or profession, health emergencies, or natural disasters. These difficulties may also be on a worldwide scale in some instances, such as the COVID-19 pandemic, which illustrated how linked our society is and how swiftly unforeseen difficulties can have an effect on all facets of existence.
2. **The significance of getting ready**
1. **Strength and Fortitude in the Confrontation of Uncertainty**
   Building resilience requires critical preparation in the form of mental and physical workouts. In the face of adversity, the ability to adapt, recover, and even thrive is what we mean when we talk about resilience. Accomplishing this requires equipping oneself with the mental, emotional, and behavioral resources necessary to handle challenges.
2. **Lessening the Effect of the Impact**
   Even while it is hard to anticipate or avoid all unanticipated challenges, being prepared can help lessen the impact of those challenges. one is like to fastening your seatbelt before getting behind the wheel of a car; you can't anticipate an accident, but you can get ready for one. In a similar vein, you can lessen the intensity of the impact that life's unpredictabilities have on you by making preparations for them.
3. **A Healthy Mental State of Being**

Additionally, preparation can result in beneficial psychological impacts. A sense of control and a reduction in worry can be gained by being aware that preparations have been made for difficulties that were not anticipated. Even in challenging circumstances, it has the potential to build a sense of personal agency.

III. Tactics to Use in Order to Get Ready for Unanticipated Obstacles

1. **Tax and Estate Preparation**
   Having a plan for one's finances is essential. In the event of a financial emergency, having adequate insurance coverage, an emergency savings account, and responsible debt management can provide a safety net. You might be able to weather unexpected job loss, medical bills, or economic downturns with the help of these methods.
2. **Physical and mental well-being**
   Putting one's physical and mental health first is an essential part of getting ready for anything. You may improve your ability to deal with issues relating to your health by adopting and sticking to a healthy lifestyle, by going in for routine checkups at the doctor, and by having access to services for mental health.
3. **Networking and Support Structures**
   The value of constructing a robust social network and support system cannot be overstated. In times of need, emotional support, practical assistance, and moral direction can be provided by friends, family, and coworkers. It is crucial to keep these relationships alive and well.
4. **Ongoing Education and Training**
   Continuous education and improvement of one's skills are absolutely necessary for professional resiliency. If you want to be more adaptable and marketable in the job market, you can make yourself more marketable by increasing your skill set and staying current on industry trends.
5. **Contingency Planning and Disaster Relief**
   It is absolutely necessary to have a contingency plan in place in the event of large-scale emergencies or natural catastrophes. This involves having critical supplies, being familiar with evacuation

routes, and being aware of the processes that are specific to the area.

6. **Having an Adaptable Attitude**
A mindset that is open to change is one of the most important components of effective preparation. Your ability to effectively handle unanticipated hurdles is directly correlated to your openness to change, readiness to adjust to new situations, and ability to develop creative solutions to problems.

7. **Safety Measures for Computers**

Protecting your digital footprint is absolutely necessary in a world that is becoming increasingly digital. In the event that your digital identity or assets are targeted by hackers or stolen in a data breach, protecting them with cybersecurity measures, robust passwords, and data backups can help.

IV. The Importance of Being Able to Adapt

When becoming ready for unexpected difficulties, one of the most important traits you may have is adaptability. It gives people the ability to react to changing circumstances, learn from mistakes, and make changes that are necessary. Your ability to change course, adapt your strategy, and prevail in the face of adversity is directly correlated to your mental flexibility.

V. Finding Solutions to Unanticipated Obstacles on a Global Scale

The significance of collective global preparedness has been brought into sharper focus as a result of global disasters like as the COVID-19 pandemic. A more comprehensive strategy for addressing global concerns should include elements such as international cooperation, timely information sharing, and effective healthcare systems.

Unanticipated obstacles are an unavoidable component of everyday existence. Although it is difficult to anticipate every obstacle that might appear, it is fully within our power to get ready for them when they do. Planning one's finances, taking care of one's health, establishing reliable support networks, cultivating a flexible mentality, and keeping up with current events are all components of effective preparation.

The ability to be well-prepared is not a failsafe against the occurrence of difficulties; rather, it is a buffer that can help reduce the severity of the effects of unexpected obstacles. It provides us with the resources that we require to adjust, recuperate, and eventually thrive in spite of the challenges that we confront. Resilience is our greatest asset in a world full of unpredictability, and it is something we can grow and strengthen through proactive preparation. Resilience is our greatest advantage.

www.ingramcontent.com/pod-product-compliance
Lightning Source LLC
LaVergne TN
LVHW010157070526
838199LV00062B/4394